mind STRETCHERS

CROSSWORDS WORD SEARCHES
LOGIC PUZZLES & SURPRISES!

mind STRETCHERS

RED EDITION

EDITED BY STANLEY NEWMAN

Reader's Digest

The Reader's Digest Association, Inc.
Pleasantville, NY / Montreal

Project Staff

EDITORS
Neil Wertheimer, Sandy Fein

PUZZLE EDITOR
Stanley Newman

PRINCIPAL PUZZLE AUTHORS
George Bredehorn, Stanley
Newman, Dave Phillips,
Peter Ritmeester

SERIES ART DIRECTOR
Rich Kershner

DESIGNERS
Tara Long, Erick Swindell

ILLUSTRATIONS
©Norm Bendell

COPY EDITOR
Diane Aronson

Reader's Digest Home & Health Books

**PRESIDENT, HOME & GARDEN
AND HEALTH & WELLNESS**
Alyce Alston

EDITOR IN CHIEF
Neil Wertheimer

CREATIVE DIRECTOR
Michele Laseau

EXECUTIVE MANAGING EDITOR
Donna Ruvituso

**ASSOCIATE DIRECTOR,
NORTH AMERICA PREPRESS**
Douglas A. Croll

MANUFACTURING MANAGER
John L. Cassidy

MARKETING
Dawn Nelson, Charlene Thatcher

The Reader's Digest Association, Inc.

**PRESIDENT AND
CHIEF EXECUTIVE OFFICER**
Mary Berner

**PRESIDENT,
CONSUMER MARKETING**
Dawn Zier

**VICE PRESIDENT,
CONSUMER MARKETING**
Kathryn Bennett

ISBN 978-0-7621-0783-4

Address any comments about *Mind Stretchers, Red Edition* to:

The Reader's Digest Association, Inc.
Editor in Chief, Books
Reader's Digest Road
Pleasantville, NY 10570-7000

To order copies of this or other editions of the *Mind Stretchers* book series, call 1-800-846-2100.

Visit our online store at **rdstore.com**.

For many more fun games and puzzles, visit www.rd.com/games.

Printed in the United States of America

1 3 5 7 9 10 8 6 4 2

US 4967/L-3

Contents

Dear Puzzler,

Have you ever wondered what goes through the mind of a puzzlemaker when creating a puzzle? Since I conduct many "Crossword Secrets Revealed" seminars every year, I get asked this a lot.

Like many puzzle professionals I know, I keep notebooks of crossword ideas. My notebooks contain two things: possibilities for puzzle themes, and interesting new words or phrases I've recently come across. These often come from reading or TV viewing. But puzzle ideas are just as likely to come to me from a snippet of conversation or a roadside billboard.

Some of the puzzle themes I have on file right now but haven't yet created: "Animal Verbs" (MONKEYING AROUND or YAKKING AWAY, for example) and "Enough About Me" (phrases with a hidden "ME," like RANDOM ERROR and STEAM ENGINE).

I keep a separate notebook with answers for "Themeless Toughies." They fall into several different categories:

- Short multiword answers (since puzzlers expect shorter answers to be one word only), like WHO ME ("Insincere denial") and GOT ID ("Security question")

- Longer answers I've already thought of tricky clues for, like PAY TO THE ORDER OF ("Check phrasing"), I GIVE UP ("Uncle's relative") and WELL DRESSED ("Smart")

- Phrases with unusual letter sequences and that don't look like "real answers" until they're nearly fully filled in, like ED MCMAHON and LOUIS XIV

In spite of all the ideas I'm constantly writing down, I frequently find myself having nothing suitable on file for a particular crossword I need to make that day. What do I do then? If I know the puzzle will appear on a particular day or time of the year, I often try for a timely theme, but with an unexpected twist. Like a "Turkey Day" puzzle for Thanksgiving, all about Turkey (the country) rather than "turkey" (the bird). Or "Spring Is Here" for late March, with the identical clue "Spring is here" for answers like POGO STICK and JACK IN THE BOX—in other words, "things with springs."

As you match wits with all the puzzlemakers whose fine work fills these pages, you may find it helpful now and then to "think like the puzzle-maker." I hope these paragraphs will give you some insight to make that "role reversal" a little easier.

Stanley Newman
Mind Stretchers Puzzle Editor

■ Foreword

Meet the Puzzles!

Mind Stretchers is filled with a delightful mix of classic and new puzzle types. To help you get started, here are instructions, tips, and examples for each.

WORD GAMES

Crossword Puzzles

Edited by Stanley Newman

Crosswords are arguably America's most popular puzzles. As presented in this book, the one- and two-star puzzles test your ability to solve straightforward clues to everyday words. "More-star" puzzles have a somewhat broader vocabulary, but most of the added challenge in these comes from less obvious and trickier clues. These days, you'll be glad to know, uninteresting obscurities such as "Genus of fruit flies" and "Famed seventeenth-century soprano" don't appear in crosswords anymore.

Our 60 crosswords were authored by more than a dozen different puzzle makers, all nationally known for their skill and creativity.

Clueless Crosswords

by George Bredehorn

A unique crossword variation invented by George, these 7-by-7 grids primarily test your vocabulary and reasoning skills. There is one

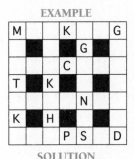

EXAMPLE

SOLUTION

simple task: Complete the crossword with common uncapitalized seven-letter words, based entirely on the letters already filled in for you.

Hints: Focusing on the last letter of a word, when given, often helps. For example, a last letter of G often suggests that IN are the previous two letters. When the solutions aren't coming quickly, focus on the shared spaces that are blank—you can often figure out whether it has to be a vowel or a consonant, helping you solve both words that cross it.

Split Decisions

by George Bredehorn

Crossword puzzle lovers also enjoy this variation. Once again, no clues are provided except within the diagram. Each answer consists of two words whose spellings are the same, except for two consecutive letters. For each pair of words, the two sets of different letters are already filled in for you. All answers are common words; no phrases or hyphenated or capitalized words are used. Certain missing words may have more than one possible solution, but there is only one solution for each word that will correctly link up with all the other words.

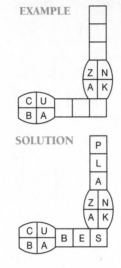

EXAMPLE

SOLUTION

Hints: Start with the shorter (three- and four-letter) words, because there will be fewer possibilities that spell words. In each puzzle, there will always be a few such word pairs that have only one solution. You may have to search a little to find them, since they may be anywhere in the grid, but it's always a good idea to fill in the answers to these first.

Triad Split Decisions

by George Bredehorn
This puzzle is solved the same way as Split Decisions, except you are given three letters for each word instead of two.

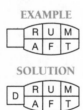

EXAMPLE

SOLUTION

Word Searches

Kids love 'em, and so do grownups, making word searches perhaps the most widely appealing puzzle type. In a word search, the challenge is to find hidden words within a grid of letters. In the typical puzzle, words can be found in vertical columns, horizontal rows, or along diagonals, with the letters of the words running either forward or backward. Usually, a list of words to search for is given to you. But to make word searches harder, puzzle writers sometimes just point you in the right direction, such as telling you to find 25 foods. Other

ANSWERS!

Answers to all the puzzles are found beginning on page 233, and are organized by the page number on which the puzzle appears.

twists include allowing words to take right turns, or leaving letters out of the grid.

Hints: One of the most reliable and efficient searching methods is to scan each row from top to bottom for the first letter of the word. So if you are looking for "violin" you would look for the letter "v." When you find one, look at all the letters that surround it for the second letter of the word (in this case, "i"). Each time you find a correct two-letter combination (in this case, "vi"), you then scan either for the correct three-letter combination ("vio") or the whole word.

NUMBER GAMES

Sudoku

by Peter Ritmeester
Sudoku puzzles have become massively popular in the past few years, thanks to their simplicity and test of pure reasoning. The basic Sudoku puzzle is a 9-by-9 square grid, split into 9 square regions, each containing 9 cells. Each puzzle starts off with roughly 20 to 35 of the squares filled in with the numbers 1 to 9. There is just one rule: Fill in the rest of the squares with the numbers 1 to 9 so that no number appears twice in any row, column, or region.

EXAMPLE

	8	2	4				9	1
7		4	9	8		6		2
1			5		3			
	9	1		7		5	8	4
2	8		4			1		3
			3			2		
8	1	6						
	4	3		2	5		1	
	7	2						8

SOLUTION

6	5	8	2	4	7	3	9	1
7	3	4	9	8	1	6	5	2
1	2	9	5	6	3	8	4	7
3	9	1	6	7	2	5	8	4
2	8	7	4	5	9	1	6	3
4	6	5	3	1	8	2	7	9
8	1	6	7	3	4	9	2	5
9	4	3	8	2	5	7	1	6
5	7	2	1	9	6	4	3	8

Hints: *Use the numbers provided to rule out where else the same number can appear. For example, if there is a 1 in a cell, a 1 cannot appear in the same row, column, or region. By scanning all the cells that the various 1 values rule out, you often can find where the remaining 1 values must go.*

Hyper-Sudoku

by Peter Ritmeester

Peter is the inventor of this unique Sudoku variation. In addition to the numbers 1 to 9 appearing in each row and column, Hyper-Sudoku has four more 3-by-3 regions to work with than the standard version, which are indicated by gray shading.

EXAMPLE

1	4	5	9			7		
		7	5	8	4	1		
3				7	2		5	
5	9		4	2	7			
	6		8					7
	7	4				2	9	5
	1					8		
	5		2			6		
6			7			5		

SOLUTION

1	4	5	9	3	6	7	2	8
9	2	7	5	8	4	1	3	6
3	8	6	1	7	2	9	5	4
5	9	3	4	2	7	8	6	1
2	6	1	8	5	9	3	4	7
8	7	4	6	1	3	2	9	5
7	1	9	3	6	5	4	8	2
4	5	8	2	9	1	6	7	3
6	3	2	7	4	8	5	1	9

LOGIC PUZZLES

Find the Ships

by Peter Ritmeester

If you love playing the board game Battleship, you'll enjoy this pencil-and-paper variation! In each puzzle, a group of ships of varying sizes is provided on the right. Your job: Properly place the ships in the grid. A handful of ship "parts" are put on the board to get you started. The placement rules:

1. Ships must be oriented horizontally or vertically. No diagonals!

2. A ship can't go in a square with wavy lines; that indicates water.

3. The numbers on the left and bottom of the grid tell you how many squares in that row or column contain part of ships.

4. No two ships can touch each other, even diagonally.

Hints: *The solving process involves both finding those squares where a ship must go and eliminating those squares where a ship cannot go. The numbers provided should give you a head start with the latter, the number 0 clearly implying that every square in that row or column can be eliminated. If you know that a square will be occupied by a ship, but don't yet know what kind of ship, mark that square, then cross out all the squares that are diagonal to it—all of these must contain water.*

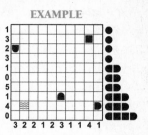

EXAMPLE

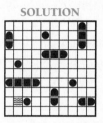

SOLUTION

ABC

by Peter Ritmeester

This innovative new puzzle challenges your logic much in the way a Sudoku puzzle does. Each row and column in an ABC puzzle contains exactly one A, one B, and one C, plus one blank (or two, in harder puzzles). Your task is to figure out where the three letters go in each row. The clues outside the puzzle frame tell you the first letter encountered when moving in the direction of an arrow.

EXAMPLE

C ↓   C ↓

←A

A→

↑
B

SOLUTION

C	B	A	
A		B	C
B	C		A
	A	C	B

Hints: *If a clue says a letter is first in a row or column, don't assume that it must go in the first square. It could go in either of the first two squares (or first three, in the harder puzzles). A good way to start is to look for where column and row clues intersect (for example, when two clues look like they are pointing at the same square). These intersecting clues often give you the most information about where the first letter of a row or column must go. At times, it's also possible to figure out where a certain letter goes by eliminating every other square as a possibility for that letter in a particular row or column.*

Circular Reasoning

by Peter Ritmeester

Lovers of mazes will enjoy these challenges. Your task: Connect all of the circles by drawing a single line through every square of the diagram. But there are a few rules:

EXAMPLE

SOLUTION

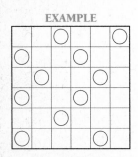

1. All right-angle turns must alternate between boxes containing a circle and boxes without a circle.

2. You must make a right-angle turn out of every square that contains a circle.

3. The line enters every square exactly once.

4. The line must end in the square that it began.

Hint: *Look for a corner with no circle in it. Since the line must make a right-angle turn in this square, according to the above rules, both sides of the line must continue straight until reaching a circle, then make a right-angle turn out of that square.*

Islands

by Peter Ritmeester

Your task: Shade in some of the blank squares (as "water"), so that each remaining white box is part of an island. Here are the rules:

EXAMPLE

SOLUTION

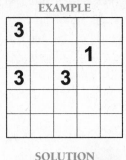

1. Each island will contain exactly one numbered square, indicating how many squares that island contains.

2. Each island is separated from the other islands by water but may touch other islands diagonally.

3. All water is connected.

4. There are no 2-by-2 regions of water.

Hints: *The most useful squares are those with 1 in them. Since an island with a "1" contains only that one square, you can black in every square adjacent to it. If you know three connected right-angle squares are water, by rule #4 above, the fourth square in the 2-by-2 region must be part of an island.*

Star Search

by Peter Ritmeester

EXAMPLE

SOLUTION

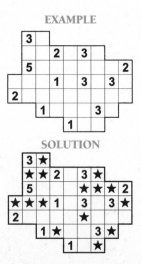

Another fun game in the same style as Minesweeper. Your task: Find the stars that are hidden among the blank squares. The numbered squares indicate how many stars are hidden in squares adjacent to them (including diagonally).

There is never more than one star in any square.

Hint: If, for example, a 3 is surrounded by four empty squares, but two of those squares are adjacent to the same square with a 1, the other two empty squares around the 3 must contain stars.

123

by Peter Ritmeester

Each grid in this puzzle has pieces that look like dominoes. You must fill in the blank squares so that each "domino" contains one each of the numbers 1, 2, and 3, according to these two rules:

EXAMPLE

SOLUTION

1. No two adjacent squares, horizontally or vertically, can have the same number.

2. Each completed row and column of the diagram will have an equal number of 1s, 2s, and 3s.

Hints: Look first for any blank square that is adjacent to two different numbers. By rule 1 above, the "missing" number of 1-2-3 must go in that blank square. Rule 2 becomes important to use later in the solving process. Knowing that, for example, a 9-by-9 diagram must have three 1s, three 2s, and three 3s in each row and column allows you to use the process of elimination to deduce what blank squares in nearly filled rows and columns must be.

VISUAL PUZZLES

Throughout *Mind Stretchers* you will find unique mazes, visual conundrums, and other colorful challenges, each developed by maze master Dave Phillips. Each comes under a new name and has unique instructions. Our best advice? Patience and perseverance. Your eyes will need time to unravel the visual secrets.

In addition, you will also discover these visual puzzles:

Line Drawings

by George Bredehorn

George loves to create never-before-seen puzzle types, and here is another unique Bredehorn game. Each Line Drawing puzzle is different in its design, but the task is the same: Figure out where to place the prescribed number of lines to partition the space in the instructed way.

Hint: Use a pencil and a straightedge as you work. Some lines come very close to the items within the region, so being straight and accurate with your line-drawing is crucial.

One-Way Streets

by Peter Ritmeester

Another fun variation on the maze. The diagram represents a pattern of streets. A and B are parking spaces, and the black squares are stores. Find a route that starts at A, passes through all the stores exactly once, and ends at B. (Harder puzzles use P's to indicate parking spaces instead of A's and B's, and don't tell you the starting and ending places.) Arrows indicate one-way traffic for that block only. No block or intersection may be entered more than once.

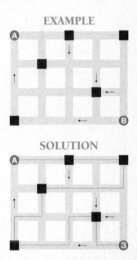

EXAMPLE

SOLUTION

Hints: The particular arrangement of stores and arrows will always limit the possibilities for the first store passed through from the starting point A and the last store passed through before reaching ending point B. So try to work both from the start and the end of the route. Also, the placement of an arrow on a block doesn't necessarily mean that your route will pass through that block. You can also use arrows to eliminate blocks where your path will not go.

BRAIN TEASERS

To round out the more involved puzzles are more than 150 short brain teasers, most written by our puzzle editor Stanley Newman. Stan is famous in the puzzle world for his inventive brain games. When necessary, an example of how to solve each puzzle appears in the puzzle's first occurrence (the page number is noted below). You'll find the following types scattered throughout the pages.

* Invented by and cowritten with George Bredehorn

** By George Bredehorn

But wait...there's more!

At the top of many of the pages in this book are additional brain teasers, organized into three categories:

• **QUICK!**: These tests challenge your ability to instantly calculate numbers or recall well-known facts.

• **DO YOU KNOW ...:** These more demanding questions probe the depth of your knowledge of facts and trivia.

• **HAVE YOU ...:** These reminders reveal the many things you can do each day to benefit your brain.

For the record, we have deliberately left out answers to the **QUICK!** and **DO YOU KNOW...** features. Our hope is that if you don't know an answer, you'll be intrigued enough to open a book or search the Internet for it!

■ Meet the Authors

STANLEY NEWMAN (puzzle editor and author) is crossword editor for *Newsday,* the major newspaper of Long Island, New York. He is the author/editor of over 100 books, including the autobiography and instructional manual *Cruciverbalism* and the best-selling *Million Word Crossword Dictionary.* Winner of the First U.S. Open Crossword Championship in 1982, he holds the world's record for the fastest completion of a *New York Times* crossword— 2 minutes, 14 seconds. Stan operates the website www.StanXwords.com and also conducts an annual crossword-themed luxury-liner cruise.

GEORGE BREDEHORN is a retired elementary school teacher from Wantagh, New York. His variety word games have appeared in the *New York Times* and many puzzle magazines. Every week for the past 20 years, he and his wife, Dorothy, have hosted a group of Long Island puzzlers who play some of the 80-plus games that George has invented.

DAVE PHILLIPS has designed puzzles for books, magazines, newspapers, PC games, and advertising for more 30 years. In addition, Dave is a renowned creator of walk-through mazes. Each year his corn-maze designs challenge visitors with miles of paths woven into works of art. Dave is also codeveloper of eBrainyGames.com, a website that features puzzles and games for sale.

PETER RITMEESTER is chief executive officer of PZZL.com, which produces many varieties of puzzles for newspapers and websites worldwide. Peter is also general secretary of the World Puzzle Federation. The federation organizes the annual World Puzzle Championship, which includes difficult versions of many of the types of logic puzzles that Peter has created for *Mind Stretchers*.

■ Master Class: **Brain Health**

15 Surprising Tips for an Even Better Functioning Noggin

Headlines over the past few years have detailed all the exciting new research into how reading, thinking, puzzle solving, and positive emotions can benefit your brain's health. But let us not forget that the brain is still a physical entity that needs unique nutrients and care to function at its peak.

With this in mind, we've interviewed the experts and read the research, and have come up with this list of "home remedies" for a healthier, more functional brain. These tips not only maintain brain health, but stimulate better memory and information processing.

1. Exercise.

Your brain uses a lot of oxygen and fuel to function. And to get it, it needs a steady flow of blood, which carries both key nutrients. Among the best ways to increase the flow of blood to the brain is to get moving. There's even some evidence that exercise may increase the number of nerve cells in the brain. Any type of regular exercise, but especially aerobic exercise like walking and biking, will do. Exercise also helps prevent illnesses like diabetes, stroke, and high blood pressure, all of which can contribute to memory lapses.

2. Consider taking 120 milligrams of ginkgo biloba a day.

The herb appears to improve blood flow to the brain, which helps brain cells get the oxygen they need to perform at their peak. In Germany, where the government's Commission E reports regularly on the effectiveness of herbal medicines, a standardized extract of ginkgo is frequently prescribed to prevent memory loss as well as stroke. If you're perfectly healthy, you probably won't see any effect from ginkgo. But if you have diminished blood flow to the brain, it may help.

3. Cut back on foods high in saturated fat.

You probably already know that it clogs the arteries that feed the heart. But high-fat foods also clog arteries that feed the brain, which reduces the supply of oxygen that reaches your noggin. Just as bad as saturated fats are the trans fats found in soft margarine and many packaged baked goods and snack foods.

4. Eat fish two or three times a week.

Cold-water fish such as salmon, mackerel, herring, and tuna contain omega-3 fatty acids. You probably know these fats are good for your heart because they help "thin" the blood and prevent clogged arteries; they're good for your brain for the same reasons.

5. Drink up.

The brain is 85 percent water. So if you're not drinking at least eight 8-ounce glasses a day, it's time to get into the habit. Dehydration leads to fatigue, which can take its toll on memory and brain function.

6. Get more B vitamins.

These include vitamins B_6, B_{12}, niacin, and thiamine. These nutrients help make and repair brain tissue, and some of them help your body turn food into mental energy. Bananas, chick-peas, and turkey are rich in vitamin B_6; whole grains and meat are good sources of all the Bs. Nuts and seeds, wheat germ, and fortified breakfast cereals are other good sources of B vitamins.

7. Take a multivitamin every day.

Make certain it has 100 percent of the DV (daily value) of folic acid and B_{12}, as it's difficult to get enough of these vitamins in your diet. Even moderate shortfalls may contribute to mental decline.

8. Count on coffee.

If you drink caffeinated beverages, you'll get a short-term boost in your ability to concentrate. And there may be long-term benefits as well. At the Faculty of Medicine in Lisbon, Portugal, researchers concluded that elderly people who drink three or four cups of coffee a day were less likely to experience memory loss than people who drank a cup a day or less.

9. Keep your blood sugar steady.

New research has uncovered a link between mild glucose intolerance and age-related memory loss. Food converted by the digestive system to glucose (blood sugar) is the main fuel that powers the organs, including the brain. But many people, especially those past their youth, have poor glucose tolerance, meaning they have trouble processing glucose out of the bloodstream and into their cells. According to the new research, even mild, non-diabetic glucose intolerance appears to reduce short-term memory in middle age and beyond.

What to do? Eat reasonably sized meals at regular hours, emphasizing fiber-rich whole grains and vegetables over "white" carbohy-drates such as white pasta, white bread, potatoes, and white rice. Also focus on good fats—those found in vegetable oils, nuts, seeds, avocados, and fish. They help keep your blood sugar steady without clogging your arteries.

10. Catch a whiff.

At a health-food store, purchase a small bottle of either rosemary or basil essential oil. Tests of brain waves show that inhaling either of these scents increases the brain's production of beta waves, which indicate heightened awareness. All you need to do is put a trace of the oil in your hair, on your wrists or clothing—any-where you can get a whiff. Or put some of the oil in a diffuser, and let it fill the air.

11. Consider taking eleuthero.

Also known as Siberian ginseng, this herb helps protect the body from the effects of stress and is said to heighten mental alertness. Buy a liquid extract and follow the dosage directions on the label.

12. Also consider this herb.

Gotu kola, an herb elephants love to consume, has been used to increase mental acuity for thousands of years. There is some research to support the use of the herb to boost memory. Buy a standardized extract and take 200 mil-ligrams three times a day.

13. Sound out the problem.

Listen to music often, and sample various types. Researchers have found that listening to music can improve your ability to concentrate and help you remember what you've learned. Some types of music actually cause brain neurons to fire more quickly. The faster the beat, the more the brain responds.

14. Make music.

If you're really motivated to sharpen your brain power, take up a musical instrument. Whether you want to play the drums or the piano, learn-ing to play will develop your motor skills while it fine-tunes your brain's ability to remember, analyze, and focus.

15. Find ways to reduce stress.

Tense people have high levels of stress hormones in their bodies. Over time, these hormones can affect the hippocampus, the part of the brain that controls memory. You don't have to chant or meditate—just do something that's simple and fun, from swinging in a hammock to finger painting with your children or grandchildren.

mental gymnastics

Try these fun exercises to challenge your brain and help you perfect the art of recall:

Memory Booster #1

Want to grow some new brain circuitry? Several times a day, use the "wrong" hand to do an everyday task. For example, if you normally brush your teeth with your right hand, use your left instead. If you always zip up your jeans with your left hand, use your right. The brain "knows" when you're using the wrong hand, because of the sensory and motor information it receives from that hand. It's that "confusion" that stimu-lates new brain circuits, as the brain struggles to master a new task. (Stick to the simple tasks, though. You don't want to try this when you're using a power drill.)

Memory Booster #2

If you're trying to remember how to spell a word, think of the word as an acronym and expand it into a sentence. Many kids learned to spell "arithmetic" by remembering the line "A Rat In The House Might Eat The Ice Cream." You can use the same trick to memorize lists. Need to stop at the Library, Post Office, and Drugstore? Make up a phrase like "Larry Plays On the Drums." Or you may have a shopping list that includes Jam, Apples, Paper towels, Eggs, Milk, and Cheese. How about "Jane And Polly Eat Moldy Cheese"?

Memory Booster #3

Need to remember which errands you have to run? Make up a short story—the more fantastic, the better—about them. Suppose your list includes bank, library, drugstore, and a stop at your friend Fred's to return a book you borrowed. The story might go like this: "Frantic Fred, a renowned drug addict, robbed the bank at gunpoint and then hid in the library."

★ Beddy-Bye by Gail Grabowski

ACROSS

1 Clean, as a floor spill
6 Marsh bird
11 Ashen
14 Oklahoma city
15 Linen fabric
16 Whitney or Wallach
17 Low-growing shrubbery
19 RN's specialty
20 Breathing room
21 Letterman nickname
22 Stinging insect
23 See 50 Across
25 "To conclude ..."
27 Disaster signal
30 Scottish garment
32 Scarlett's home
33 In one piece
35 Currency in Spain
37 Penny-__ poker
40 Data, for short
41 Measuring stick
42 Saturday Night Live feature
43 Small children
44 "Take __ from me!"
45 Luster
46 Roadway rig
48 Lima's locale
50 With 23 Across, singing syllables
51 Mattress part
53 Pork cut
55 Knight's title
56 Sgts., e.g.
58 Big-billed bird
61 Diamonds __ Forever
62 Baker's utensil
65 Hot drink
66 Soothed
67 Dug for gold
68 Wind up
69 Cooks slowly
70 Waist-length jackets

DOWN

1 Office conference: Abbr.
2 Yours and mine
3 Raindrop sound
4 Run-of-the-mill
5 Flapjack
6 And so forth: Abbr.
7 Well-behaved
8 Opponent
9 Skyscraper need
10 Singer Brewer
11 Party pooper
12 Bowling lane
13 Pleasant
18 Supermarket section
24 Alaskan native
26 Landfill input
27 Loretta of M*A*S*H
28 Words of dismay
29 Tub margarine, for example
31 Cup-shaped flower
34 Defeated one
36 Force back
38 Stadium level
39 Sicilian peak
41 Waterproof garment
45 "I'm agreeable to that!"
47 Chops, as garlic
49 Thorny flower
51 Warning signal
52 Swan relative
54 Like a perfect game
55 Fully satisfy
57 Distort
59 Gambling mecca
60 Quick-witted
63 Psyche parts
64 NFL scores

★ Color Paths

Find the shortest path through the maze, entering at the top left and exiting at the bottom right, by using paths in this color order: yellow, red, blue, yellow, red, etc. Change path colors through the white squares. It is okay to retrace your path.

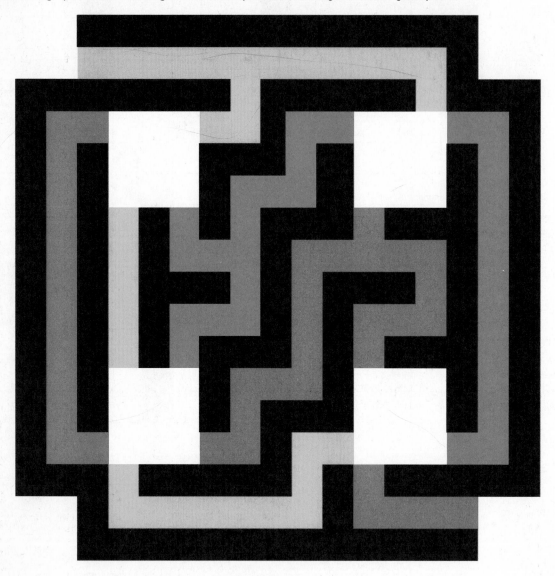

ADDITION SWITCH

Switch the positions of two of the digits in the incorrect sum at right, to get a correct sum.
Example: 955+264 = 411. Switch the second 1 in 411 with the 9 in 955 to get: 155+264 = 419

$$\begin{array}{r} 775 \\ +150 \\ \hline 862 \end{array}$$

★ United Nations

Find the 23 world nations that are hidden in the diagram either across, down, or diagonally.

```
N  G  R  E  E  C  E  Y  Y  W  T  E
E  I  N  D  I  A  N  X  A  L  G  L
D  K  A  Q  K  A  I  L  A  M  T  I
E  A  I  P  M  Y  E  K  R  U  T  H
W  B  I  R  S  S  W  F  M  I  O  C
S  T  E  L  P  O  R  T  U  G  A  L
U  G  U  N  A  E  M  A  T  L  A  M
R  I  N  N  F  R  H  E  B  E  D  W
E  T  O  S  I  U  T  P  X  B  Z  L
P  A  R  Q  N  S  O  S  A  I  I  E
O  L  W  G  L  L  I  B  U  Z  C  U
A  Y  A  C  A  H  U  A  A  A  F  O
V  R  Y  N  C  L  R  N  D  P  H
Y  C  D  R  D  J  B  T  P  Y  G  E
```

COMMON SENSE

What three-letter word can be found in the dictionary definitions of all of these words:

BOWLING, DECADE, RUMMY, and DIME STORE?

— — —

★ Sudoku

Fill in the blank boxes so that every row, column, and 3x3 box contains all of the numbers 1 to 9.

	4	5	2		9	1		3
	9					2		8
7	1	2	4					
1	3						2	4
2	8	7	3	9			6	1
	5		6		2	8		7
5		8		7	3		1	
			5		1		8	9
			8	4		3		

MIXAGRAMS

Each line contains a five-letter word and a four-letter word that have been mixed together (the order of the letters in each word has not been changed). Unmix the two words on each line and write them in the spaces provided. When you're done, find a two-part answer to the clue by reading down the letter columns in the answers. Example: D A R I U N V E T = DRIVE + AUNT

CLUE: It's fit to be tied

M O W A L I S E T = _ _ _ _ _ + _ _ _ _

M O P U S A H L Y = _ _ _ _ _ + _ _ _ _

B A M I R O C A N = _ _ _ _ _ + _ _ _ _

F I L E N N E D R = _ _ _ _ _ + _ _ _ _

★ Hot Day by Sally R. Stein

ACROSS

1 Garbage boat
5 Accumulate
10 Nonwritten test
14 Press for
15 Susan of *All My Children*
16 __, *Nanette*
17 Cabbage Patch Kid, e.g.
18 Mythical giant
19 Chorus member
20 Hot, as weather
22 Appear to be
23 Army assent
24 Fully prepared
26 Dollar fractions
30 Time-out
34 Short skirt
38 *The World According to __* (Irving novel)
39 Girl at a ball
40 Computer owner
41 Aromas
43 PDQ relative
44 Rips (up)
46 Wicked
47 *Daily Planet* reporter
48 Spooky
49 TV host Philbin
51 Roofing material
53 London's river
58 Couch
61 Hot, as a fashion
65 *Moby-Dick* captain
66 Mary Tyler __
67 Brontë heroine
68 Aspirin unit
69 Earlier
70 Have to have
71 Fillet fish
72 Puts in the mail
73 __ and sciences

DOWN

1 Full of lather
2 *Gladiator* star
3 Stares at
4 *The Time Machine* author
5 Superman, to 47 Across
6 *The Ghost and Mrs. __*
7 Start of a play
8 Read electronically
9 Croons
10 Hot, as a sports team
11 Performer's part
12 Poker-game starter
13 Weaver's machine
21 __-tac-toe
25 Recede
27 Third-party candidate of 2000
28 Hidden treasure
29 Parsley piece
31 Otherwise
32 Actor Alda
33 Held onto
34 TV remote button
35 Conversation filler
36 In the area
37 Hot, as a grump
42 Moves like a snake
45 Sailor's locale
50 That woman
52 Freeway exits
54 Sports venue
55 Metro-Goldwyn-__
56 White heron
57 Spring plantings
58 Drains energy from
59 Where Dayton is
60 Lose altitude
62 Traditional knowledge
63 Beef cut
64 Walked on

★ Circular Reasoning

Connect all of the circles by drawing a single continuous line through every square of the diagram. All right-angle turns of your line must alternate between boxes containing a circle and boxes not containing a circle. You must make a right-angle turn out of every square that contains a circle. Your line must end in the same square that it begins, and it cannot enter any square more than once.

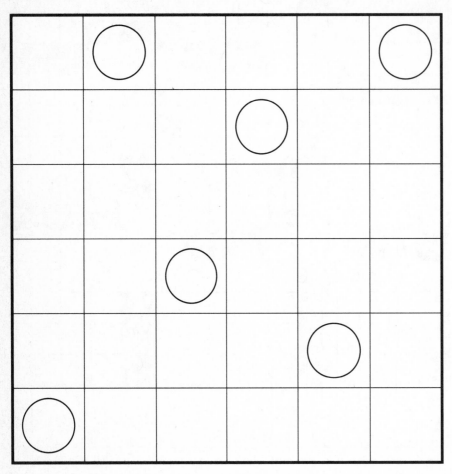

COUNTDOWN

Inserting plus signs and minus signs, as many as necessary, in between the digits from 9 to 1 below, create a series of additions and subtractions whose final answer is 66. Any digits without a sign between them are to be grouped together as a single number.
Example: 9 8 + 7 6 - 5 4 - 3 + 2 1 = 138

| 9 | 8 | 7 | 6 | 5 | 4 | 3 | 2 | 1 | = | 66 |

★★ Line Drawing

Draw two straight lines, each from one edge of the square to another edge, so that the letters in each of the four regions spell a single word.

LED

S

TIF

ER

PE

MO

AM

LE

FU

SS

EL RE

INITIAL REACTION

The "equation" below contains the initials of words that will make it correct, forming a numerical fact. Solve the equation by supplying the missing words. Example: 60 = M. in an H. (Minutes in an Hour)

8 = S. on a S.S. _____

★ Picnic Puzzle

Find the 24 different items that you might bring to a picnic. They are hidden either across, down, or diagonally. Answers include four plurals. For an extra challenge, find the word that appears four times.

```
C F L T U M B L E R S H G E H I
H H L R X P E A C H A A H G C Z
I C O U E M E B H N T C L N I T
C S R C O T A U A C I V Y A W I
K A A N O S A N D W I C H R D U
E I A U K L A W D P R W J O N C
N D W E S B A N H C I W D N A S
E W T K Q A A T E L P P A E S I
U G Q A I S G S E T A L P B I B
L C A C E S E E H C F O R K S P
S H K N I V E S O M S N O O P S
```

TONGUE TWISTER

From what language are all of these words derived:

ALGEBRA, SHERBET, SPINACH, and SULTAN?

A) Japanese B) Hindi C) Arabic D) Swahili

★ Squeeze Play by Gail Grabowski

ACROSS

1 Sand-trap club
6 Admired celebrity
10 Ticket portion
14 Perfect
15 Something prohibited
16 Fictional plantation
17 Angers
18 Soda flavor
19 Gymnast Korbut
20 Battalion or brigade
23 Above, in poetry
24 Chicago-to-Detroit dir.
25 Reach across
28 Sound of discomfort
31 Chains of hills
35 Ancient
36 Toledo's lake
38 *Mea __*
39 Shangri-Las song of '64
43 Enthusiastic
44 Chianti, e.g.
45 Fish eggs
46 Enter
48 Carpenter's tool
49 Veterinary patient
50 Score 100% on
51 Airport information: Abbr.
53 Toast topping
60 Gravy holder
61 Feel concern
62 Less colorful
64 Author __ Stanley Gardner
65 Arkin or Alda
66 Overact
67 Homeowner's document
68 Take a breather
69 Went out with

DOWN

1 Hairpiece
2 Dutch cheese
3 Food store
4 Four quarts
5 Commercial cow
6 Ancient South American
7 Cabinet cover
8 Part of SRO
9 Slip-on shoe
10 Accumulated
11 Perfumed powder
12 Craving
13 Lamb's sound
21 More faithful
22 Confined, slangily
25 Boot bottoms
26 Skirt fold
27 Proverb
29 Get bigger
30 '60s stereos
32 Blinding light
33 Orlando attraction
34 "Land __ alive!"
37 Sicilian erupter
40 Left the premises
41 Author Jong
42 Ax wielder
47 Big game-show prize
49 __ party (sleepover)
52 Used a keyboard
53 Feeling peeved
54 Folk story
55 Hay unit
56 Chapters of history
57 Monthly payment
58 Substantially
59 Dole (out)
60 Cradle, e.g.
63 Primary color

★ **Islands**

Shade in some of the white squares in the diagram with "water," so that each remaining white box is part of an island. Each island will contain exactly one numbered square, indicating how many squares that island contains. Each island is separated from the other islands by water but may touch other islands diagonally. All water is connected, but there are no 2x2 regions of water in the diagram.

1				
4				**3**
1				**3**

AND SO ON

Unscramble the letters in the phrase RED ROLE, to form two words that are part of a common phrase that has the word AND between them. Example: The letters in LEATHER HAY can be rearranged to spell HALE and HEARTY.

_____ and _____

★ Shades of Meaning

Find the five shades of one particular color hidden in the honeycomb. Form your words by moving from one letter tile to another as long as they share a side in common. All tiles must be used exactly once.

SUDOKU SUM

Without repeating any digits, complete the sum at right, by filling one digit in each of the five blanks.

```
    5 _ 3
+   _ 7 _
─────────
    _ _ 2
```

★ Canine Clothing by Sally R. Stein

ACROSS

1 Dietary component, for short
5 Paris' subway
10 Health resort
13 Stan Laurel's partner
14 Had a charley horse
15 Two-year-old
16 *Superman* star
17 Opted for
18 Everyone
19 Briefs alternative
21 Drink with crumpets
22 Lieutenant Kojak
23 Evaluate
25 Prepare leftovers, perhaps
28 Big name in TV talk
30 Spin
31 Land unit
32 Canine cry
36 Canine healer
37 Chemist's wear
40 Compete
41 "Hey, you!"
43 Purple fruit
44 Green fruit
46 Berth choice
48 Like some sweaters
49 Maine city
52 Attend
53 __ Baba
54 '50s women's fashion
60 TV news hour
61 Country singer Tucker
62 Emanate
63 Golf starting point
64 Group of eight
65 Hunted for morays
66 Extremity
67 Dial up
68 Acorn, essentially

DOWN

1 Nile queen, for short
2 Emcee Trebek
3 Construction worker
4 Oktoberfest locale
5 Manly
6 Cave effect
7 Norse god
8 Highway stopping place
9 Ukraine city
10 Cabinet department
11 Skier's supports
12 Book of maps
13 Sphere
20 Full collection
24 Timid
25 Invitation letters
26 Rams' mates
27 Top-rated songs
28 Come to pass
29 Gym dance
31 Well-qualified
33 Sinful
34 "As I __ and breathe!"
35 Hammer part
38 Get close to
39 Feet, slangily
42 Harbor boat
45 Glance, so to speak
47 Soda-can device
48 Misfortune
49 Moisten, as a turkey
50 Sci-fi visitor
51 Vetoed
52 Forest clearing
55 Not fooled by
56 Actress Cannon
57 Capri, for one
58 Felt sorry about
59 Senator Kennedy

★ One-Way Streets

The diagram represents a pattern of streets. A and B are parking spaces, and the black squares are stores. Find the route that starts at A, passes through all stores exactly once, and ends at B. Arrows indicate one-way traffic for that block only. No block or intersection may be entered more than once.

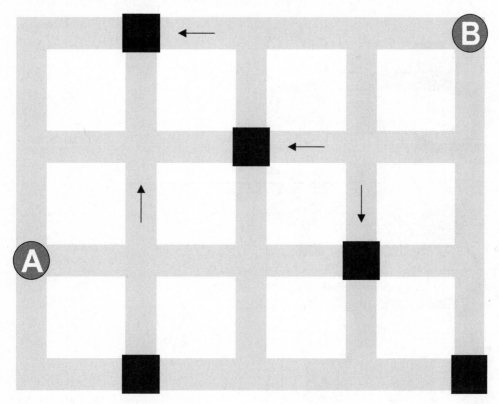

THREE AT A RHYME

Rearrange these letters to form three one-syllable words that rhyme.
Example: A A A B C E K S W X X = AXE, BACKS, WAX

E E F H I M R R R R W Y

_____   _____   _____

★ Split Decisions

In this clueless crossword puzzle, each answer consists of two words whose spellings are the same, except for the consecutive letters given. All answers are common words; no phrases or hyphenated or capitalized words are used. Some of the clues may have more than one solution, but there is only one word pair that will correctly link up with all the other word pairs.

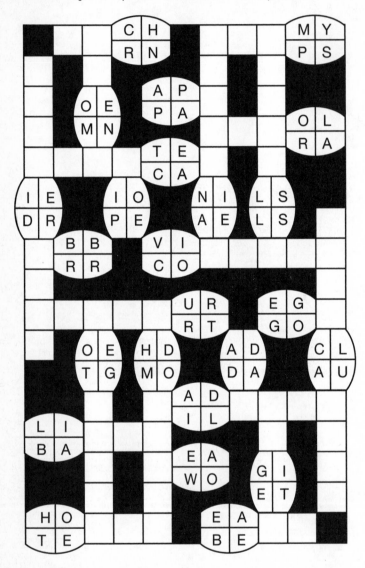

TWO-BY-FOUR

The eight letters in the word CHEERFUL can be rearranged to form a pair of common four-letter words in only one way, if no four-letter word is repeated. Can you find the two words?

— — — — — — — —

★ Star Search

Find the stars that are hidden in some of the blank squares. The numbered squares indicate how many stars are hidden in the squares adjacent to them (including diagonally). There is never more than one star in any square.

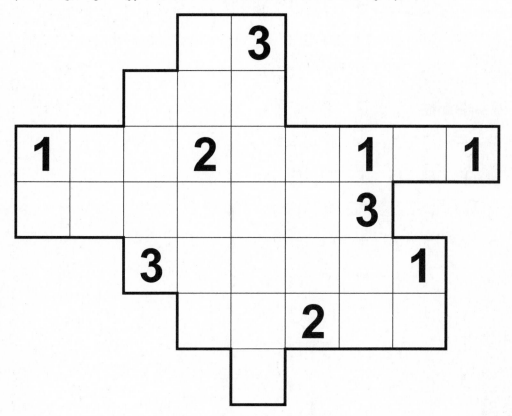

MIXAGRAMS

Each line contains a five-letter word and a four-letter word that have been mixed together (the order of the letters in each word has not been changed). Unmix the two words on each line and write them in the spaces provided. When you're done, find a two-part answer to the clue by reading down the letter columns in the answers.

CLUE: Frozen assets

C O T U R A L C T = _ _ _ _ _ + _ _ _ _

M O P A T I M A C = _ _ _ _ _ + _ _ _ _

L E T M O H U N S = _ _ _ _ _ + _ _ _ _

D O M U S A S H E = _ _ _ _ _ + _ _ _ _

★ Building Blocks

Find the 23 types of buildings, structures, and establishments housed in buildings, that are hidden in the diagram either across, down, or diagonally.

```
L A T I P S O H D U E R
M C M U S E U M N G E E
U A A B U D A I A S L C
I S O F P M V R T T L A
D T Q P E E A A L A I L
A L H N R G U T I B M A
T E I S M R A Q G L D P
S C I B A Z A T H E N N
C T R N R N L N T G I O
Y S T I K A A O H O W S
K N A B E Y R L O B C I
U F A C T O R Y U H X R
A I R P O R T P S M C P
E R T A E H T E E V J S
```

TELEPHONE TRIOS

	ABC	DEF
1	**2**	**3**
GHI **4**	JKL **5**	MNO **6**
PRS **7**	TUV **8**	WXY **9**
*	**0**	**#**

Using the numbers and letters on a standard telephone, what three seven-letter words from the same category can be formed from these telephone numbers?

225-5666   _ _ _ _ _ _ _

247-5263   _ _ _ _ _ _ _

247-7447   _ _ _ _ _ _ _

★ Cut to the Chase by Gail Grabowski

ACROSS

1 Got up
6 Does sums
10 Win, place or __
14 Poultry purchase
15 Prepare presents
16 It's not allowed
17 Robbery
18 Poker ritual
19 Part of U.S.A.: Abbr.
20 Locomotive pathway
23 Lincoln's nickname
25 Caviar
26 Type of seaweed
27 Reply to an impatient person
29 Hearts or clubs
32 Get it wrong
33 *The Thin Man* dog
34 Saloon bill
36 Candidate's itinerary
41 Glistens
42 Barbershop sound
44 New York ballplayer
47 Pimlico postings
48 More submissive
50 Drained of color
52 EMT specialty
53 __-Cone (summer snack)
54 Party game
59 Awoke, with "to"
60 Prefix meaning "against"
61 Fuzzy fruit
64 __ for business
65 Kitchen utensils
66 Overused, as expressions
67 Exam
68 Even trade
69 __ and Cher

DOWN

1 Do something
2 College cheer
3 *H.M.S. Pinafore* is one
4 TV room furniture
5 Unabbreviated
6 In the know
7 James Bond foe
8 Statistical info
9 Exceeded the limit
10 Traffic jam
11 Public tribute
12 Like a small garage
13 Employee
21 Parking place
22 Mongol invader
23 Santa __, CA
24 Kind of pear
28 Alternative to potatoes
29 Wise ones
30 Coffee brewers
31 *The Addams Family* cousin
34 Tie tightly
35 Headquarters
37 Word before book or booth
38 Pitch in
39 Laundry challenge
40 Legal claim
43 Golf instructor
44 Navy goat, e.g.
45 Break out of captivity
46 London's river
48 Speedometer letters
49 Bursts forth
51 Banquet or tournament
52 Crunchy
55 Afternoon snoozes
56 Chew like a beaver
57 Sicilian peak
58 Infamous Roman emperor
62 Wholesale qty.
63 "You there!"

★ Hyper-Sudoku

Fill in the blank boxes so that every row, column, 3x3 box, *and* each of the four
3x3 gray regions contains all of the numbers 1 to 9.

		3		9			8	
		1	6	3	4			
	4		5		8		3	
4	3			5				
	2		9		6	3	4	1
9			4	7	3	2	5	
6			8	2	9	4		
		2		4				5
3				6	5		9	

TRANSDELETION

Delete one letter from the word ACROBATICS and rearrange the rest, to get the two-word name of
a world nation.

_____

★ Loops

The diagram depicts a group of interconnected, unbroken loops. Carefully trace out all the paths, and determine how many different loops there are.

BETWEENER

What five-letter word belongs between the word at left and the word at right, so that the first and second word, and the second and third word, each form a common two-word phrase?

TALL __ __ __ __ __ BLANK

★ 123

Fill in the diagram so that each rectangular piece has one each of the numbers 1, 2, and 3, under these rules: 1) No two adjacent squares, horizontally or vertically, can have the same number. 2) Each completed row and column of the diagram will have an equal number of 1s, 2s, and 3s.

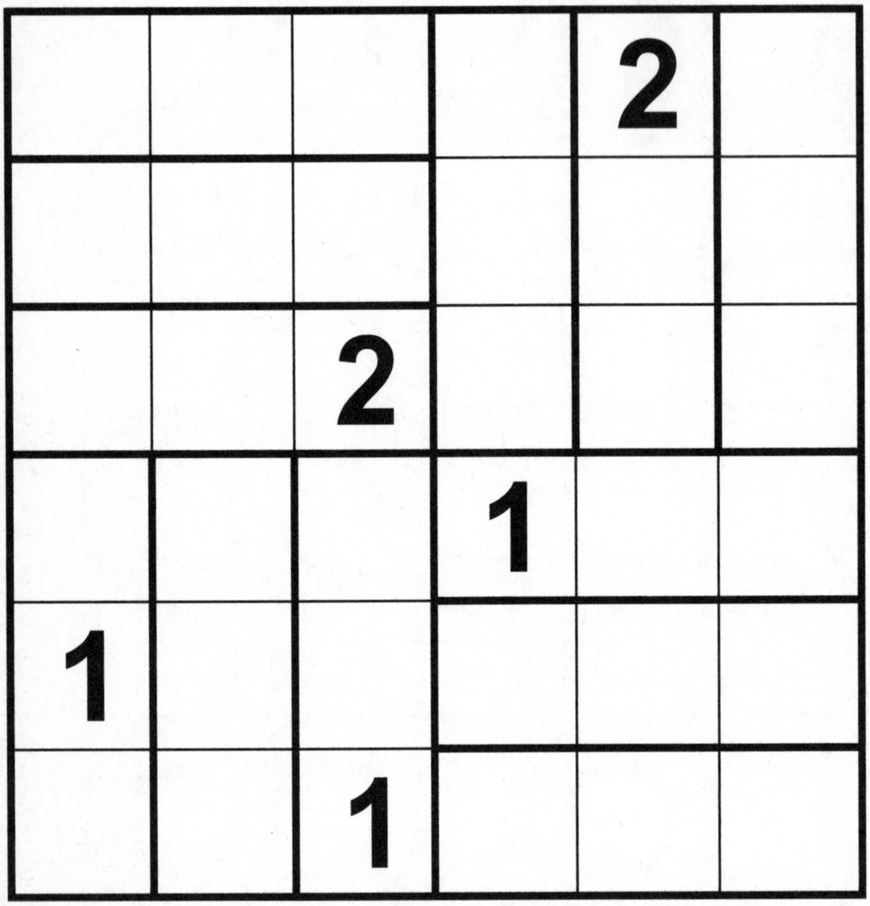

				2	
		2			
			1		
1					
		1			

THREE OF A KIND

Find the three hidden words in the sentence that, read in order, go together in some way.
Example: I <u>s</u>old Nor<u>ma new</u> screwd<u>rivers</u> (answer: "old man river").

Many students are mad—English Literature exam is taken on Thursday.

★ Auto-Graph by Norma Steinberg

ACROSS

1 Molten rock
5 Moisten, as a roast
10 Stage manager's concern
14 Realtor's measurement
15 "Sound the __!"
16 Rich vein
17 Ability to appal
19 Fairy tale's second word
20 Also
21 Vane reading
22 Astaire partner
24 Gloomy
26 Long stories
28 Motel room
30 In reality
34 Blossom's support
37 In re
39 Hawk's move
40 Night-table light
41 Storefront signs
43 Oodles
44 Sign of the Ram
46 Stumble
47 Tibetan bovines
48 Repeats verbatim
50 Actress Ward
52 Central parts
54 Acid in oranges
58 Athens' ancient rival
61 Utah ski resort
63 Yoko __
64 Dagwood's young neighbor
65 Nonstop talker
68 Lacking stiffness
69 Call up
70 Arthur of tennis
71 Durocher et al.
72 Crooner's repertoire
73 Driver's ed student, usually

DOWN

1 Stands the test of time
2 Sound of a sneeze
3 Race-car engine sound
4 Former nuclear monitor: Abbr.
5 From Munich
6 "Too bad!"
7 Adds seasoning to
8 Play about Capote
9 Come into view
10 Keeps trying to do
11 Lasso
12 Nasal appraisal
13 Barnyard enclosures
18 Sharp
23 Cloddish ones
25 Farmers' abundances
27 Handsome young man
29 African fly
31 Soft drink
32 Filched
33 Makes a choice
34 Strike with open hand
35 Skater Lipinski
36 Mideast leader
38 Rocky outcropping
42 Ghosts in Gloucester
45 Chimney residue
49 Hobos
51 Actor Neeson
53 Used as a cushion
55 Awaken
56 "What __ world!"
57 Clinton defense secretary
58 Order to a broker
59 Ballerina's bend
60 Bullets, e.g.
62 Yearn (for)
66 Taunting exclamation
67 Feedbag grain

★ ABC

Enter the letters A, B, and C into the diagram so that each row and column has exactly one A, one B, and one C. The letters outside the diagram indicate the first letter encountered, moving in the direction of the arrow. Keep in mind that after all the letters have been filled in, there will be one blank box in each row and column.

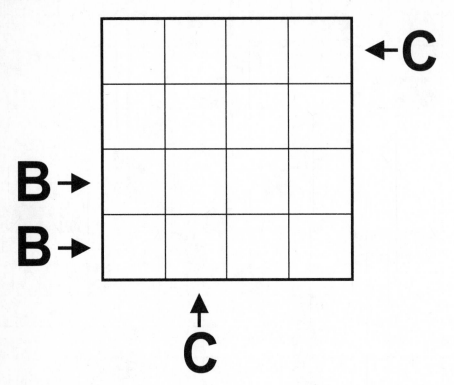

CLUELESS CROSSWORD

Complete the crossword with common uncapitalized seven-letter words, based entirely on the letters already filled in for you.

	M			R		D
		X				
		P		D		
G						T
O		E				O
				T		
	U		P			T

★ Find the Ships

Determine the position of the 10 ships listed to the right of the diagram. The ships may be oriented either horizontally or vertically. A square with wavy lines indicates water and will not contain a ship. The numbers at the edge of the diagram indicate how many squares in that row or column contain parts of ships. When all 10 ships are correctly placed in the diagram, no two of them will touch each other, not even diagonally.

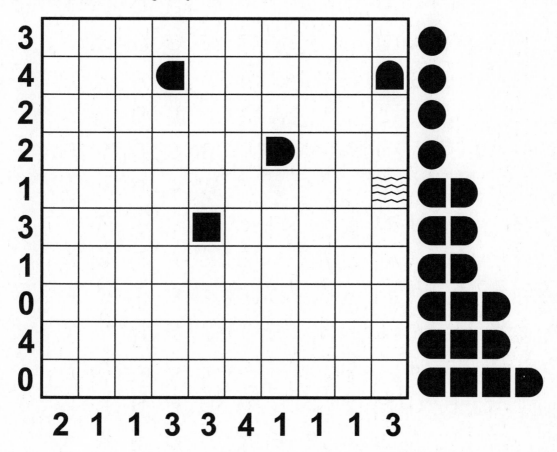

SOUND THINKING

We can think of four common uncapitalized words whose only consonant sounds are D, S, P, and L, in that order. How many can you think of?

_____   _____

_____   _____

★ Light Reading

Find the 29 words associated with "light" that are hidden in the diagram either across, down, or diagonally. Answers include four compound words ending in LIGHT, four verbs ending in ING, and one plural.

```
F I R E L I G H T S K E T N H N
L G N A R L M T T I C B H O H I
G F N E Q A U A E N S E G C G F
P L P I T B R M A C T A I A I F
Z A O C M L L I I A E L L E L A
T M H W I A D A N N M R S B S R
X E I G I A E I Z D O W A H A A
S C H A R N M L J E E S G L G P
K T V A W U G C G S B L I R G R
T H G I L P M A L C R A D T Q R
U B C L T F A H S E I N H N Y Y
Y C I W S H I N I N G T C W A R
G N I N R U B Z D C H E R R A C
B R I G H T T A P E Y R O W W X
B E A M G H S A L F I N T W A F
```

IN OTHER WORDS

There are only two common uncapitalized words (and one capitalized trademark) that contain the consecutive letters YGR. Can you think of them all?

_____   _____   _____

★ Fruity Remarks by Gail Grabowski

ACROSS

1 Fearless
5 Not quite right
10 Dairy-case purchase
14 Aroma
15 Winter coat
16 Grasped in one's hand
17 In the know
18 Shy
19 Connecticut university
20 Fiancée's suggestion
23 Blood components
24 Breakfast bread
27 Caesar's language
30 Boise's state: Abbr.
33 Scarlett of fiction
35 Not moving
37 Wedding phrase
39 Possesses
40 Complimentary comment
44 Naval Academy graduate: Abbr.
45 Received
46 Unit of temperature
47 Pave again
50 Curvy letter
52 "Omigosh!"
53 Folk singer Bob
55 Slippery swimmers
57 Indifferent one's remark
63 Largest continent
66 Hang like a hummingbird
67 Queue
68 On-board shout
69 Teheran native
70 Actor Alda
71 Female fowls
72 On edge
73 Fender-bender result

DOWN

1 Soup holder
2 *Garfield* dog
3 Needing directions
4 More fancy
5 More likely
6 Rum cocktail
7 __ *la Douce*
8 Slip and slide
9 Anwar of Egypt
10 "Is that so?"
11 Pasture
12 House extension
13 Poem of praise
21 Touch or taste
22 __ close for comfort
25 African desert
26 Followed, as footprints
27 Wedding-cake feature
28 Made amends
29 Reliable
31 Cuts calories
32 Tooth-care org.
34 Fireplace remains
36 Kids' running game
38 Ancient
41 Caviar
42 Banana coverings
43 Sandwich filler
48 Forever
49 College cheer
51 Dice rolls
54 Pitch extremely well
56 Like a haunted house
58 Clinton's vice president
59 Lendl of tennis
60 Manicurist's tool
61 __ instant (quickly)
62 Polite fellow
63 Sound of satisfaction
64 That woman
65 Charged particle

★ Go With the Flow

Enter the maze at right center, pass through all the starred circles, then exit the maze at bottom. You must go with the flow, making no sharp turns. Your path can cross itself, but you may not retrace your path.

TWO-BY-FOUR

The eight letters in the word INVENTOR can be rearranged to form a pair of common four-letter words in two different ways, if no four-letter word is repeated. Can you find both pairs?

— — — —   — — — —

— — — —   — — — —

★★ Circular Reasoning

Connect all of the circles by drawing a single continuous line through every square of the diagram. All right-angle turns of your line must alternate between boxes containing a circle and boxes not containing a circle. You must make a right-angle turn out of every square that contains a circle. Your line must end in the same square that it begins, and it cannot enter any square more than once.

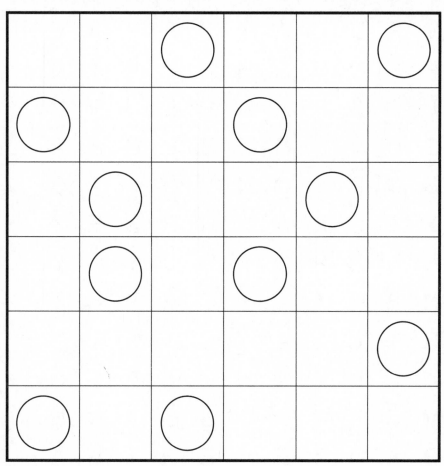

ADDITION SWITCH

Switch the positions of two of the digits in the incorrect sum at right, to get a correct sum.

$$
\begin{array}{r}
3\,4\,8 \\
+1\,0\,9 \\
\hline
5\,4\,7
\end{array}
$$

★ Beastly

Find the 22 animals hidden in the diagram, either across, down, or diagonally.

```
A W R K C S T S U P Y T A L P
W N O U F O L N C C O E E J Z
A I T L M R U R A K O F I R E
L W O E P E O G A H F U E I B
L W G E L C L P A A P L G P R
A L B O O O I R F Z E D A A
B E I D R N P I O N M C L T R
Y L I O X I G E A V O H B E Z
L L T T N H L P O A N E Y H Z
E E I O N R M I T I G E R H E
M Z G O R I L L A Y O T G Y B
U A E C H E E T A H O A P E R
C G U C M O N G O O S Q A N H
C H I M P A N Z E E E R T S A
```

CITY SEARCH

Use the letters in PASADENA to form common uncapitalized five-letter words. Plurals ending in S or verbs ending in S aren't allowed. We found five words. How many can you find?

_ _ _ _ _   _ _ _ _ _   _ _ _ _ _

_ _ _ _ _   _ _ _ _ _

★ Three Headed Relatives by Randall J. Hartman

ACROSS

1 Vocal
5 Small amounts
9 Lunch time, perhaps
14 *Peter Pan* dog
15 Land unit
16 __ around (asked questions)
17 Ballet skirt
18 Superman's alter ego
19 Russian rulers of yore
20 Beat the throw to first base
23 With it
24 72, at Augusta
25 Toward the rudder
28 Vesuvius output
31 Words of comprehension
36 Profound
38 Puerto __
40 Actress Verdugo
41 More than ready for battle
44 Syrup flavor
45 *Hi and* __ (comic strip)
46 French cash
47 Catches some z's
49 Decays
51 *The Raven* poet
52 Made in the __
54 Extremely long time
56 Paid for everything
63 Singer Page
64 Rich soil
65 Chicken's home
67 Bandleader Shaw
68 Not working
69 "I __ a dream"
70 Surly
71 Dark type of typeface
72 Adam and Eve locale

DOWN

1 Ottawa's prov.
2 Actor Julia
3 Card game fee
4 Comic's goal
5 Join in
6 Scored 100 on an exam
7 James Bond adversary
8 Establish
9 Accurately aimed
10 Have a snack
11 Morales of *La Bamba*
12 Saucy
13 AMA members
21 Hodges of baseball
22 Mai __
25 Second president
26 Not domesticated
27 City near Phoenix
29 Stringed instrument
30 Cast member
32 Gen. Robert __
33 Get ready, in golf
34 Opening comments
35 Western border lake
37 Brazilian soccer star
39 Cleveland's state
42 Sheriff's aides
43 Highly regarded
48 Memphis-to-Mobile dir.
50 Weep audibly
53 Off-the-cuff remark
55 Suitable place
56 Jamie of *M*A*S*H*
57 Director Preminger
58 Singer Redding
59 Fuss
60 Anteroom
61 Take on cargo
62 Zero, in tennis
63 Expanse west of Calif.
66 Signer's need

★ Sudoku

Fill in the blank boxes so that every row, column, and 3x3 box contains all of the numbers 1 to 9.

	3		7	9	2			
7		2		1	8			
	9	1				8	7	
1			9	8		6		
8	2		1		3	7		
			2	7		1		8
9		4	3	6	1			5
	1	5			9		3	
			4		7			6

SUDOKU SUM

Without repeating any digits, complete the sum at right, by filling one digit in each of the five blanks.

```
    3 _ 9
+   _ 0 _
    _ _ 6
```

★ 123

Fill in the diagram so that each rectangular piece has one each of the numbers 1, 2, and 3, under these rules: 1) No two adjacent squares, horizontally or vertically, can have the same number. 2) Each completed row and column of the diagram will have an equal number of 1s, 2s, and 3s.

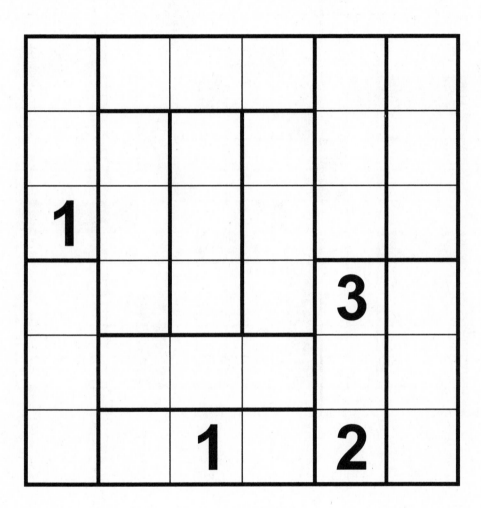

AND SO ON

Unscramble the letters in the phrase EMU FANGS, to form two words that are part of a common phrase that has the word AND between them.

_____ and _____

★ In Place by Norma Steinberg

ACROSS

1 Writing implements
5 Ali __
9 Glimmer
14 Time and again
15 Takes advantage of
16 Copier additive
17 Grow weary
18 Camera part
19 Exterior
20 Catcher's base
22 Nudges
23 Paper-clip alternative
24 Little branch
26 Elevator inventor
29 "Finally!"
33 Overly sentimental
37 Shout out to
39 Jalopy
40 Jai __
41 Give the __ his due
42 Glitch
43 Retained
44 15th of March
45 Houston baseball player
46 Track bet
48 To-do
50 Visibility problem
52 Perches
57 Coral formations
60 Tournament trophy
63 Divvy up
64 Poetic works
65 Copenhagen native
66 Emergency signal
67 Read closely, with "over"
68 Director Kazan
69 Chats
70 Historical periods
71 Bottle part

DOWN

1 Hiking trails
2 Writer T.S.
3 __ Rae
4 Expensive
5 Crime-lab specimen
6 Making a sailing
7 Twisted
8 Valuable possession
9 "Cut that out!"
10 Sand-filled timepiece
11 Long-division word
12 Prerequisite
13 Goofs up
21 Stratagem
25 Side of a room
27 Topped with frosting
28 Puts in the bank
30 Mom's sister
31 Constellation component
32 Diner order
33 "For Pete's __!"
34 Emcee Trebek
35 Hemingway nickname
36 Hay implement
38 Agenda
41 Actress Cameron
45 Elvis __ Presley
47 Samples, as soup
49 Garden flowers
51 Avoid a big wedding
53 Poet Nash
54 Weighing device
55 Long blouse
56 Command to Fido
57 Huck's transportation
58 Singer Fitzgerald
59 Israeli airline
61 Fragrance
62 Aloe __

★ One-Way Streets

The diagram represents a pattern of streets. A and B are parking spaces, and the black squares are stores. Find the route that starts at A, passes through all stores exactly once, and ends at B. Arrows indicate one-way traffic for that block only. No block or intersection may be entered more than once.

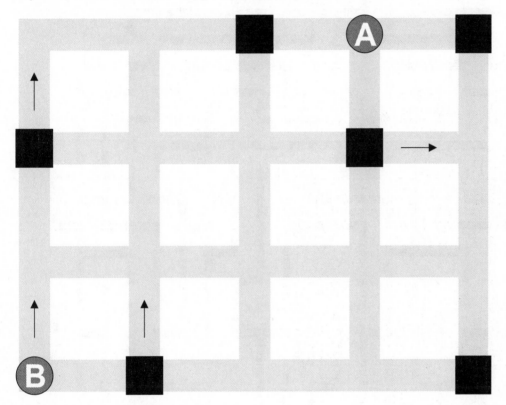

MIXAGRAMS

Each line contains a five-letter word and a four-letter word that have been mixed together (the order of the letters in each word has not been changed). Unmix the two words on each line and write them in the spaces provided. When you're done, find a two-word answer to the clue by reading down the letter columns in the answers.

CLUE: Shredder's output

D E L U S C E A T = _ _ _ _ _ + _ _ _ _

S O B I O L E S T = _ _ _ _ _ + _ _ _ _

S I N P L A R E T = _ _ _ _ _ + _ _ _ _

K E V I E W N I T = _ _ _ _ _ + _ _ _ _

★ Star Maze

Enter the maze at bottom, pass through each of the four small stars, and end on the large star in the center. You may not retrace your path.

COMMON SENSE

What three-letter word can be found in the dictionary definitions of all of these words:

PEN PAL, OVERSHOOT, AFIELD, and DEEP DISCOUNT?

— — —

★ Star Search

Find the stars that are hidden in some of the blank squares. The numbered squares indicate how many stars are hidden in the squares adjacent to them (including diagonally). There is never more than one star in any square.

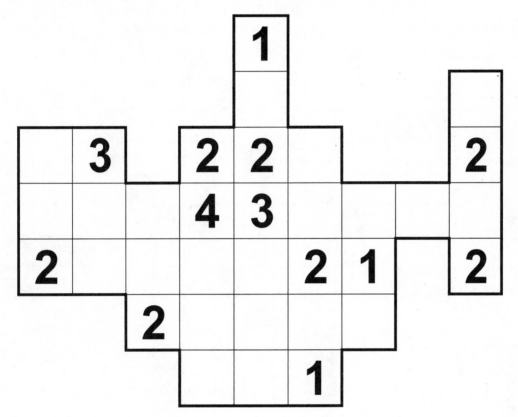

TELEPHONE TRIOS

Using the numbers and letters on a standard telephone, what three seven-letter words from the same category can be formed from these telephone numbers?

243-3824 _ _ _ _ _ _ _

536-7273 _ _ _ _ _ _ _

726-7437 _ _ _ _ _ _ _

★ Noble Names by Gail Grabowski

ACROSS

1 Coffee-shop purchase
6 Fencing blade
10 Jai __
14 Senator Hatch
15 Dice toss
16 Frying medium
17 Legendary jazz bandleader
19 Sandwich cookie
20 Thoughtful sound
21 Got up
22 "Men" or "women"
24 Each
26 Like a tree-lined trail
27 Hats or helmets
29 Boxing stats
32 Choir section
35 Corporal or captain
36 Oath taker's words
37 Ooze
38 Point of view
40 Oklahoma city
41 Minuscule amount
42 Supplements, with "out"
43 __ Carta
44 Pose a question
45 Puts in a showcase
48 Carpenter's fasteners
50 Bee or beetle
53 Sculptor's tool
55 Borscht ingredient
56 Bowl over
58 Fireplace fillers
59 '60s Supreme Court leader
62 Tennis great Arthur
63 Threesome
64 Went ballistic
65 Shea baseballers
66 Meal in a pot
67 Dalmatian markings

DOWN

1 __ Ness monster
2 Pleasant scent
3 Declaration in bridge
4 Anchovy container
5 Menu items
6 Wiped clean
7 Sit for a portrait
8 Actor Wallach
9 Circus animal
10 Vocally
11 CNN talk host
12 Vicinity
13 Rock star, to teens

18 __ Raton, FL
23 Merry escapade
25 Denny's competitor
26 Connery of film
28 Clutch
30 Norse god of war
31 Soft drink
32 Hammett hound
33 Meadows
34 *Mary Tyler Moore Show* star
38 Frying pans
39 Not as much
40 Soothe

42 Singer Adams
43 "Good heavens!"
46 Stay out of sight
47 Over again
49 Beasts of burden
51 Trucker's load
52 Bird sound
53 Chowder ingredient
54 Garden accessory
55 French cheese
57 Football linemen
60 Singer Garfunkel
61 MTV genre

★★ Three-for-One Word Search

Find the seven hidden words in each of the three diagrams, either across, down, or diagonally. A hint to each group of words is found above each diagram.

SUN ____

```
B R S Y T O F
J A E H T A B
I W G W I K E
L I R T O N H
L N O E Z L E
T G O S C X F
P D F Y A D S
```

____ MOON

```
O L Z T F A P
W L Y S D G A
E U W E N V P
H F U V N M E
U L C R J O R
B F L A H B H
N I T H Q P L
```

STAR ____

```
W A D S B V T
R E U N H B D
F I S H O I N
N O T A U R P
Z G R M U I F
S D I T K Q H
W A R S J G C
```

BETWEENER

What four-letter word belongs between the word at left and the word at right, so that the first and second word, and the second and third word, each form a common two-word phrase?

MOTOR __ __ __ __ FREE

bRAin BREAtHER
QUIPS ON COMPUTERS

There's perhaps no invention that's as convenient—and as utterly frustrating—as your personal computer. If ever you've experienced password problems, hard disk drama, or Internet annoyances, you'll empathize with these wise and wary words.

The first rule of intelligent tinkering is to save all the parts.

—PAUL EHRLICH

* * *

Never trust a computer you can't throw out a window.

—STEVE WOZNIAK

* * *

A computer lets you make more mistakes faster than any invention in human history—with the possible exceptions of handguns and tequila.

—MITCH RATLIFFE

* * *

My favorite thing about the Internet is that you get to go into the private world of real creeps without having to smell them.

—PENN JILLETTE

* * *

To err is human, but to really foul things up you need a computer.

—PAUL EHRLICH

* * *

To err is human—and to blame it on a computer is even more so.

—ROBERT ORBEN

I think computer viruses should count as life. I think it says something about human nature that the only form of life we have created so far is purely destructive. We've created life in our own image.

—STEPHEN HAWKING

* * *

The danger from computers is not that they will eventually get as smart as men, but we will meanwhile agree to meet them halfway.

—BERNARD AVISHAI

* * *

The real problem is not whether machines think but whether men do.

—B.F. SKINNER

* * *

The great thing about a computer notebook is that no matter how much you stuff into it, it doesn't get bigger or heavier.

—BILL GATES

* * *

The most likely way for the world to be destroyed, most experts agree, is by accident. That's where we come in; we're computer professionals. We cause accidents.

—NATHANIEL BORENSTEIN

★★ Line Drawing

Draw three straight lines, each from one edge of the square to another edge, so that there is the same amount of money in each of the four regions, and each region has a different combination of coins.

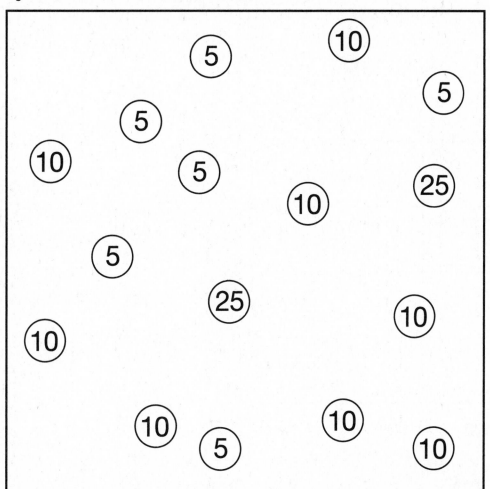

THREE AT A RHYME

Rearrange these letters to form three one-syllable words that rhyme.

A B E E F N N N R R R U Y

_____ _____ _____

★ ABC

Enter the letters A, B, and C into the diagram so that each row and column has exactly one A, one B, and one C. The letters outside the diagram indicate the first letter encountered, moving in the direction of the arrow. Keep in mind that after all the letters have been filled in, there will be one blank box in each row and column.

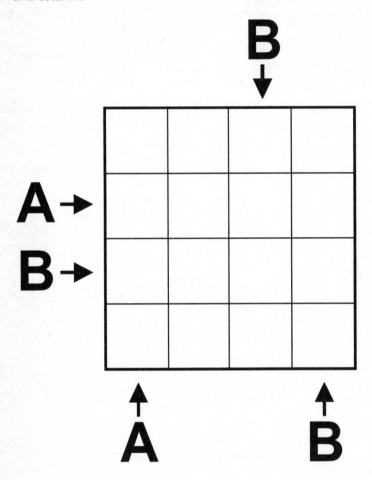

SOUND THINKING

We can think of three common uncapitalized words (one hyphenated) whose only consonant sounds are F, L, S, and F, in that order. How many can you think of?

_____   _____   _____

★ Basic Beverages by Gail Grabowski

ACROSS

1 Racetrack postings
5 '80s–'90s NBC drama
10 Small-size bed
14 Brazil neighbor
15 Scarlett's surname
16 Take risks
17 Mideast ruler
18 Part of USNA
19 Luminous heavenly body
20 Living-room piece
23 Finish
24 Bachelor parties
25 Cut off
27 Becomes less hot
30 Archer's sighting
33 Carnival offering
36 Catcher's glove
38 Liquid-Plumr competitor
39 Onassis' nickname
40 Garden bloom
42 Soft metal
43 U.S. Grant's foe
45 Far from polite
46 Give up rights to
47 Talked on and on
49 Year fraction
51 Port of Italy
53 Garbage
56 Good buddy
58 Saltine
62 "Oh my!"
64 __ Lama
65 Stay out of sight
66 Mislay
67 Open-mouthed
68 See 59 Down
69 Small plateau
70 Fender benders
71 Shut loudly

DOWN

1 Oil cartel
2 Audition tapes
3 Wander aimlessly
4 Rise, as a submarine
5 Wanting company
6 At the drop of __
7 Volcanic output
8 Many Riyadh residents
9 Billfold
10 Super Bowl scores, for short
11 D.C. hotel
12 Shah's land
13 Bookish one
21 Freudian subject
22 Escape from
26 Mess up
28 Deceitful one
29 Play a guitar lightly
31 Oklahoma city
32 Vocal quality
33 Actor Cooper
34 Vicinity
35 Opaque vase material
37 Commotion
40 Most high schoolers
41 Military guards
44 __ out a living
46 Latin dances
48 Gadget
50 Singing syllable
52 Traditional saying
54 Ability
55 Gossipy Hopper
56 Tropical tree
57 Lotion ingredient
59 With 68 Across, M*A*S*H actor
60 Cook or Hook: Abbr.
61 Paper purchase
63 Baltic or Bering

★ Looped Path

Draw a continuous, unbroken loop that passes through each of the red, blue, and white squares exactly once. Move from square to square in a straight line or by turning left or right, but never diagonally. You must alternate passing through red and blue squares, with any number of white squares in between.

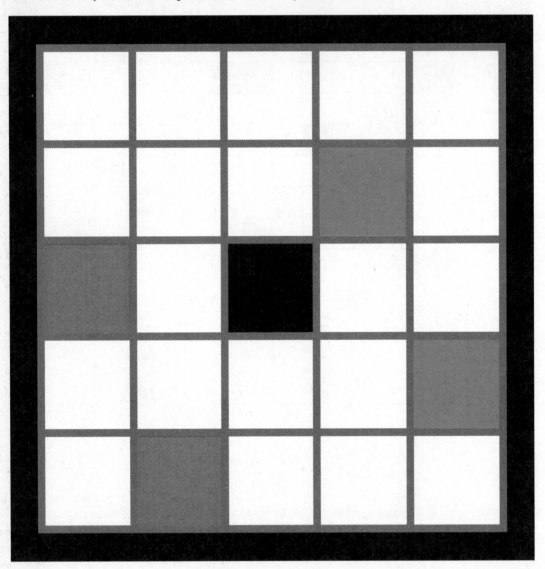

TWO-BY-FOUR

The eight letters in the word CHARMING can be rearranged to form a pair of common four-letter words in two different ways, if no four-letter word is repeated. Can you find both pairs of words?

— — — —   — — — —

— — — —   — — — —

★★ Presidential Jigsaw

The names of 25 U.S. presidents are arranged in jigsaw puzzle shapes in the diagram. Can you piece the puzzle together? One piece is shown to get you started.

ABRAHAM LINCOLN
BENJAMIN HARRISON
BILL CLINTON
CALVIN COOLIDGE
CHESTER ALAN ARTHUR
FRANKLIN PIERCE
GEORGE WASHINGTON
GEORGE W BUSH
GERALD FORD

GROVER CLEVELAND
HARRY S TRUMAN
HERBERT HOOVER
JAMES BUCHANAN
JAMES KNOX POLK
JIMMY CARTER
JOHN ADAMS
JOHN F KENNEDY
MARTIN VAN BUREN

RICHARD NIXON
RONALD REAGAN
THEODORE ROOSEVELT
~~THOMAS JEFFERSON~~
ULYSSES SIMPSON GRANT
WOODROW WILSON
ZACHARY TAYLOR

```
J A M G R O V W O O D R G E R A L B E N J
B S E L C R E C A L W O H A R F D N I M A
U C H E V E L A N V W I L Y R O R H A R R
A N A T H O M A D I N O S S T R D F R S I
N U L Y F E J S H N C O O A M U K N A O N
S E S S F E R R E G D I L N R I L I N P I
S I M P N O S B E E B I L L C C H E C R E
G N O S O O H T R N O T N I L R A J O H N
R A J A V E R J I M M J O H N D S M A D A
T N E M R E T R A C Y K F N I X O N C H E
A B S K N G E O R R O E N N E D Y R E T S
A R P X O B W E G A N Z A C H A R A L A N
H A O L K U S H D L R O L Y A T Y M A R A
L M T H E O D O R E A B N A V N I T R T H
I N C O O R E R N A G U R E N G E O R G U
N L O S E V E L T N O T G N I H S A W E R
```

TRANSDELETION

Delete one letter from the word ORNAMENTED and rearrange the rest, to get the two-word name of a well-known American university.

_____

★ Find the Ships

Determine the position of the 10 ships listed to the right of the diagram. The ships may be oriented either horizontally or vertically. A square with wavy lines indicates water and will not contain a ship. The numbers at the edge of the diagram indicate how many squares in that row or column contain parts of ships. When all 10 ships are correctly placed in the diagram, no two of them will touch each other, not even diagonally.

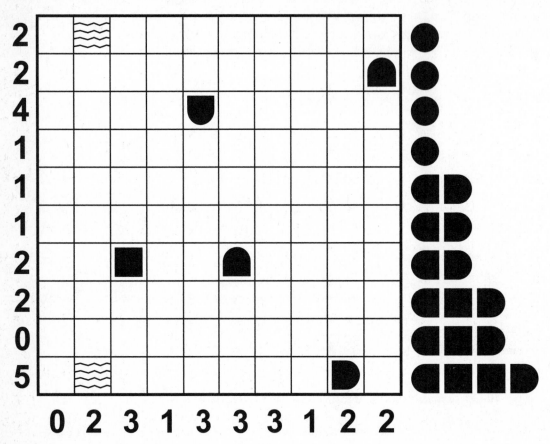

TONGUE TWISTER

From what language are all of these words derived:

HONCHO, KETCHUP, KOWTOW, and TYPHOON?

A) French   B) Chinese   C) Greek   D) Spanish

★★ Sudoku

Fill in the blank boxes so that every row, column, and 3x3 box contains all of the numbers 1 to 9.

1		5		7	9			
		6	4	1	3			5
	7		5	8		4		
3	6	1	9					
	8	4	3				6	9
		7		6		5		
					4		5	
4					2	9	7	3
6	5			3	8		4	

MIXAGRAMS

Each line contains a five-letter word and a four-letter word that have been mixed together (the order of the letters in each word has not been changed). Unmix the two words on each line and write them in the spaces provided. When you're done, find a two-part answer to the clue by reading down the letter columns in the answers.

CLUE: Part of marine life

D I C O U B E S T = _ _ _ _ _ + _ _ _ _

P E D A K O U B E = _ _ _ _ _ + _ _ _ _

B E A L M O I W D = _ _ _ _ _ + _ _ _ _

S U L P O A T E N = _ _ _ _ _ + _ _ _ _

★ Just Kidding by Sally R. Stein

ACROSS

1 Behaves
5 Corp. leaders
9 "Santa ___ Is Coming to Town"
14 Actress Elisabeth
15 Syringe, for short
16 Wall-calendar page
17 Sailors, slangily
18 Biblical paradise
19 Not very specific
20 Children
23 Caveman discovery
24 Remnant
25 Lawyer's customer
27 Racetrack alternative: Abbr.
28 Do an usher's job
30 One of the Redgrave sisters
33 Children
37 Ghost exclamation
38 Meara's partner
40 ___ de Janeiro
41 Children
43 Change for a twenty
44 Window parts
45 "So long!"
47 Quit, as one's job
50 Long-necked beast
54 Aussie birds
55 Children
58 The Odd Couple playwright
60 Hoity-toity one
61 Some nest eggs: Abbr.
62 Escape the pursuit of
63 Citrus fruit
64 Horse's hair
65 Used a word processor
66 Kitchen appliance
67 Moose relatives

DOWN

1 Fur magnate John Jacob
2 Rub the wrong way
3 Gangs' domains
4 Legislative meeting
5 Sweet kid
6 Chanteuse Gorme
7 Unbolt
8 Selection for 6 Down
9 905, in old Rome
10 Doing nothing
11 Actress Harmon
12 Road-test maneuver
13 Piece of paper
21 Summer clock setting in L.A.
22 Act 1, ___ 1
26 Untrustworthy sort
28 Tennis star Monica
29 Electrified fish
30 JFK successor
31 "___ Are My Sunshine"
32 Election Day mo.
33 Linoleum alternative
34 Poetic "before"
35 ___ Tin Tin
36 Distress signal
38 Unexpected impediment
39 Like a honky-tonk piano
42 TV series segment
43 4 p.m., in Britain
45 British Parliament tower bell
46 Decade parts: Abbr.
47 Move back to 0, perhaps
48 Poet Dickinson
49 Give a recap of
50 Grimm character
51 Not tame
52 Candid
53 Tee preceders
56 Capital of Norway
57 Center of higher educ.
59 Beatty of Superman

★★ Circular Reasoning

Connect all of the circles by drawing a single continuous line through every square of the diagram. All right-angle turns of your line must alternate between boxes containing a circle and boxes not containing a circle. You must make a right-angle turn out of every square that contains a circle. Your line must end in the same square that it begins, and it cannot enter any square more than once.

COUNTDOWN

Inserting plus signs and minus signs, as many as necessary, in between the digits from 9 to 1 below, create a series of additions and subtractions whose final answer is 40. Any digits without a sign between them are to be grouped together as a single number.

$$9 \quad 8 \quad 7 \quad 6 \quad 5 \quad 4 \quad 3 \quad 2 \quad 1 \quad = \quad 40$$

★ Triad Split Decisions

In this clueless crossword puzzle, each answer consists of two words whose spellings are the same, except for the consecutive letters given. All answers are common words; no phrases or hyphenated or capitalized words are used. Some of the clues may have more than one solution, but there is only one word pair that will correctly link up with all the other word pairs.

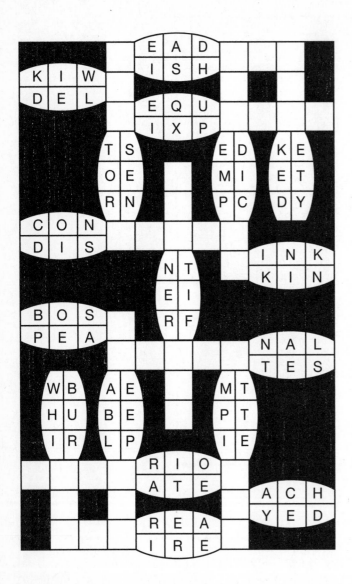

ADDITION SWITCH

Switch the positions of two of the digits in the incorrect sum at right, to get a correct sum.

```
  3 7 2
+ 5 6 8
-------
  6 4 3
```

★★ 123

Fill in the diagram so that each rectangular piece has one each of the numbers 1, 2, and 3, under these rules: 1) No two adjacent squares, horizontally or vertically, can have the same number. 2) Each completed row and column of the diagram will have an equal number of 1s, 2s, and 3s.

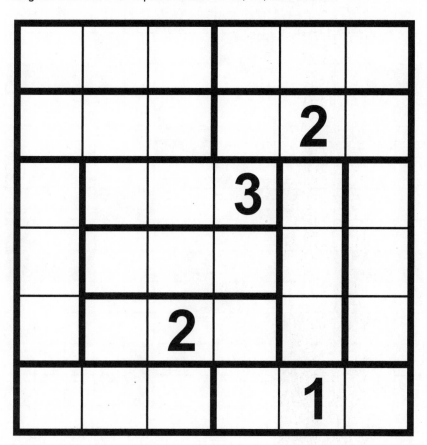

BETWEENER

What four-letter word belongs between the word at left and the word at right, so that the first and second word, and the second and third word, each form a common two-word phrase?

COUNTRY __ __ __ __ SODA

★ In the Jungle by Gail Grabowski

ACROSS

1 Craving
5 Golf hazard
9 Jeans fabric
14 D.C. 100: Abbr.
15 Country singer McEntire
16 Rub out
17 Dice throw
19 Buckets
20 Put down a new floor
21 Bygone airline
23 Pasture
24 Ran into
25 Stein beverage
26 Insincere show of sorrow
33 "__ have to?"
34 Peas holder
35 Bizarre
36 Stalemate
39 Run longer than expected
41 Film critic Roger
42 __-mo replay
43 Cot or crib
44 Mischievous behavior
49 Lowly worker
50 Bounding main
51 Doctor's org.
54 Wise bird
55 "Okay with me!"
59 Hair stylist's shop
61 Spring bloom
64 Teheran resident
65 Goofs up
66 Part of EMT: Abbr.
67 Balance-sheet plus
68 Move suddenly
69 Golfer Ballesteros

DOWN

1 Khrushchev's country: Abbr.

2 Actress Russo
3 Small fly
4 Mukluks wearer
5 Lofty branches
6 The Bridge of San Luis __
7 Lincoln's nickname
8 Subdued color
9 Went away
10 Period of note
11 Finger feature
12 Spot in the ocean
13 Elevated land formation
18 Home utility: Abbr.

22 Very small
25 Contractor's proposal
26 Small jazz band
27 Become more mature
28 Female deer
29 Wriggly swimmer
30 Many Middle Easterners
31 Formal ceremonies
32 Gardener's purchase
33 Per __ (daily)
37 Noah's creation
38 Hurry up
39 Aboveground railroads

40 Most raucous
42 Daily riser
45 Type of evergreen
46 Ran away
47 Close by
48 Soaring birds
51 Largest continent
52 Fourth planet
53 "Woe is me!"
56 Icy coating
57 Height: Abbr.
58 Brontë governess
60 A fourth of four
62 Nest-egg letters
63 Canine warning

★ Islands

Shade in some of the white squares in the diagram with "water," so that each remaining white box is part of an island. Each island will contain exactly one numbered square, indicating how many squares that island contains. Each island is separated from the other islands by water but may touch other islands diagonally. All water is connected, but there are no 2x2 regions of water in the diagram.

		2		
1		**2**		**3**

SOUND THINKING

We can think of two common uncapitalized words whose only consonant sounds are T, D, and R, in that order. Can you think of them both?

_____   _____

★ Circle Links

Find the three circles, linked to each other, that could be lifted away from all the others.

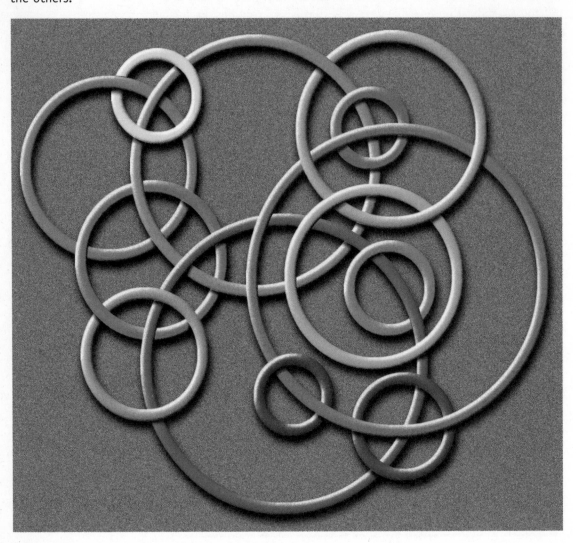

INITIAL REACTION

The "equation" below contains the initials of words that will make it correct, forming a numerical fact. Solve the equation by supplying the missing words.

9 = J. of the S.C. _____

★★ Elementary

Find the 41 chemical elements hidden in the diagram, either across, down, or diagonally.

```
O M N O C I L I S M M
X U C B A R I U M U A
Y N O O L S E U I I C
G I B R I U I C B M T
E T A O F P N M I D I
N A L K O E C U S A N
O L T R R M H I M C I
N P U W N U L L U J U
E E A Z I I O U T G M
X L G V U N R H H C L
O N L O M I I T I E V
Y O M D R E N N K A B
G R L U N T E C N B P
M O U O I S I A K A O
G B G C R N D N L H S
C R E A R I I L Q U M
A H R R U E A M L G I
R L R M Y D M P F O U
B X C O I L H I T A M
O N F U M U L A E U B
N A M E R I C I U M M
F R A N C I U M U O U
S A M A R I U M P M I
B R O M I N E M Y R B
R E V L I S I L M E R
M U I R U L L E T P E
N E T S G N U T C P T
M U I M L O H S D O T
M U I C L A C W D C Y
```

COMMON SENSE

What three-letter word can be found in the dictionary definitions of all of these words:

BUSINESS CARD, MULTITASKING, PUBLIC SERVANT, and TRAVEL TIME?

— — —

★ Handyman Special by Norma Steinberg

ACROSS

1 Etching need
5 Hitter's turn
10 *Damn Yankees* character
14 Ranch visitor
15 "__ you are!"
16 Heroic tale
17 Precision marchers
19 Express one's anger
20 Author Tolstoy
21 Electrified particles
22 Motes
24 Old Testament heroine
26 Vocal quaver
28 Actress Paquin
30 Donkey sounds
34 Smile broadly
37 Therefore
39 Accounting entry
40 Grad
41 Gridiron measures
43 __ mater
44 Contract addendum
46 Witches' creation
47 Corporate div.
48 Kenya's capital
50 Identical
52 Parking spot
54 As of now
58 Says
61 Art __
63 Cambridge sch.
64 Electrical cord
65 Wasn't fooled by
68 "__ Want for Christmas ..."
69 Cream of the crop
70 Sailing, perhaps
71 Storefront sign
72 Prongs
73 *Show Boat* composer

DOWN

1 Confuse
2 Makes all better
3 Dostoyevsky title character
4 Pa. neighbor
5 Member of the bar
6 At that time
7 Beauty's love
8 Supply with weapons
9 Entertainer O'Shea
10 Sensible
11 Oil grp.
12 Connect
13 Performs in a play
18 Mortgage, e.g.
23 Implored
25 *Show Boat* lyricist
27 __ Scholar
29 Koran's language
31 Competent
32 Weakling
33 Immediately, in the OR
34 Rural building
35 Director Kazan
36 Mercedes rival
38 "Stay away from my dog food!"
42 Decorator's samples
45 Lariat
49 Breed of hound
51 Secure in a berth
53 Telejournalist Newman
55 Tickle
56 Woods of golf
57 Actor Hawke
58 Ugly Duckling, eventually
59 Scrabble letter
60 Singer Guthrie
62 Diminutive suffix
66 __ Baba
67 Desk wood

★ One-Way Streets

The diagram represents a pattern of streets. A and B are parking spaces, and the black squares are stores. Find the route that starts at A, passes through all stores exactly once, and ends at B. Arrows indicate one-way traffic for that block only. No block or intersection may be entered more than once.

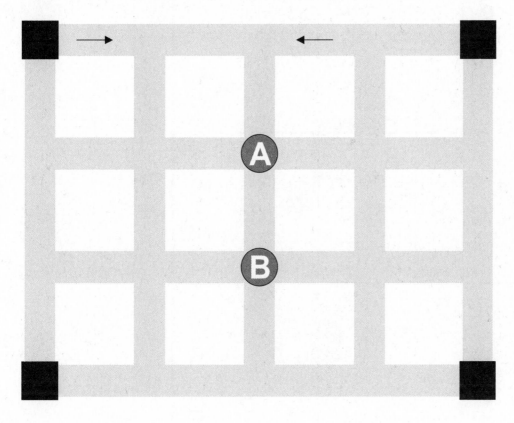

TWO-BY-FOUR

The eight letters in the word MAGICIAN can be rearranged to form a pair of common four-letter words in only one way. Can you find the two words?

— — — —   — — — —

★★ Hyper-Sudoku

Fill in the blank boxes so that every row, column, 3x3 box, *and* each of the four 3x3 gray regions contains all of the numbers 1 to 9.

1		6	5		4	8	9	
	8	3	1			5		
5				3		4		2
				8		9		1
		1	9		3	6	2	
9	3		2			7		8
	1	5	7		9			
	6	9						5
	4						7	9

TELEPHONE TRIOS

1	ABC 2	DEF 3
GHI 4	JKL 5	MNO 6
PRS 7	TUV 8	WXY 9
*	O	#

Using the numbers and letters on a standard telephone, what three seven-letter words from the same category can be formed from these telephone numbers?

782-3486   _ _ _ _ _ _ _

268-8243   _ _ _ _ _ _ _

626-7466   _ _ _ _ _ _ _

★★ Star Search

Find the stars that are hidden in some of the blank squares. The numbered squares indicate how many stars are hidden in the squares adjacent to them (including diagonally). There is never more than one star in any square.

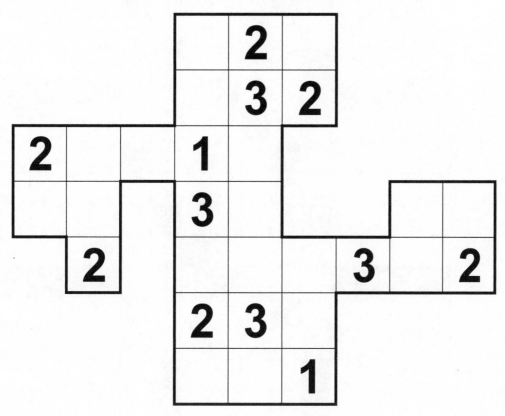

SUDOKU SUM

Without repeating any digits, complete the sum at right, by filling one digit in each of the five blanks.

```
      3  7  8
  + _  1  _
  _  _  4
```

★ Clothes to You by Sally R. Stein

ACROSS

1 Sahara caravan beast
6 Fresh talk
10 Oyster relative
14 Make a speech
15 Part of the foot
16 Sector
17 In charge, in a household
20 All the __ (nevertheless)
21 Make simpler
22 Lobbies for
23 Word on some towels
24 Newsman Rather
26 Wedding locale
30 Advertising addressed to "Occupant"
35 *Bonanza* or *Stagecoach*
36 President James K. __
37 *Born Free* lioness
38 Broadway rituals
41 Do manuscript work
42 Bed-and-breakfasts
43 Brings under control
44 Plot summary
46 Spanish explorer
47 Author Deighton
48 Had been
49 Sneeze sound
53 Exercise establishments
55 Money in Marseilles
59 "Be patient!"
62 Mental picture
63 Considerably
64 Window covering
65 Singer Carter
66 Renown
67 Campfire residue

DOWN

1 Dairy animals
2 Neck of the woods
3 Polite term of address
4 Raison d'__
5 Hawaiian garland
6 Epic stories
7 Patron of the __
8 Timetables
9 That lady
10 Business bigwig
11 Yearn (for)
12 Poker-game starter
13 Untidy place
18 Astronaut Armstrong
19 Young hoodlum
23 Word on some towels
25 Pop singer Paul
26 Secret messages
27 Laurel's partner
28 Stayed home for dinner
29 Green sauce
30 __ Hopkins University
31 Butte relatives
32 Davy Crockett's last stand
33 Small spot of land
34 Lariat
36 Florida or Iberia
39 Increase
40 Traveler's paths: Abbr.
45 Ruse
46 Short race
48 Squander
49 Similar (to)
50 Sign away
51 Sock part
52 Whitish gem
54 High-school dance
55 Slips up
56 Nevada neighbor
57 Lariat
58 Small bills
60 Clumsy person
61 Boise locale: Abbr.

★★ ABC

Enter the letters A, B, and C into the diagram so that each row and column has exactly one A, one B, and one C. The letters outside the diagram indicate the first letter encountered, moving in the direction of the arrow. Keep in mind that after all the letters have been filled in, there will be one blank box in each row and column.

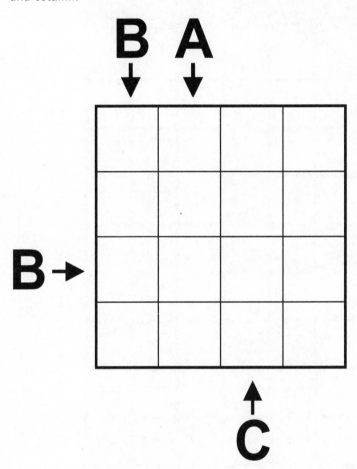

AND SO ON

Unscramble the letters in the phrase MOAT CUES, to form two words that are part of a common phrase that has the word AND between them.

_____ and _____

★ Alternating Tiles

Starting in the upper left, alternate between yellow and red tiles, and end in the middle yellow tile at right. You may move horizontally or vertically from tile to tile, but never diagonally.

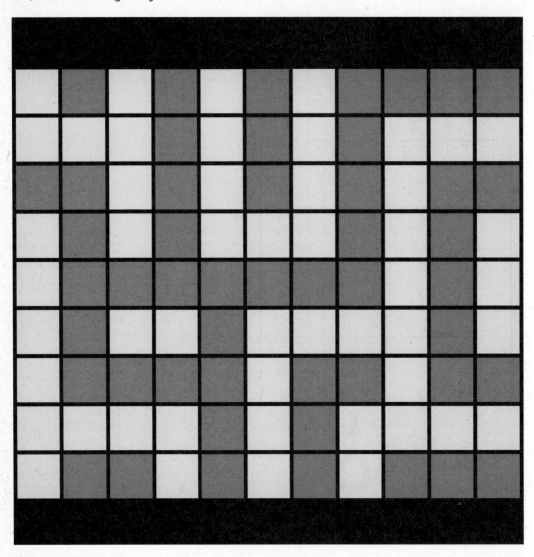

BETWEENER

What four-letter word belongs between the word at left and the word at right, so that the first and second word, and the second and third word, each form a common two-word phrase?

EGG __ __ __ __ CALL

★★ Sudoku

Fill in the blank boxes so that every row, column, and 3x3 box contains all of the numbers 1 to 9.

6				7	9			
2	7			5	8	4	1	3
	1				2			
	5	2		1			7	
3			8				4	2
	4		7					8
1	9	3				6		
					7	2	9	

MIXAGRAMS

Each line contains a five-letter word and a four-letter word that have been mixed together (the order of the letters in each word has not been changed). Unmix the two words on each line and write them in the spaces provided. When you're done, find a two-part answer to the clue by reading down the letter columns in the answers.

CLUE: Astronomical rarity

S E B R I A B M E = _ _ _ _ _ + _ _ _ _

C O V U E L T O D = _ _ _ _ _ + _ _ _ _

S P O T R U L O M = _ _ _ _ _ + _ _ _ _

A R O B L E A R N = _ _ _ _ _ + _ _ _ _

★ Put on the Dog by Gail Grabowski

ACROSS

1 Be concerned
5 Topnotch
9 Call up
14 "Oh my!"
15 Hawaiian island
16 Vessel carrying petroleum
17 German shepherd of TV
19 Passover meal
20 Agree (to)
21 Animal skin
23 Football measurements: Abbr.
24 Giggling sound
25 Spaghetti topping
27 Ice-cream drinks
31 Dentists' tools
34 Utter
37 Slugger Sammy
38 Sell, as merchandise
39 Australian bird
40 Super-intelligent movie mutt
42 Zsa Zsa's sister
43 *Jeopardy!* contestants
46 Birch or beech
48 Salesperson, for short
49 Observe
50 Desirable quality
52 "When pigs fly!"
54 Actress Rene
58 Furniture wood
60 Playwright Levin et al.
62 Kitchen implement
63 From the Orient
65 Jack London's wolf/dog mix
67 Yard barrier
68 Old stories
69 *Born Free* lioness
70 Wise advisors
71 Leak slowly
72 High schooler

DOWN

1 Jeweler's measure
2 Ralph Kramden's wife
3 Salad dressing flavor
4 Regard highly
5 Tibia or clavicle
6 Consume
7 Send off a package
8 Ditties
9 Body stance
10 Hasten
11 Labrador in a Disney film
12 Requirement
13 Goes astray
18 Notions
22 Scottish boys
26 Spy org.
28 Seafood selection
29 Mao __-tung
30 North Pole resident
32 Dwell
33 Ginger cookie
34 Aquatic mammal
35 Playground reply
36 Sergeant Preston's Alaskan husky
41 Eleventh graders, for short
44 Supplement, with "out"
45 Steep valleys
47 Very strange
51 Miss Muffet's seat
53 Soul singer Lou
55 No longer fresh
56 Sight or smell
57 Church instrument
58 Bunglers
59 Under sail
61 Sandal, e.g.
62 Short distance
64 Expert
66 Make angry

★★ Line Drawing

Draw two straight lines, each from one edge of the square to another edge, so that the five words in each of the three regions go together in some way.

MAROON   CARMINE   RUBY

WINE   CHERRY

JADE

OLIVE

LIME

PISTACHIO

EMERALD

NAVY

SAPPHIRE

PEACOCK

AZURE   COBALT

THREE AT A RHYME

Rearrange these letters to form three one-syllable words that rhyme.

A B E E E F F F G I L R

_____   _____   _____.

★ Find the Ships

Determine the position of the 10 ships listed to the right of the diagram. The ships may be oriented either horizontally or vertically. A square with wavy lines indicates water and will not contain a ship. The numbers at the edge of the diagram indicate how many squares in that row or column contain parts of ships. When all 10 ships are correctly placed in the diagram, no two of them will touch each other, not even diagonally.

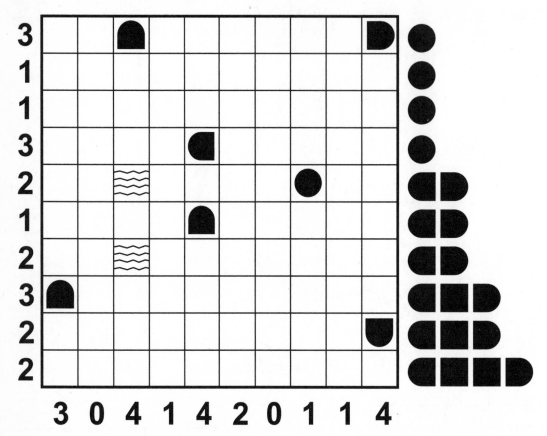

3 1 1 3 2 1 2 3 2 2

3 0 4 1 4 2 0 1 1 4

CLUELESS CROSSWORD

Complete the crossword with common uncapitalized seven-letter words, based entirely on the letters already filled in for you.

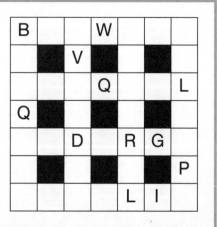

★★ Circular Reasoning

Connect all of the circles by drawing a single continuous line through every square of the diagram. All right-angle turns of your line must alternate between boxes containing a circle and boxes not containing a circle. You must make a right-angle turn out of every square that contains a circle. Your line must end in the same square that it begins, and it cannot enter any square more than once.

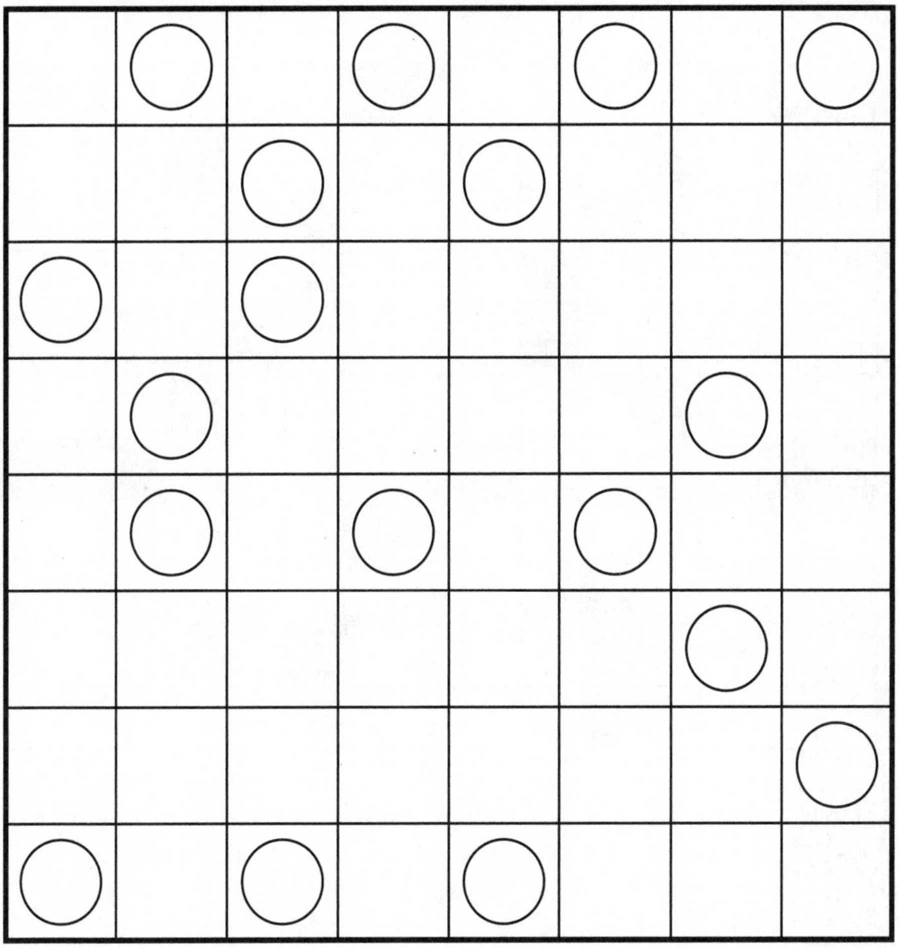

SOUND THINKING

We can think of five common uncapitalized words whose only consonant sounds are B, G, and L, in that order. How many can you think of?

_____   _____   _____

_____   _____

★ At the Beach by Shirley Soloway

ACROSS

1 French hat
6 High cards
10 Make a trade
14 Painter's pigment
15 Laotian neighbor
16 Domesticate
17 Sailor's time off
19 On the summit of
20 Trig ratio
21 Antsy
23 *The __ of Night* (soap opera)
25 Cake layer
26 '80s TV alien
29 He'll put you to sleep
32 Hit the slopes
35 Common condiment
37 Former Italian coin
38 Henry VIII's royal house
40 Undeniable evidence
42 Rummy variety
43 Pollen bit
44 A former Mrs. Trump
45 Convene
47 Long-necked bird
48 Tabby or calico
49 Had an easy time
52 Wind dir.
53 More than impressed
55 Irritated state
57 Having the best manners
61 Rules of conduct
65 Mail-chute opening
66 Use a Web browser
68 Subway rider's hope
69 Elitist
70 Wear away
71 Stage award
72 __ spumante
73 Extend a subscription

DOWN

1 Pear variety
2 Resound
3 Greek letters
4 Spooky
5 Current fashions
6 Consumed
7 Burn somewhat
8 Roof overhang
9 Afternoon nap
10 No longer fresh
11 Dilutes
12 "Famous" cookie guy
13 Enlivens, with "up"
18 Within the law
22 Colors slightly
24 Puzzle or riddle
26 Savory jelly
27 Young insect
28 Raise funds, perhaps
30 Helps with the dishes
31 Impressionist works
33 Islamic sacred text
34 Actress Dunne
36 Freight weight
39 Postal Service alternative
41 Gem surface
46 Group principle
50 Ukrainian seaport
51 Flustered state
54 Verbally clever
56 In that spot
57 "Hey, you!"
58 Table spread
59 Centers of solar systems
60 Moderate gait
62 Let __ (tell about)
63 Formally surrender
64 Slow-cooked meal
67 Most Wanted List org.

★★ Sets of Three

Group all of the symbols into sets of three, with each set having either all the same shape or all the same color. The symbols in each set must all be connected to each other by a common horizontal or vertical side.

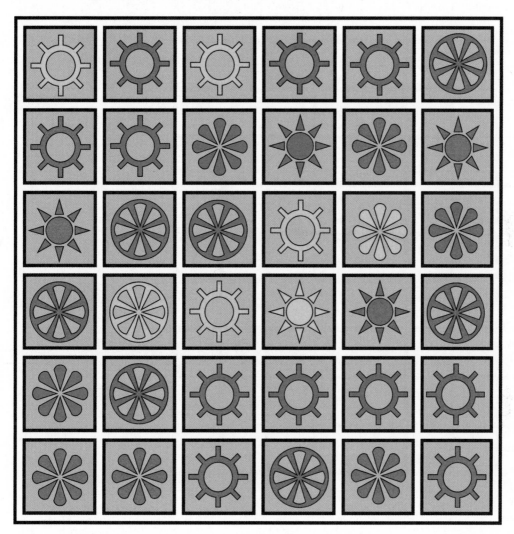

CITY SEARCH

Use the letters in WORCESTER to form common uncapitalized six-letter words. Plurals or verbs ending in S aren't allowed. We found nine words. How many can you find?

— — — — — —   — — — — — —   — — — — — —

— — — — — —   — — — — — —   — — — — — —

— — — — — —   — — — — — —   — — — — — —

★★ 123

Fill in the diagram so that each rectangular piece has one each of the numbers 1, 2, and 3, under these rules: 1) No two adjacent squares, horizontally or vertically, can have the same number. 2) Each completed row and column of the diagram will have an equal amount of 1s, 2s, and 3s.

TRANSDELETION

Delete one letter from the word ORIENTING and rearrange the rest, to get a chemical element.

_____

★★ Islands

Shade in some of the white squares in the diagram with "water," so that each remaining white box is part of an island. Each island will contain exactly one numbered square, indicating how many squares that island contains. Each island is separated from the other islands by water but may touch other islands diagonally. All water is connected, but there are no 2x2 regions of water in the diagram.

3				
1				**4**
		2	**1**

TWO-BY-FOUR

The eight letters in the word PHARMACY can be rearranged to form a pair of common four-letter words in two different ways. Can you find both pairs of words?

_ _ _ _   _ _ _ _

_ _ _ _   _ _ _ _

★ Feeling Blue by Gail Grabowski

ACROSS

1 City official
6 Eastern Europeans
11 Stew cooker
14 Got up
15 Bother continuously
16 Yoko __
17 Queen Elizabeth, Prince Charles, etc.
19 Clever one
20 True-blue
21 Purple fruit
22 Female deer
23 Wineglass feature
25 Final part
27 Qt. fractions
30 Company VIP
32 Endure
33 Had a crush on
35 Verbal exam
37 Take a card
40 Cameo stone
41 Stockholm resident
42 Traditional knowledge
43 Stinging insect
44 Actor Morales
45 Lubricate again
46 Snowman's eye, maybe
48 City near Phoenix
50 Angry
51 Dinner-plate garnish
54 Part of UCLA: Abbr.
56 Menu phrase
57 Battery fluid
59 Tatum of *Paper Moon*
62 Absorb, with "up"
63 Bridge builder
66 Fill in __ blank
67 *Singin' in the Rain* star
68 Togetherness
69 Teacup handle
70 Confuse
71 High-strung

DOWN

1 Do damage to
2 GI offense
3 Spool-like toy
4 Gives the nod to
5 Linked by blood
6 Large body of water
7 Item on an end table
8 At an angle
9 Worth a lot
10 Frustrate
11 Place to touch up makeup
12 Pizza topping
13 Hauled
18 Show off, as muscles
24 Feline sounds
26 Soup server
27 Farm tool
28 Singer Turner
29 Lofty building
31 Dairy product
34 Montreal baseballers
36 Farewell, in France
38 Opera solo
39 Actress Tuesday
41 Chose
45 Canceled baseball game
47 49th state
49 Winter precipitation
51 Scrapbooking need
52 Hawaiian greeting
53 Triangular road sign
55 Captain Nemo creator
58 Wooded valley
60 Similar (to)
61 __ go (releases)
64 Caustic substance
65 Sandwich bread

★★ Color Squares

Enter the maze at top right, pass through all the color squares once and then exit the maze at bottom right, all without retracing your path. You must pass through the color squares in this order: blue, red, yellow, blue, red, yellow, blue, red, yellow.

ADDITION SWITCH

Switch the positions of two of the digits in the incorrect sum at right, to get a correct sum.

$$\begin{array}{r} 6\;1\;9 \\ +\;2\;1\;4 \\ \hline 3\;8\;3 \end{array}$$

★★ Split Decisions

In this clueless crossword puzzle, each answer consists of two words whose spellings are the same, except for the consecutive letters given. All answers are common words; no phrases or hyphenated or capitalized words are used. Some of the clues may have more than one solution, but there is only one word pair that will correctly link up with all the other word pairs.

COMMON SENSE

What four-letter word can be found in the dictionary definitions of all of these words:

TELEPHONE BOOTH, AHOY, DEMAND, and WHIPPOORWILL?

— — — —

★ Hyper-Sudoku

Fill in the blank boxes so that every row, column, 3x3 box, *and* each of the four 3x3 gray regions contains all of the numbers 1 to 9.

	2		3		8		9	1
1	7	9		2	5	3		
	3			4		2		6
3		5						
	6	1				4	5	9
	5						6	
		4	5	7				3
8	1			3		7	2	5

MIXAGRAMS

Each line contains a five-letter word and a four-letter word that have been mixed together (the order of the letters in each word has not been changed). Unmix the two words on each line and write them in the spaces provided. When you're done, find a two-part answer to the clue by reading down the letter columns in the answers.

CLUE: Lob, for instance

D U C H E M B E R = _ _ _ _ _ + _ _ _ _

C R O I F D A L E = _ _ _ _ _ + _ _ _ _

B A G O R W E E L = _ _ _ _ _ + _ _ _ _

T H O R E P E A L = _ _ _ _ _ + _ _ _ _

★ Lion Around by Sally R. Stein

ACROSS

1 Last but not __
6 Crunchy sandwiches, for short
10 *Herr*'s wife
14 Eskimo dwelling
15 *Star Wars* princess
16 Lubricates
17 Frames of mind
18 Senior citizens' org.
19 Flying saucers, for example
20 Shade of gray
21 Newsroom trainee
24 Worship from __
26 Close, as a window
27 Butte relative
29 Hoopsters' grp.
32 Cornell University locale
36 Prefix for violet
38 Video-game name
40 AMA members
41 *Great Gatsby* decade
44 Likely (to)
45 "Ring around the __ ..."
46 Gaggle member
47 Ogle
49 Digital recordings
51 Helper: Abbr.
52 Reverberate
54 Alan of *M*A*S*H*
56 One's child, often
61 Periodical, for short
64 H. __ Perot
65 Ancient Roman emperor
66 Germany's major river
68 Butter alternative
69 Neighbor of Nebr.
70 Rarin' to go
71 Bend, as muscles
72 Plumlike fruit
73 Author Harriet Beecher __

DOWN

1 Capital of Peru
2 Self-images
3 Hawaii nickname
4 Outfield material
5 Puccini opera
6 Tell everything
7 Shakespearean king
8 Station wagon's wheels
9 Blue gemstone
10 July holiday
11 Fissure
12 Lotion ingredient
13 Cold War letters
22 Coffee brewer
23 Hike or picnic
25 Costar of 54 Across
27 Large painting
28 Take the honey and run
30 Skycap's concerns
31 Storage room
33 Fernando's friendly farewell
34 Salad vegetable
35 Balance-sheet entry
37 Hotshot pilot
39 More than impressed
42 Polite turndown
43 Frog relative
48 Boston baseballers
50 __ Paulo, Brazil
53 Ryan or Tatum
55 Ancient stringed instruments
56 Coll. teacher
57 Dice toss
58 Conversation filler
59 First James Bond film
60 San __, CA
62 All over again
63 *Pretty Woman* actor
67 At the drop of a __

★★ C as in "Cat"

Find all these words and phrases associated with cats hidden in the diagram in various C shapes. One "C" is shown to get you started.

```
T O M O H Z S P M E N P U T E S P
U G P E W G O C T H A U M X C E R
S E R Z A U L L T I E S U O G W D
T E R W L G N I R I K D A J N N X
N A L R L Q A R E H K G R Z E I G
G U H E Z I K M T L Y U U P M A Q
N W L S T A C A D T A C A R M T S
O E B F N L F H D G J L D O R E J
B T G D U Q R R K U C L G T O A C
D D K K F O H S B L S N O C T K E
S O O F R F Y T E R E D Y A N E R
J J F I T Y H A E N O A I V T I P
I U S Q H B E B K P Y L I L T Z B
V A O X R A I R S V F A C S Y I L
X T I V J P W N F I H W M I H C O
V O Y R U C N I N A A N C R E T M
V N E A C E K G C M T S R S L U B
I C L G E L H O S R Y Y I C W O T
L L I I B I X F R A I B T Y X Q J
R E F C O Q V E S A Y S R O R Y W
```

ANGORA
BENGAL
BIRMAN
CALICO
CATERWAUL
CATNIP
CATTERIES
COLLAR
COUGAR
CUDDLY
CURIOSITY
FELINE
FLUFFY
FOOD BOWLS
~~GINGER~~
HIMALAYAN
HUNTER
JAGUAR
KITTEN
LITTER
MOUSER
NINE LIVES
OCELOT
SHORTHAIR
SLEEPY
STRAYS
STROKE
TERRITORY
WHISKERED

TONGUE TWISTER

From what language are all of these words derived:

BRANDY, FURLOUGH, WALRUS, and YACHT?

A) Dutch B) Japanese C) Italian D) Scottish

bRAiN BREATHEr
TOMATO TRICKS

Do you love America's favorite vegetable, which is actually a fruit? Here are surprising ways to make the most of this red, saucy gem!

Store tomatoes at room temperature.

Ripe, juicy, just-picked tomatoes have a rich, vibrant taste and texture. Putting them in the refrigerator will completely ruin this texture, and turn them into mealy, tasteless versions of their former glory. Keep tomatoes in the pantry in a basket so that air can circulate around them.

Capture the flavor of tomatoes at their peak.

Our forebears often canned tomatoes for future use, but canning takes a long time and makes a big mess. Instead, try freezing tomatoes: "Just cut out the tough part of the core, put the whole tomatoes on a baking sheet and in the freezer," writes Jyl Steinback, author of *The Busy Mom's Slow Cooker Cookbook*. After they're frozen, transfer them to a plastic zipper bag and put them back into the freezer. Use them in recipes for any cooked dish.

Avoid crushed and ground canned tomatoes.

They're often packed in poor-quality tomato paste that has a metallic aftertaste.

Use whole canned tomatoes instead. If you're making sauce in a hurry and don't have time to cook down all that juice, just pour it off and save it. And instead of cutting up the whole tomatoes, just break them up with your hands or mash them with a wooden spoon as you add them to the sauce.

Keep the tomato seeds and skin.

A sauce with peels and seeds in it—horrors! That's what some people think, and they're entitled to their opinion. But it's all a matter of taste. The skin and seeds both contribute a great deal to the flavor of a tomato sauce. Another sauce tip: When you've tasted one tomato, you haven't tasted them all. Different varieties have different flavors, and even a single tomato has several aspects to its character. It can be sweet, sour, and salty, all at the same time. Different spices will bring out the fruit's different facets, too: Basil, chives, sweet peppers, and even mint will bring out sweetness. Wine, citrus, capers, and vinegars will bring out the sour. The salty aspect will respond to anchovies, olives, capers, and cured meats.

★★ One-Way Streets

The diagram represents a pattern of streets. P's are parking spaces, and the black squares are stores. Find the route that starts at a parking space, passes through all stores exactly once, and ends at the other parking space. Arrows indicate one-way traffic for that block only. No block or intersection may be entered more than once.

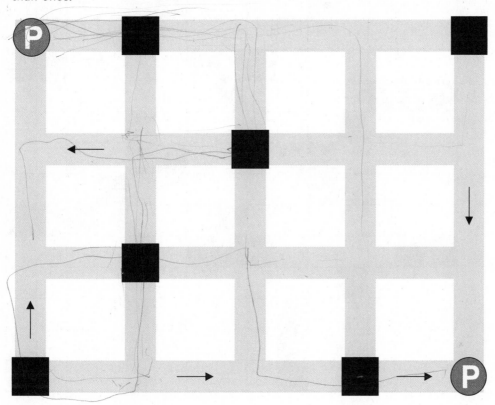

TRANSDELETION

Delete one letter from the word SHOWERING and rearrange the rest, to get the last name of an American composer.

_____

★ Materialization by Gail Grabowski

ACROSS

1 Easter entrées
5 Shade sources
9 Army officer
14 Author Wiesel
15 Ark builder
16 Music drama
17 "__ of your business!"
18 Have the courage
19 Annual Kentucky horserace
20 Very light dessert
23 U-turn from NNW
24 Less difficult
25 Author __ Stanley Gardner
27 Thomas Hardy heroine
29 Riled
32 Taxpayer ID
35 Abhor
37 Land measure
38 Designer Cassini
40 Amazed exclamation
41 Capitol feature
42 Fixed charge
43 "That's the truth!"
46 Armed conflict
47 Smallish sleeping spot
49 Open-handed hit
51 Close by
52 Fully ready
56 __-tac-toe
58 Carnival confection
62 Fragrance
64 Not straight
65 Something to do
66 "Ship of the desert"
67 Stuff to excess
68 Shoe stretcher
69 Bell sound
70 Egg on
71 Snakelike swimmers

DOWN

1 From now on
2 Luau greeting
3 Short skirts
4 Believe it proper
5 Support, as a candidate
6 Homebuyer's aid
7 __ Antony
8 Mets' stadium
9 Contemporary
10 Chimp or gorilla
11 Dairy-farm beast
12 Globes
13 Comedienne Martha
21 Provide dinner for
22 Lois Lane coworker
26 Laundry measure
28 Got (up)
29 Campsite residue
30 Author Bombeck
31 Stag or doe
32 Classify
33 Shredded side dish
34 Bottom line, in business
36 Very long time
39 Autry of oaters
43 Medal recipient
44 Like some handwriting
45 After-shower powder
48 Mrs. Bogart
50 Nebraska river
53 Trap
54 '50s Ford
55 Youngsters
56 Bulletin-board item
57 Teheran's country
59 Cookbook amt.
60 Rip
61 "I'm __ your tricks!"
63 Brooks or Tormé

★★ Think Straight

Enter the grid at the right edge between the two black squares, pass through the four yellow squares, then leave the grid somewhere at the top. You may travel only horizontally or vertically in a straight line, and may turn only to avoid passing through a black square. It is okay to pass through a square more than once.

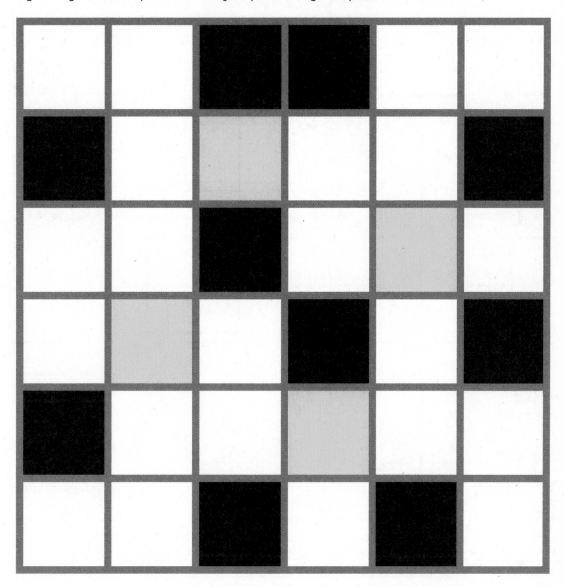

THREE OF A KIND

Find the three hidden words in the sentence that, read in order, go together in some way.

A toxic, horrid ether ails one of the ward's patients.

★★ Star Search

Find the stars that are hidden in some of the blank squares. The numbered squares indicate how many stars are hidden in the squares adjacent to them (including diagonally). There is never more than one star in any square.

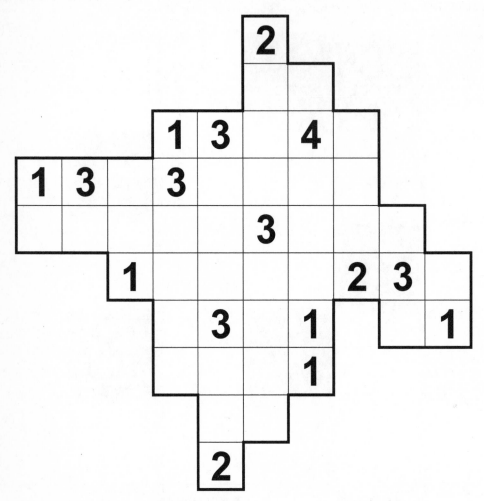

TELEPHONE TRIOS

Using the numbers and letters on a standard telephone, what three seven-letter words from the same category can be formed from these telephone numbers?

738-3683   _ _ _ _ _ _ _

227-4825   _ _ _ _ _ _ _

365-5277   _ _ _ _ _ _ _

★★ Triad Split Decisions

In this clueless crossword puzzle, each answer consists of two words whose spellings are the same, except for the consecutive letters given. All answers are common words; no phrases or hyphenated or capitalized words are used. Some of the clues may have more than one solution, but there is only one word pair that will correctly link up with all the other word pairs.

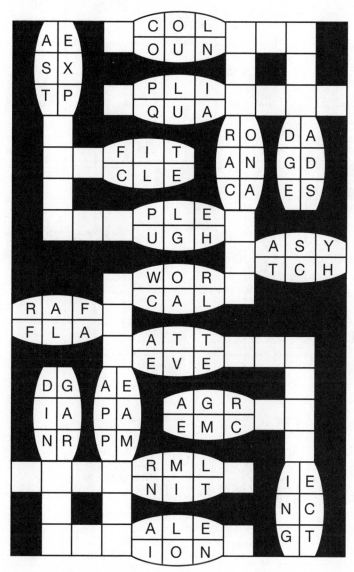

IN OTHER WORDS

There is only one common uncapitalized word that contains the consecutive letters GHC. What is that word?

_____

★★ Gnawing Issue by Fred Piscop

ACROSS

1 Goldman's Wall Street partner
6 Military priest
11 Family drs.
14 God of Islam
15 Invalidate
16 Mudder's morsel
17 Oregon nickname
19 Architect I.M.
20 Speed the progress of
21 Taj __
23 When the sun is up
24 Keep from happening
26 OPEC, for one
30 Near-ringer
31 Radio-studio sign
32 Intended
33 Air-gun ammo
36 Umlaut elements
37 Artichoke center
38 Colorado resort
39 Santa __, CA
40 Hang back
41 French textile city
42 Submit, as homework
44 Saved, with "out"
45 Libertarian adversary
47 Census datum
48 Tribal emblem
49 M*A*S*H star
54 Industrious bug
55 Annette or Cubby
58 Place to graze
59 Borden bovine
60 Brown ermine
61 Guessed-at fig.
62 Postgame wrap-up
63 Welcome forecast

DOWN

1 Kemo __
2 The A in A-Rod
3 Thunder sound
4 Give birth to
5 Dog, periodically
6 Pallid
7 Part of a.m.
8 Genetics focus
9 Unchanging grind
10 Hydrogen or helium
11 Pitch hit for a homer
12 Hymn of praise
13 Circus prop
18 Iranian money
22 Forum greeting
24 Arctic explorer
25 Talk wildly
26 Final section in music
27 Unknown auth.
28 Woodpecker's rhythm
29 "__ the season ..."
30 Get wind of
32 Be worthy of
34 Liver product
35 Husky's burden
37 Brinker of fiction
38 7, on a sundial
40 Barber's gadget
41 Negligence
43 Western Indian
44 Rooster's nose
45 Like old bread
46 Musical sounds
47 Sack out
49 Nepal's locale
50 Aleutian island
51 Novelist Uris
52 University official
53 Overly stylish
56 Bullfight bravo
57 Trojans' sch.

★★ ABC

Enter the letters A, B, and C into the diagram so that each row and column has exactly one A, one B, and one C. The letters outside the diagram indicate the first letter encountered, moving in the direction of the arrow. Keep in mind that after all the letters have been filled in, there will be two blank boxes in each row and column.

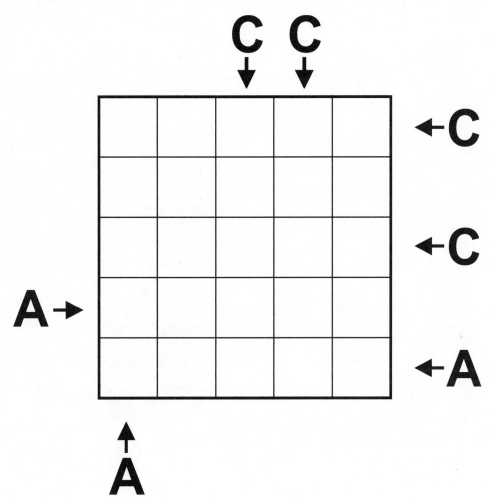

SUDOKU SUM

Without repeating any digits, complete the sum at right, by filling one digit in each of the five blanks.

```
  _ 2 _
+ 4 _ 7
-------
  _ 9 _
```

★★ Find the Ships

Determine the position of the 10 ships listed to the right of the diagram. The ships may be oriented either horizontally or vertically. A square with wavy lines indicates water and will not contain a ship. The numbers at the edge of the diagram indicate how many squares in that row or column contain parts of ships. When all 10 ships are correctly placed in the diagram, no two of them will touch each other, not even diagonally.

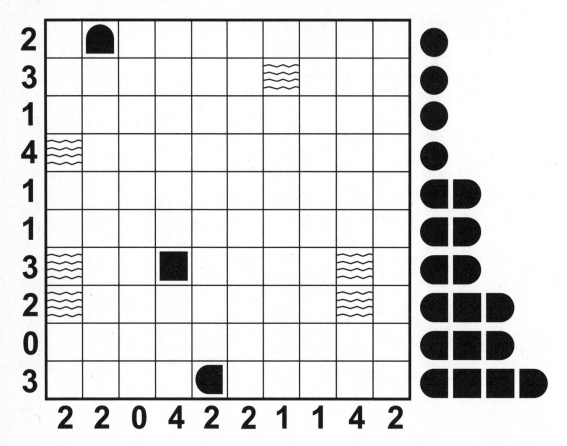

AND SO ON

Unscramble the letters in the phrase ARBOR MOOD, to form two words that are part of a common phrase that has the word AND between them.

_____ and _____

★★ Brake Job by Daniel R. Stark

ACROSS

1 Blonde shade
4 Purple hue
9 Tough question
14 Greek letter
15 Microscopic swimmer
16 Dragon of '50s TV
17 Bank robber
19 Veldt prowlers
20 All through
21 Give the go-ahead for
23 Wave sites
24 Tolerate
27 Warm up for a bout
30 Live in
33 Vexation
34 Work force
37 City near Helena
39 Self-absorbed person
40 Sign maker's aid
42 Bird that honks
43 Looks high and low
44 Indiana Jones quest
45 Operagoer's reference
48 Wear well
50 Sierra __
51 Eye layer
55 Canary comment
57 Articles
58 Treat wood
60 Out-of-stock coupon voucher
64 Conversation starter
65 Think alike
66 Dakota Indian
67 Cheerleading routines
68 Shaw contemporary
69 Repair a seam

DOWN

1 Workout woes
2 Was all aglow
3 Poet Doolittle
4 Pay tribute to
5 Little devil
6 Apollo craft
7 Lawyers' org.
8 Northwest Passage locale
9 Collect views
10 Mixed bags
11 Kind of softball
12 Aachen article
13 Scale notes
18 Tyrants
22 Tennis do-over
24 Tarzan companions
25 Lancaster of films
26 They, in Calais
28 Clarinetist Shaw
29 Movie spools
31 Picture window
32 Roeper's partner
34 Copier setting
35 Socrates' hangout
36 Bibliophile's source
38 Impolite
40 Viewed
41 London art gallery
43 Box-office sign
46 Suffix for percent
47 Sell out
49 Jacket fabric
52 Turns aside
53 Game-show host
54 Out of kilter
56 Baseball great Slaughter
57 Treats a sprain
58 Bashful
59 Plumbing joint
61 Census info
62 Keogh relative
63 Make after taxes

★★ Twelve-Letter Word

Using each letter in the diagram exactly once, form a twelve-letter word by starting with the first letter, and spelling the remaining letters in the word in order, by moving through the gaps in the walls.

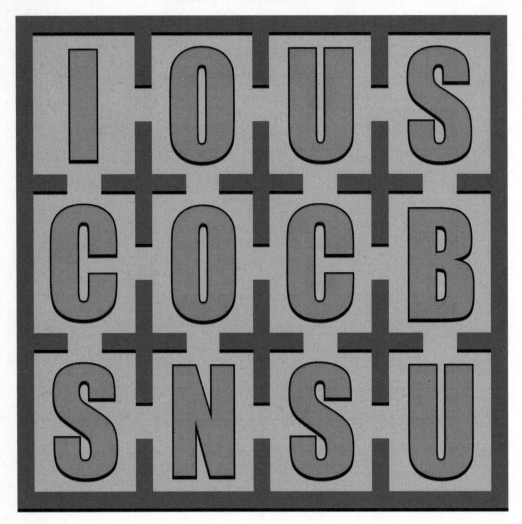

BETWEENER

What four-letter word belongs between the word at left and the word at right, so that the first and second word, and the second and third word, each form a common two-word phrase?

SMALL __ __ __ __ SHOW

★★ Sudoku

Fill in the blank boxes so that every row, column, and 3x3 box contains all of the numbers 1 to 9.

6		2	4					
		1	5				7	4
4	5		7	6				9
		9		1		7		2
	3					8		
			3				9	
						9	5	
3	9	4				2		
1				7	3			8

MIXAGRAMS

Each line contains a five-letter word and a four-letter word that have been mixed together (the order of the letters in each word has not been changed). Unmix the two words on each line and write them in the spaces provided. When you're done, find a two-word answer to the clue by reading down the letter columns in the answers.

CLUE: Kind of reaction

J E K A I D N E G = _ _ _ _ _ + _ _ _ _

S E M I N A T R E = _ _ _ _ _ + _ _ _ _

W E R I O T R E D = _ _ _ _ _ + _ _ _ _

K N E A L W E L Y = _ _ _ _ _ + _ _ _ _

★★ Circular Reasoning

Connect all of the circles by drawing a single continuous line through every square of the diagram. All right-angle turns of your line must alternate between boxes containing a circle and boxes not containing a circle. You must make a right-angle turn out of every square that contains a circle. Your line must end in the same square that it begins, and it cannot enter any square more than once.

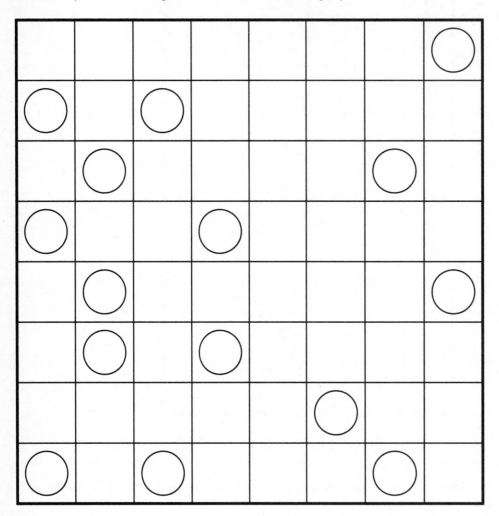

THREE AT A RHYME

Rearrange these letters to form three one-syllable words that rhyme.

A A C E E G H I I R R S T T T W

_____   _____   _____

★★ At the Bank by Robert H. Wolfe

ACROSS

1 Stick in one's __
5 Wood cutters
9 To this point
14 Baby's woe
15 Gen. Robert __
16 Cloth pattern
17 Ancient Peruvian
18 Ring slowly
19 Moved in a circular path
20 Fibber
23 Superman insignia
24 Batch of soup
25 Environmental concern
27 Guide to the summit
31 Cause to fail
34 Hardwood tree
38 Theater honor
39 Borge, for one
40 Wind instruments
41 Actor Wallach
42 Sealy competitor
43 Composer Bartók
44 Reducing regimen
45 Intense feeling
46 Fr. religious figures
47 Make lovable
49 Cutlet meat
51 Piston ring
56 Neighbor of Miss.
58 Low-tech dryer
62 Seles milieu
64 Layered cookie
65 Kappa preceder
66 Spherical dwelling
67 Knitting stitch
68 Wool sources
69 Discourage
70 Spring planting
71 Hardly ever seen

DOWN

1 Like some cereals
2 Raced in the direction of
3 Wide neckwear
4 Liner's landing spot
5 Come to terms
6 Succulent plant
7 Rural water source
8 Offer at retail
9 Move in large numbers
10 Above, to poets
11 Footballer's protection
12 Birds: Lat.
13 Beatty film
21 Noels
22 Catch sight of
26 Command
28 Dined at home
29 Gave (out)
30 Become one
32 Keen on
33 Just about
34 Unruly groups
35 Assist, as in a heist
36 Track event
37 Rental contract
42 Teasdale et al.
44 Farmer's place, in a song
48 Ancient
50 Role player
52 More knavish
53 Southwest Native American
54 Computer key
55 Badger with banter
56 Base neutralizer
57 Theater section
59 Word after a mishap
60 Right on target
61 Roll-call response
63 Fish eggs

★★ Islands

Shade in some of the white squares in the diagram with "water," so that each remaining white box is part of an island. Each island will contain exactly one numbered square, indicating how many squares that island contains. Each island is separated from the other islands by water but may touch other islands diagonally. All water is connected, but there are no 2x2 regions of water in the diagram.

		2			
3		**3**		**3**	
	2				**1**

COMMON SENSE

What four-letter word can be found in the dictionary definitions of all of these words:

SNIFFLE, THAW, MILK SHAKE, and THERMOS?

— — — —

★★ Hyper-Sudoku

Fill in the blank boxes so that every row, column, 3x3 box, *and* each of the four 3x3 gray regions contains all of the numbers 1 to 9.

				6	8			
	9	1				5		
6			5	1				7
	3			2	1			
		8	7	9				1
				3	4			
		5					9	4
					2	8		
4		6					7	5

TRANSDELETION

Delete one letter from the word UNRAVELED and rearrange the rest, to get a flowering plant.

_____

★★ From A to B by Fred Piscop

ACROSS

1 School orgs.
5 Whitish gem
9 Relay race hand-off
14 Mardi Gras follower
15 Junction point
16 Really like
17 "Inner" starter
18 Lake bird
19 Big goof
20 Insecticide medium
23 Zeus or Thor
24 "__ by Starlight"
25 Praise highly
27 Part of IRS
29 SAT section
33 *George M!* subject
37 Time past
40 Greek vowel
41 Seafood serving
44 Start another hitch
45 Oscar superlative
46 Oboe pair
47 Nabokov novel
49 Sharp __ tack
51 __ Rica
54 Apt to erupt
59 Get mellower
62 Ray Stevens song of '62
64 Takes a bath
66 NYC cultural center
67 Bit of roofing
68 Movie star's rep
69 Partner of anon
70 Cold War initials
71 Koufax of Cooperstown
72 Author Jaffe
73 Track event

DOWN

1 "Guilty" and "nolo"
2 Basic principle
3 Netman Agassi
4 Milker's seat
5 Out, at the library
6 Hustler's game
7 Pueblo home
8 Wedgwood alternative
9 Talk nonsense
10 Commotion
11 Chinese gang
12 Two-tone cookie
13 Geeky guy
21 Move furtively
22 Expert
26 Brief moment
28 Newcastle's river
30 Tiresome one
31 Just __ (slightly)
32 Chem classes
33 Sagan of *Cosmos*
34 Pancake topper
35 Do a trucker's job
36 Jellied garnish
38 Says "yes" to
39 Actress Moreno
42 Put to shame
43 Pre-meal prayer
48 Warm and comfy
50 Much of North Africa
52 Ringling employee
53 From the beginning
55 Ms. O'Neal
56 Angelou's "Still __"
57 French dance
58 Thumb-moving critic
59 "How sad!"
60 Totally smitten
61 Fifty-fifty
63 Some Feds
65 Phase out

★★ AND Enders

Find the 24 different words that end with AND that are hidden in the diagram either across, down, or diagonally. Answers include a man's first name and the names of five countries.

```
B  I  N  C  D  U  P  L  A  N  D  H
K  A  S  U  K  N  D  S  D  Q  B  O
H  V  N  L  D  N  A  M  E  R  D  L
Y  V  W  D  A  P  O  L  A  N  D  L
G  A  R  L  A  N  D  N  G  T  E  A
D  D  B  A  I  X  D  C  H  N  G  N
D  N  A  L  T  E  W  O  U  B  E  D
E  A  A  J  D  D  U  M  R  R  N  L
X  L  T  W  N  S  N  M  R  A  P  D
P  E  D  N  A  R  G  A  L  O  N  N
A  R  C  N  H  T  N  N  L  A  B  A
N  I  D  Y  F  D  I  D  R  O  E  M
D  P  Q  F  F  F  Z  T  A  L  R  E
M  H  I  G  O  S  S  T  A  N  D  D
```

INITIAL REACTION

The "equation" below contains the initials of words that will make it correct, forming a numerical fact. Solve the equation by supplying the missing words.

30 = D. in S., A., J., and N. _____

★★ Four-Letter Word Routes

Using each of the 24 letters exactly once, find the six routes that form the six four-letter words hidden in the diagram. For each route, start with the first letter in each word and spell the remaining letters in the word in order, by moving through the gaps in the walls.

AND SO ON

Unscramble the letters in the phrase OLD FUTONS, to form two words that are part of a common phrase that has the word AND between them.

_____ and _____

★★ Starting Line by Fred Piscop

ACROSS

1 Discover by chance
6 Beer ingredient
10 Star in Lyra
14 __ Rogers St. Johns
15 Nonwritten test
16 Skater's leap
17 Up to the task
20 Just gets by
21 Metal marble
22 Dada pioneer
24 Less restrained
25 Politician's promise, perhaps
30 Lloyd Webber musical
33 Japanese dog
34 Bard's "soon"
35 Sigma follower
38 Observe the end of Daylight Savings Time
42 Ltr. add-ons
43 Wooden wedge
44 *The Great Dictator* star
45 Shoelace tip
47 Turns to confetti
48 Iraqi port
51 Language suffix
53 Like some protests
56 Verve
62 Dismissal from Dad
64 Do some lawn work
65 Lioness of film
66 Versatile aide
67 Journey parts
68 County center
69 Sarcastic

DOWN

1 Do damage to
2 Inventor's start
3 Deck wood
4 Ye __ Shoppe
5 Dissenting votes
6 Pay tribute to
7 Former California fort
8 Cat feet
9 Cut open
10 Eamon de __
11 Napoleon's fate
12 Wish granter
13 Author Horatio
18 Ponderosa son
19 Took a powder
23 Compact illuminator
25 Coarse file
26 Barely manages, with "out"
27 Is the right size
28 Mel of Cooperstown
29 Stadium shout
31 "Va-va-__!"
32 Corporation abbr.
34 Feel sore
35 Help oneself to
36 Etcher's need
37 Hawaiian strings
39 Alien's subj.
40 __-i-noor diamond
41 Soap unit
45 Gets up
46 Rubberneck
47 Tailor's line
48 Holey roll
49 Battery terminal
50 Football coach Amos Alonzo __
52 Nursery-rhyme surname
54 Affirmative votes
55 Part to play
57 Auction assents
58 "This weighs __!"
59 Hebrew letter
60 Hung on to
61 Perry's creator
63 Letters on a stamp

★★ One-Way Streets

The diagram represents a pattern of streets. P's are parking spaces, and the black squares are stores. Find the route that starts at a parking space, passes through all stores exactly once, and ends at the other parking space. Arrows indicate one-way traffic for that block only. No block or intersection may be entered more than once.

ADDITION SWITCH

Switch the positions of two of the digits in the incorrect sum at right, to get a correct sum.

$$\begin{array}{r} 779 \\ +179 \\ \hline 150 \end{array}$$

★★ 123

Fill in the diagram so that each rectangular piece has one each of the numbers 1, 2, and 3, under these rules: 1) No two adjacent squares, horizontally or vertically, can have the same number. 2) Each completed row and column of the diagram will have an equal number of 1s, 2s, and 3s.

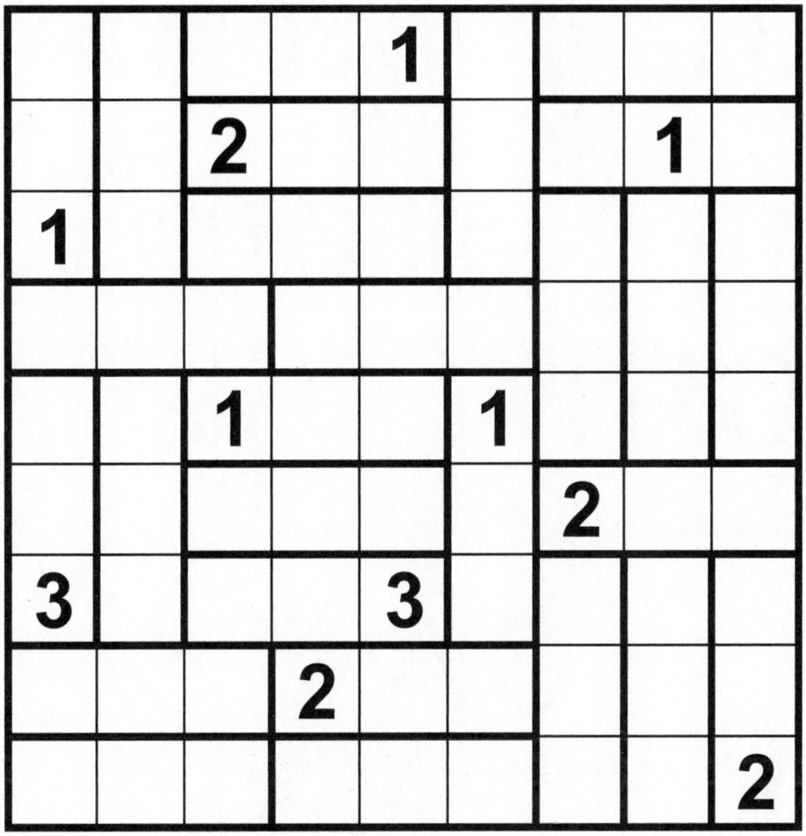

				1				
		2					1	
1								
		1			1			
						2		
3				3				
			2					
								2

TELEPHONE TRIOS

1	ABC 2	DEF 3
GHI 4	JKL 5	MNO 6
PRS 7	TUV 8	WXY 9
*	o	#

Using the numbers and letters on a standard telephone, what three seven-letter words from the same category can be formed from these telephone numbers?

745-4266   _ _ _ _ _ _ _

276-6463   _ _ _ _ _ _ _

225-2486   _ _ _ _ _ _ _

★★ Line Drawing

Draw two straight lines, each from one edge of the square to another edge, so that the letters in each of the three regions spell a single word.

ER   T

NG   RP

RI   CHI

CHI   CA

           OR

SOUND THINKING

We can think of six common uncapitalized words whose only consonant sounds are J, L, and T, in that order. How many can you think of?

_____   _____   _____

_____   _____   _____

★★ Cleanup Crew by Fred Piscop

ACROSS

1 Teen idols, slangily
6 "Well, __-di-dah!"
9 Editor's "keep it"
13 __ fours (crawling)
14 Japanese ring sport
15 Roof overhang
16 "I give up!"
17 Touched down
18 Plane measure
19 Donald Duck nephew
20 Desert phenomenon
22 As far as
24 Tallow source
25 USN bigwigs
27 Thanksgiving Day: Abbr.
30 Fragrant fir
34 Sampras of tennis
35 Trike riders
37 Hajji's destination
38 Post-ER place
39 Beatle haircuts
41 Same old thing
42 Duke or earl
44 Highway rig
45 Adorable
46 Hall of Famers
48 Meth. or Luth.
49 Follow orders
50 Pittsburgh Pirates, in headlines
52 French city
54 Wristwatch feature
59 Slip past
62 Quad building
63 Lamb's alias
64 Weight deductions
65 Toledo's lake
66 Canasta play
67 Map within a map
68 Hotfooted it
69 Language suffix

70 Parts of instructions

DOWN

1 Malodorous
2 __ Domini
3 Component of early computers
4 Orbital shape
5 Wintry forecast
6 Lollapalooza
7 Out of kilter
8 Home-spa device
9 Space Needle city
10 Source of poi
11 Partner of anon

12 Jets, Mets, or Nets
14 In the doldrums
21 Skirt features
23 Sergeant Snorkel's dog
25 Talking like
26 Interior design
28 Beer ingredient
29 Out-and-out
31 Surgeon's aide
32 Sharp as a tack
33 Sea dog's buddy
36 A handful of
39 Ran into, with "with"

40 Dosage unit
43 Stuck a tag on
45 Radiator fluid
47 Plot deviously
51 Mall events
53 Hairy Himalayans
54 "__ a Lady" (Tom Jones song)
55 Bend out of shape
56 Author Wiesel
57 Cairo's river
58 Ward, to Beaver
60 Like a bass voice
61 Repairer's figs.

★★ Star Search

Find the stars that are hidden in some of the blank squares. The numbered squares indicate how many stars are hidden in the squares adjacent to them (including diagonally). There is never more than one star in any square.

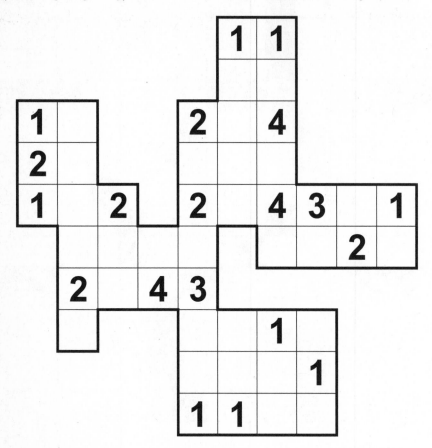

MIXAGRAMS

Each line contains a five-letter word and a four-letter word that have been mixed together (the order of the letters in each word has not been changed). Unmix the two words on each line and write them in the spaces provided. When you're done, find a two-part answer to the clue by reading down the letter columns in the answers.

CLUE: Where to get dates

P I T R I T P Y E = _ _ _ _ _ + _ _ _ _

E S C A R R N A P = _ _ _ _ _ + _ _ _ _

B L U R E L Y E K = _ _ _ _ _ + _ _ _ _

K N E A R E M A D = _ _ _ _ _ + _ _ _ _

★★ Bead Maze

Enter the maze at right center, pass through all beads exactly once, and then exit at bottom center. You may not pass through three consecutive beads of the same color.

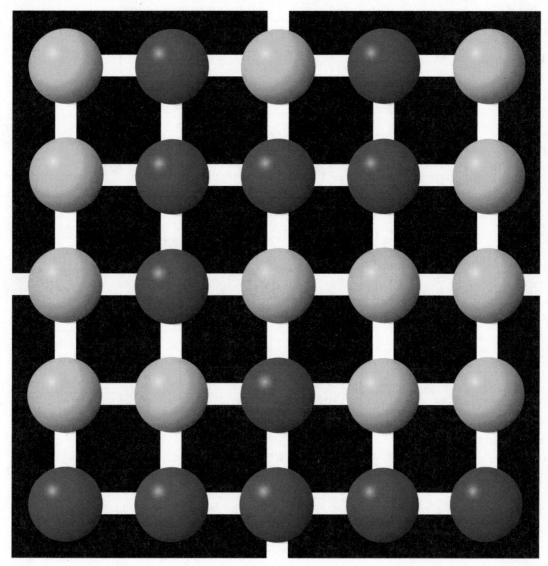

SUDOKU SUM

Without repeating any digits, complete the sum at right, by filling one digit in each of the five blanks.

$$
\begin{array}{r}
5\ \_\ 1 \\
+\ \_\ 2\ \_ \\
\hline
\_\ \_\ 7
\end{array}
$$

★★ Imitative by Daniel R. Stark

ACROSS

1 Search thoroughly
5 Dust particle
10 Unwelcome obligation
14 Lamb's pen name
15 Miss Universe prize
16 Monthly expense
17 Tiny stream
18 Happen
19 Showroom model
20 Kids' game
23 Cousteau's middle name
24 Johnny Mathis tune
25 Midwest metropolis
28 Port in a storm
31 Green Hornet's assistant
32 Appointed
34 Hair mousse alternative
37 Collectible book
40 Feminine force
41 More uncanny
42 Author Wister
43 Feats
44 Building wing
45 Pizza topping
48 Clobber
50 Burroughs creation
57 Price increase
58 Districts
59 Improv gear
60 Not bumpy
61 Lipstick holder
62 __-fixe dinner
63 Some wines
64 Installs in office
65 Backpacker's gear

DOWN

1 *What's My Line?* wit
2 Hodgepodge
3 Pepper grinder
4 Hype
5 Vermont ski resort
6 Ancient Scots
7 Per person
8 Mötley __
9 Malden or Marx
10 Predetermine
11 Must-haves
12 Like some goals
13 Building floor
21 Biologist's eggs
22 Fix, as a manuscript
25 Sign off on
26 Hawaiian island
27 Memo abbr.
28 Kachina makers
29 Queens tennis stadium
30 Go off at an angle
32 Hudson Bay Indian
33 Stony
34 Formal wear
35 Pentathlon need
36 Wild cat
38 Actress Davis
39 Court violation
43 Doughnut orders
44 Jungfrau, e.g.
45 Significant __
46 Unsophisticated
47 Vexed
48 Jungle creature
49 Facilitates
51 Takes a snooze
52 Quiz choice
53 Jealous wife of myth
54 Quicksand
55 Very similar
56 First in line

★★ Hyper-Sudoku

Fill in the blank boxes so that every row, column, 3x3 box, *and* each of the four 3x3 gray regions contains all of the numbers 1 to 9.

		6			3	2		7
								5
			9		4			1
						2		
8			2				1	6
5		1		7				
					9			2
		9		8				
	8	7	1	4	5		9	

COUNTDOWN

Inserting plus signs and minus signs, as many as necessary, in between the digits from 9 to 1 below, create a series of additions and subtractions whose final answer is 100. Any digits without a sign between them are to be grouped together as a single number.

| 9 | 8 | 7 | 6 | 5 | 4 | 3 | 2 | 1 | = | 100 |

★★ ABC

Enter the letters A, B, and C into the diagram so that each row and column has exactly one A, one B, and one C. The letters outside the diagram indicate the first letter encountered, moving in the direction of the arrow. Keep in mind that after all the letters have been filled in, there will be two blank boxes in each row and column.

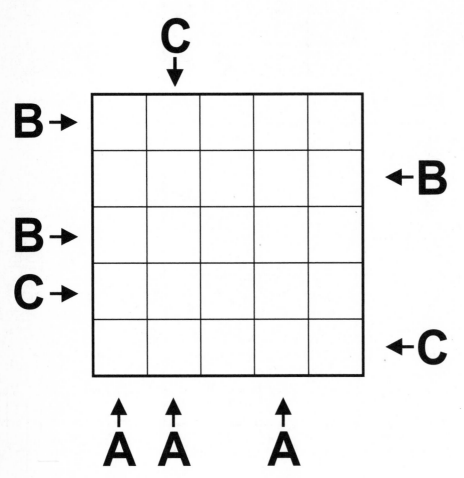

IN OTHER WORDS

There are only two common uncapitalized words that contain the consecutive letters KJA. What are they? For extra credit, what world capital city has the same consecutive letters?

_____   _____   _____

★★ On Top by Daniel R. Stark

ACROSS

1 Strong wind
5 Have __ (enjoy oneself)
10 Nickel fraction
14 Biblical brother
15 Shire of *Rocky*
16 Stead
17 High-level meeting
19 Shah's land
20 GI hangout
21 Competes
22 Decadent
24 Writers' tools
26 Coral creation
27 Genetic letters
28 Construction workers
32 Capable people know them
35 Name for a poodle
36 Yves' girlfriend
37 Singer Tori
38 Strong suit
39 Leaf juncture
40 Pretzel topping
41 Former spouses
42 Very mean ones
43 Brief biographies
45 Exist
46 Uses a calculator
47 Mighty loud
51 Home of the Cowboys
54 Rhythmic swing
55 __'wester
56 Not written
57 Busy time
60 "Well done!"
61 Go along (with)
62 Ladder step
63 Idyllic locale
64 Honor with insults
65 Oater backdrop

DOWN

1 Fill the tank
2 Maltreatment
3 Iced-tea garnish
4 House shader
5 Hun of note
6 *Psycho* villain
7 "That's too bad!"
8 __ *Abner*
9 Buffalo's water
10 Close contest
11 Gaelic republic
12 "Well done!"
13 Ditty
18 Columnist Molly
23 Not hungry
25 Discouraged
26 River floaters
28 Rents, as a limo
29 Eros, in Rome
30 Ebb or neap
31 Catches a glimpse of
32 Coarse file
33 Actor Sharif
34 Equestrian sport
35 Wild canines
38 Mineral in granite
42 Speak publicly
44 Muckraker Tarbell
45 Ready to go
47 Items in a rack
48 Publish
49 Lunch periods
50 __ *Din*
51 Completed
52 Like the Kalahari
53 Curtain material
54 *Tomb Raider* heroine
58 Id companion
59 Sofa section

★★ Pencil Pile

Which one of the 11 pencils was the sixth dropped in the pile?

CITY SEARCH

Use the letters in CAMBRIDGE to form common uncapitalized seven-letter words. We found four of them. How many can you find?

_ _ _ _ _ _ _   _ _ _ _ _ _ _

_ _ _ _ _ _ _   _ _ _ _ _ _ _

★★ Find the Ships

Determine the position of the 10 ships listed to the right of the diagram. The ships may be oriented either horizontally or vertically. A square with wavy lines indicates water and will not contain a ship. The numbers at the edge of the diagram indicate how many squares in that row or column contain parts of ships. When all 10 ships are correctly placed in the diagram, no two of them will touch each other, not even diagonally.

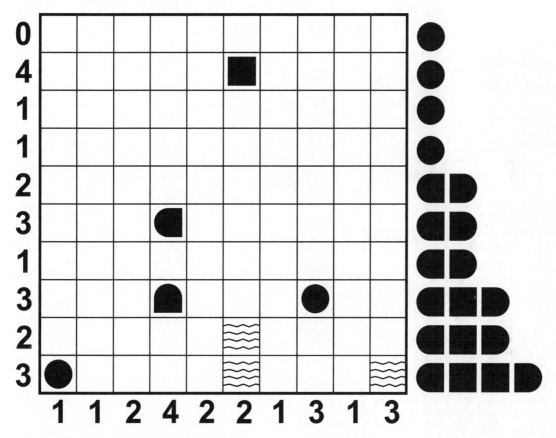

CLUELESS CROSSWORD

Complete the crossword with common uncapitalized seven-letter words, based entirely on the letters already filled in for you.

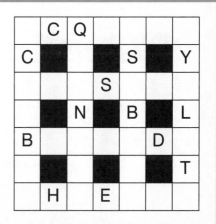

★★ Triad Split Decisions

In this clueless crossword puzzle, each answer consists of two words whose spellings are the same, except for the consecutive letters given. All answers are common words; no phrases or hyphenated or capitalized words are used. Some of the clues may have more than one solution, but there is only one word pair that will correctly link up with all the other word pairs.

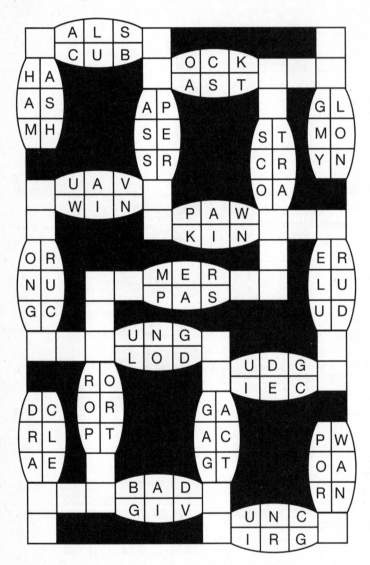

THREE AT A RHYME

Rearrange these letters to form three one-syllable words that rhyme.

A E E F G G I I I N N V

_____   _____   _____

★★ Meal Time by Fred Piscop

ACROSS

1 Irene of *Fame*
5 Be next to
11 Spanish Mrs.
14 Foretoken
15 Simple shelter
16 Whole bunch
17 Rustic stopover
20 Chicken __ king
21 Pedometer reading
22 Actor Barrymore
23 Lollipop tastes
25 Scot's refusal
28 Netman Agassi
29 "Toodle-oo!"
30 Bleachers seating
32 Management level
33 Deadlock
35 Horn sound
37 Radical '60s grp.
38 Informal invitation
41 __ Paulo, Brazil
43 "As __ on TV"
44 Genetic initials
45 Limburger quality
47 Coin-toss call
49 Laundry cycle
53 __ it out (fought)
55 Shad delicacy
56 French sci-fi pioneer
57 "__ Restaurant"
59 President pro __
61 __ snail's pace
62 Romantic date
66 One with a J.D.
67 Unlike today's gasoline
68 Cornfield measure
69 Word form for "recent"
70 National Guard center
71 Be flexible

DOWN

1 Shade of blue
2 Aviator Earhart
3 Edit
4 Santa __, CA
5 Actor __ Ray
6 Make a fillet of
7 Pickle holder
8 Small bill
9 Slanted type: Abbr.
10 Motorola competitor
11 Miles of Plymouth
12 Pinkish hue
13 Female reindeer have them
18 Figs.
19 Helvetica bold, e.g.
24 *Taming of the Shrew* nickname
26 Actor Banderas
27 Environmental sci.
30 Attack from all sides
31 Work time
34 Part of TGIF
36 Spike TV's former name
38 Investigate
39 Diary entry starter
40 Gumshoe's job
41 Recyclable item
42 Praise to the skies
46 Shipping dept. stamp
48 Varsity award
50 Strut like a pony
51 New physician
52 Closed in on
54 Perry's aide
56 Keydets' sch.
58 Palm reader
60 Water swirl
63 Hasty escape
64 Altar declaration
65 Slap cuffs on

★★ 123

Fill in the diagram so that each rectangular piece has one each of the numbers 1, 2, and 3, under these rules: 1) No two adjacent squares, horizontally or vertically, can have the same number. 2) Each completed row and column of the diagram will have an equal number of 1s, 2s, and 3s.

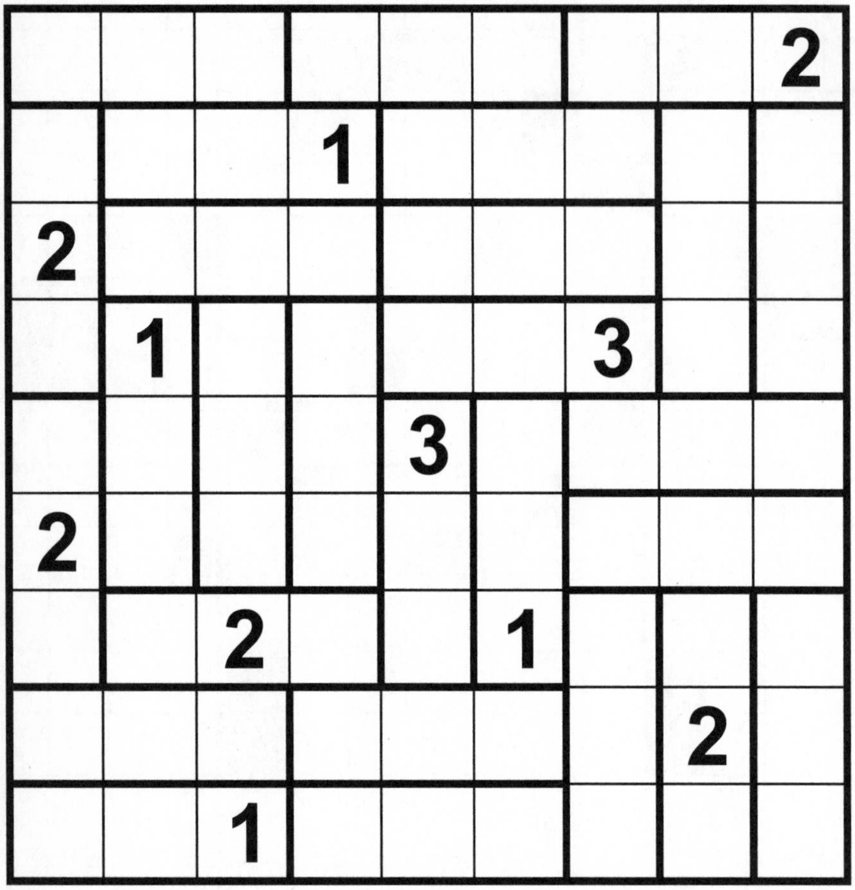

								2
			1					
2								
	1					3		
				3				
2								
		2			1			
							2	
		1						

TWO-BY-FOUR

The eight letters in the word HEREDITY can be rearranged to form a pair of common four-letter words in three different ways, if no four-letter word is repeated. Can you find all three pairs of words?

— — — —   — — — —

— — — —   — — — —

— — — —   — — — —

★★ Circular Reasoning

Connect all of the circles by drawing a single continuous line through every square of the diagram. All right-angle turns of your line must alternate between boxes containing a circle and boxes not containing a circle. You must make a right-angle turn out of every square that contains a circle. Your line must end in the same square that it begins, and it cannot enter any square more than once.

COMMON SENSE

What four-letter word can be found in the dictionary definitions of all of these words:

CHRISTMAS CARD, GENIE, COVET, and GESUNDHEIT?

— — — —

★★ Means of Support by Fred Piscop

ACROSS

1 Plowmaker John
6 Pub offerings
10 Shopper's mecca
14 Burns' partner
15 Hung on to
16 Emmy winner Falco
17 Big rigs
18 Pastry prettifier
19 PED __
20 Spreadsheet label, maybe
23 Place to graze
24 Plan detail, for short
25 Red gem
28 __-night doubleheader
31 Rubbernecked
35 Mineral suffix
36 Sierra __
38 Actress Verdugo
39 Exemplary one
42 Crime fighter Ness
43 Vaulted
44 Mallorca Mrs.
45 Keanu of Speed
47 Same old thing
48 New driver, often
49 "Within" word form
51 The elder Gershwin
53 Place for mail
59 Longish skirt
60 Reclined
61 Was slack-jawed
63 Colossal, as films
64 First governor of Alaska
65 Dunne or Ryan
66 Soup vegetable
67 Ends up with
68 Ike's two-time opponent

DOWN

1 __ Kapital
2 A util.
3 Ticklish Muppet
4 Comic Charles Nelson __
5 Come next
6 Closely related
7 Solidarity name
8 Olympic blades
9 Guitar attachments
10 Baja's capital
11 Score after deuce
12 Ding-a-__
13 Turkey portion

21 Alma __
22 Pick up
25 More developed
26 Serving a purpose
27 Prove false
29 Fabric from fleece
30 Draw a conclusion
32 Actress Witherspoon
33 __ nous
34 Six-Day War hero
36 Like some fingerprints
37 Jacob's twin
40 Like a teen with a crush, perhaps

41 Eye-related
46 Like a fence's goods
48 Knight's garment
50 Old enough
52 Aqua __ (gold dissolver)
53 Popeye's tooter
54 Garfield's foil
55 Royal decree
56 B&Bs
57 German auto
58 Warrior Princess of TV
59 Actor Gibson
62 "Agnus __"

★★ Right Turn Only

Enter the maze at bottom, and reach the center by making right turns only; no left turns allowed. You may retrace your path.

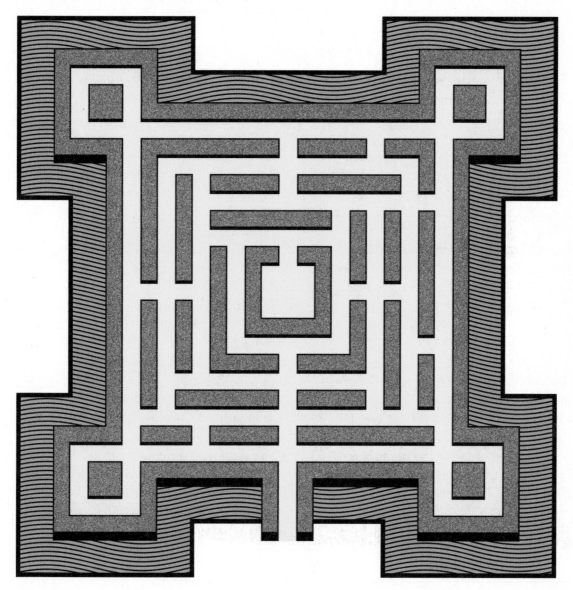

THREE OF A KIND

Find the three hidden words in the sentence that, read in order, go together in some way.

Trash or treasure? The drab bronze relic: a showpiece to a dealer.

bRaIn BReaTHer
GOTTA HAVE FAITH

Most people take their religious beliefs very seriously, but that's not to say that follow-ing a higher calling causes those of the cloth (and members of their flocks) to lose their senses of humor altogether. Here are our favorite wisecracks from the faithful:

Every Catholic church in town but one had its Mass schedule posted in front. The exception announced the time weekly bingo started. I phoned the priest to com-plain.

"My son," he replied, "our parishioners know when we hold Mass, but we have to be sure the Protestants know when we hold bingo."

—JAMES A. DAILY

* * *

Toward the close of a banquet held during an Episcopal Church convention some years ago, the bishop of the diocese stood up and quite disrupted the entire affair by announcing, "We will reserve the enter-tainment of the evening until the wait-resses have taken everything off."

—WILBUR L. LEAR

* * *

The teenager asked his father for a car. "Not until you start studying your Talmud and get your hair cut," his father said.

A month later the boy approached his father again. "Well," the father said, "I know you've been reading the Talmud quite diligently, but your hair's still long."

"You know, Dad," the boy replied, "I've been thinking about that. All the prophets had long hair."

"That's true," the boy's father said. "And everywhere they went, they walked."

* * *

The ordination of women as Episcopal ministers occasionally presents awkward situations as to what to call us. "Father" sounds inappropriate to some; "Mother" is traditionally used for unordained women overseeing religious communities.

Last year, one of my colleagues, dressed in her clerical garb, was in an airport. A man summoned the courage to ask her, "Pardon me, but what do you call a female father?"

My colleague smiled mischievously and replied, "Ambisextrous."

—MARY ELLEN APPLETON

* * *

Did you hear that the atheists have pro-duced a Christmas play? It's called *Coincidence on 34th Street.*

—JAY LENO

★★ Anatomical

Find the 46 anatomical words that are hidden in the diagram either across, down, or diagonally. Answers include 15 plurals, one of which is also the singular form of the word.

```
I  A  S  P  D  J  L  A  S  C  S  P  U  L  S  E  R
K  N  T  E  L  L  P  M  H  E  H  E  W  C  W  U  N
Z  I  E  I  V  P  I  E  I  E  T  T  Y  B  M  E  T
R  T  V  V  E  R  S  R  C  M  E  Q  U  E  M  T  X
V  E  I  N  S  T  E  M  T  U  E  F  F  O  L  N  M
R  R  D  W  M  T  F  N  R  S  T  R  D  F  M  I  V
P  I  X  G  R  J  U  A  A  C  O  B  H  I  O  O  D
X  W  H  A  C  P  X  L  E  L  A  N  R  S  E  J  H
K  N  E  E  S  A  A  L  H  E  E  O  N  T  P  D  C
Q  U  P  A  N  C  R  E  A  S  S  Y  E  N  D  I  K
S  I  C  F  E  Q  G  T  E  Y  E  B  R  O  W  N  T
S  W  O  B  L  E  B  A  I  D  N  A  L  G  I  A  N
S  V  Y  I  K  I  E  P  N  L  C  A  B  Q  O  V  B
T  P  U  Z  C  F  E  E  T  D  A  F  I  R  Y  E  T
W  B  I  E  U  F  N  O  A  S  L  G  H  L  A  L  R
C  A  P  H  N  E  S  W  G  H  V  T  E  O  S  I  M
H  S  I  L  K  C  N  R  G  Z  E  L  L  U  K  S  N
E  V  S  S  A  J  L  I  J  K  S  J  G  I  H  T  J
E  U  K  L  T  Y  H  S  P  S  G  N  U  L  P  A  G
K  X  P  Y  B  T  K  T  R  S  E  C  A  F  W  S  Z
```

TRANSDELETION

Delete one letter from the word SOAPSTONE and rearrange the rest, to get a unit of measure.

_____

★★ Hyper-Sudoku

Fill in the blank boxes so that every row, column, 3x3 box, *and* each of the four 3x3 gray regions contains all of the numbers 1 to 9.

5								
				6				1
2				7		8	9	
	1	8				6		
				5				
		7		4			3	
1	2	9	3			4		6
3			1			9		
7				8			1	

BETWEENER

What three-letter word belongs between the word at left and the word at right, so that the first and second word, and the second and third word, each form a common two-word phrase?

POP __ __ __ FORM

★★★ Off the Ground by Bob Frank

ACROSS

1 Pot covers
5 Macbeth's title
10 Not fem. or neut.
14 Troop group
15 Hayes or Hunt
16 On a voyage
17 Down Under greeting
18 Do a double take
19 H.S. junior's exam
20 Texas tea
21 African crawling fish
23 Pert
25 Systematic study
26 For all to see
30 Like some pigments
31 Lambaste
33 Shoe width
34 Short-distance planes
39 Poetic nighttime
40 Quell
41 Twenty Questions category
45 Baby birdie
49 Singer Brewer et al.
51 Novices
52 Heavy shoes
56 Buckeyes' sch.
57 Pasta, in product names
58 Princess' headpiece
59 __ B'rith
60 Grp. that includes Venezuela
61 Letter curlicue
62 Delta deposit
63 Takes a spouse
64 Poster verb
65 Crackerjacks

DOWN

1 Oscar role for Landau
2 Delhi denizen
3 Call
4 Swine spot
5 Route word
6 Pay attention to
7 Word of regret
8 Points of land
9 Draw in
10 Chartmaker
11 Agreeable one
12 Looks high and low
13 Colorful marble
21 "Oops, sorry! "
22 Actress Zadora
24 Tidbit for Muffet
27 Adjective for Abner
28 Locales in *la mer*
29 Louisiana cuisine
32 Tunnel, essentially
34 Wife of Odysseus
35 Yet to be pressed
36 OR figures
37 Tiger's taps
38 Slithery
39 Dine on humble pie
42 Corpsmen
43 Volcano dust
44 Taoism founder
46 Poignantly wry
47 Register key
48 NASA outerwear
50 Sales pitch
53 Whittle (down)
54 Comic Idle
55 Whole slew
59 Troop grp.

★★ One-Way Streets

The diagram represents a pattern of streets. P's are parking spaces, and the black squares are stores. Find the route that starts at a parking space, passes through all stores exactly once, and ends at the other parking space. Arrows indicate one-way traffic for that block only. No block or intersection may be entered more than once.

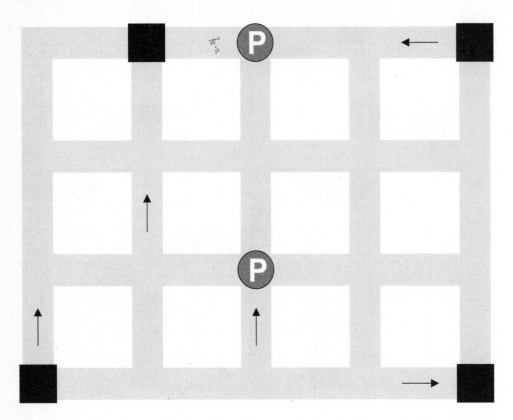

ADDITION SWITCH

Switch the positions of two of the digits in the incorrect sum at right, to get a correct sum.

$$\begin{array}{r} 1\,2\,5 \\ +\,1\,7\,6 \\ \hline 6\,0\,4 \end{array}$$

★★ Star Search

Find the stars that are hidden in some of the blank squares. The numbered squares indicate how many stars are hidden in the squares adjacent to them (including diagonally). There is never more than one star in any square.

MIXAGRAMS

Each line contains a five-letter word and a four-letter word that have been mixed together (the order of the letters in each word has not been changed). Unmix the two words on each line and write them in the spaces provided. When you're done, find a two-word answer to the clue by reading down the letter columns in the answers.

CLUE: Asian entrée

C O V I M S I C E = _ _ _ _ _ + _ _ _ _

F R O L E S H U T = _ _ _ _ _ + _ _ _ _

F O B L I R E D O = _ _ _ _ _ + _ _ _ _

K E T U L Y I S P = _ _ _ _ _ + _ _ _ _

★★★ Sound-Alike Celebs by Fred Piscop

ACROSS

1 For all to hear
6 It pours from pores
11 Trig abbr.
14 Popeye creator
15 Devil Rays' home
16 "Rope-a-dope" pugilist
17 Noted saloon raider
19 Rule, for short
20 Enzyme suffix
21 Eggy quaffs
22 Reenlist
24 Nags
26 Comic actor Arnold
27 Stubborn __ mule
28 Shatner's claim to fame
31 Amulets
34 *Oro y* __ (Montana motto)
35 Oklahoma city
36 "Bearded" bloom
37 Queeg's ship
38 Make bootees
39 Get-up-and-go
40 Throw, slangily
41 Simple tune
42 Salad green
44 Sunday seat
45 Hi-fi pioneer Fisher
46 Will add-on
50 Butter, for one
52 Holier-than-__
53 Astronomical altar
54 Ventilate
55 "Butterfly" singer
58 Pinky or Spike
59 Some jackets or collars
60 Biblical possessive
61 Have a go at
62 Jam-packed
63 Dueler's sword

DOWN

1 Songwriters' org.
2 Landlord's contract
3 Brutish sorts
4 '50s Mideast initials
5 Wine quality
6 Antlered animals
7 Bulk-rate phone line: Abbr.
8 UK record label
9 Cause abandoner
10 Trumpet blast
11 *North by Northwest* star
12 Toast topper
13 Make an X, maybe
18 Director Ephron
23 Colony insect
25 Greek T's
26 Smelled awful
28 Pizza serving
29 Cut and paste
30 "K-K-K-__"
31 Talk nonsense
32 *The Haj* novelist
33 *The Cable Guy* star
34 Shore of *Encino Man*
37 Member of a certain biological phylum
38 Fuzzy fruit
40 Prepared peas, perhaps
41 Takes off
43 Broad st.
44 Milne bear
46 Action-film highlight
47 West Indies native
48 Peace goddess
49 Cake stratum
50 Pretzel topper
51 Mooring spot
52 Pie holders
56 L. __ Hubbard
57 "I've got it!"

★★ Candy Corn

Enter the maze at bottom, pass through all candy corn, and then exit at top. You may not retrace your path.

AND SO ON

Unscramble the letters in the phrase FOSSIL PORT, to form two words that are part of a common phrase that has the word AND between them.

_____ and _____

★★ Sudoku

Fill in the blank boxes so that every row, column, and 3x3 box contains all of the numbers 1 to 9.

2						7		3
4			2	3				9
	3						8	
			4					
3	7	4	5	6				
	6				3			
	5	6	1	4				2
	9							4
		3	9		8	5		7

SUDOKU SUM

Without repeating any digits, complete the sum at right,
by filling one digit in each of the five blanks.

```
    _  6  _
+   2  _  5
_____
    _  7  _
```

★★★ Saintliness by Fred Piscop

ACROSS

1 Jai alai basket
6 Cowboy's pal
10 Dog shelter org.
14 REM stage activity
15 Creative spark
16 Go tumbling
17 Annual visitor
18 Lord's mate
19 Comic Rudner
20 Ultra-quiet vintage auto
23 Defective fireworks
24 Born first
25 Runway surface
29 *Wheel of Fortune* buy
30 Director Kazan
31 Military takeover
34 Lift with a crane
39 Yule trinket
42 Church's cut
43 End of a sneeze
44 Taxi charge
45 Compete
47 Pump levy
49 Invites to enter
53 Somali-born model
55 Cookware alloy
60 Put in groups
61 Dry as dust
62 "I've __ up to here!"
64 Robt. __
65 Something prohibited
66 Madonna film role
67 Cash register slot
68 Boxers and pugs
69 Allotted, with "out"

DOWN

1 DJ's stack
2 Historic times
3 Shipped off
4 "Toodle-oo!"
5 Actress Plummer
6 Like velvet
7 All in __ work
8 Some wines
9 Wright brothers' hometown
10 Valuable violin
11 First-rate
12 Refers to
13 In pieces
21 Susan of soaps
22 Yale or Root
25 Trial run
26 Word form for "height"
27 Knee-slapper
28 __ 1 (speed of sound)
29 Lhasa __
32 Fairy tale opener
33 "That's yucky!"
35 Switch positions
36 "__ first you ..."
37 Hospital fluids
38 Prehistoric predator
40 Costner or Kline
41 Forum garments
46 Away from shore
48 "O Canada," e.g.
49 Selling point
50 Ripped off
51 One of the Carpenters
52 Places to build
53 "Of Thee __"
54 Pre-Windows system
56 Suffix for stink
57 Roof overhang
58 Cut and paste, perhaps
59 Lo-cal
63 Smidgen

★★★ Split Decisions

In this clueless crossword puzzle, each answer consists of two words whose spellings are the same, except for the consecutive letters given. All answers are common words; no phrases or hyphenated or capitalized words are used. Some of the clues may have more than one solution, but there is only one word pair that will correctly link up with all the other word pairs.

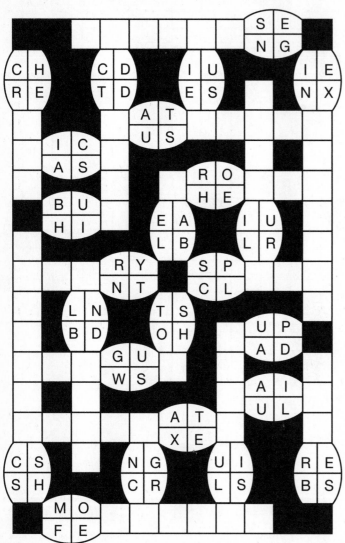

SOUND THINKING

We can think of four common uncapitalized words whose only consonant sounds are P, S, and L, in that order. How many can you think of?

_____   _____

_____   _____

★★ Islands

Shade in some of the white squares in the diagram with "water," so that each remaining white box is part of an island. Each island will contain exactly one numbered square, indicating how many squares that island contains. Each island is separated from the other islands by water but may touch other islands diagonally. All water is connected, but there are no 2x2 regions of water in the diagram.

3		**2**			
					2
		4			
					3
		1			

TELEPHONE TRIOS

1	ABC 2	DEF 3
GHI 4	JKL 5	MNO 6
PRS 7	TUV 8	WXY 9
*	o	#

Using the numbers and letters on a standard telephone, what three seven-letter words from the same category can be formed from these telephone numbers?

743-7238   _ _ _ _ _ _ _

783-3464   _ _ _ _ _ _ _

435-2846   _ _ _ _ _ _ _

★★★ Best Friends by Sheldon Benardo

ACROSS

1 Sinclair Lewis title character
5 Agatha Christie, for one
9 Roundtree role
14 What the suspicious smell
15 "I'll say!"
16 The __ Spoonful
17 Full of information
19 Torpid
20 "I'm So Excited" group
22 Let
23 Exist
24 Sault __ Marie
26 Marvin or Meriwether
27 "__ De-Lovely"
30 Freshwater fishes
33 Stayed home for brunch
35 Tatty
36 Quest in a Hammett novel
39 Weasel relative
40 Pay a call on
41 Circulatory word form
43 Fed. purchasing agcy.
44 *Super Millionaire* network
47 Building add-on
48 Recede
50 Quotable catcher
52 1898 uprising
57 Dumpy dwelling
58 Shortly
59 Gladiator venue
60 Army members
61 Ratio words
62 Upright
63 Big Board initials
64 Venison source

DOWN

1 __ tunnel
2 Small space
3 __ Row (London garment district)
4 Pitman person
5 Chip's toon partner
6 Mideast potentate
7 High-IQ group
8 Surround
9 Narrow cut
10 Whet
11 Against
12 Just released, as a film
13 Cable channel
18 Fluttering
21 Flounder alternative
25 Sixth sense
28 Comparatively wee
29 Bro's sib
31 To be counted on
32 Diplomacy
33 *Der* __ (Adenauer)
34 Black Rock Desert st.
36 Vermont college
37 Esthete
38 Fruit tree
39 Fannie __
42 '50s Wyatt Earp portrayer
44 Melodic
45 Heathcliff's creator
46 Forthrightness
49 Bandleader Goodman
51 Moor fighter
53 Warrior princess of TV
54 Flier to Ben-Gurion
55 Dugout display
56 *In* __ (really)
57 Stage hog

★★ ABC

Enter the letters A, B, and C into the diagram so that each row and column has exactly one A, one B, and one C. The letters outside the diagram indicate the first letter encountered, moving in the direction of the arrow. Keep in mind that after all the letters have been filled in, there will be two blank boxes in each row and column.

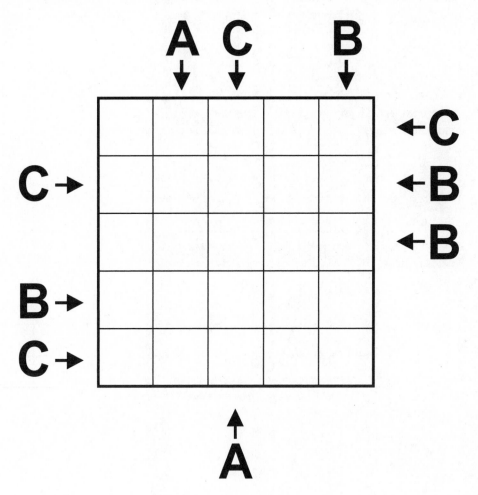

TWO-BY-FOUR

The eight letters in the word LATCHKEY can be rearranged to form a pair of common four-letter words in only one way. Can you find the two words?

— — — —   — — — —

★★ Card Maze

Starting on one of the four corner cards, pass through all the other cards exactly once by moving horizontally or vertically. Each card you visit must be either the same suit or the same rank as the card you just visited.

INITIAL REACTION

The "equation" below contains the initials of words that will make it correct, forming a numerical fact. Solve the equation by supplying the missing words.

3 = B. per M. in W.T. _____

★★ Line Drawing

Draw three straight lines, each from one edge of the square to another edge, so that the letters in each of the five regions spell a five-letter word.

MIXAGRAMS

Each line contains a five-letter word and a four-letter word that have been mixed together (the order of the letters in each word has not been changed). Unmix the two words on each line and write them in the spaces provided. When you're done, find a two-word answer to the clue by reading down the letter columns in the answers.

CLUE: Barbie has one

F L A S A I D E W = _ _ _ _ _ + _ _ _ _

R O A R I B O A T = _ _ _ _ _ + _ _ _ _

S C U R I L L E Y = _ _ _ _ _ + _ _ _ _

F E G A G U L S T = _ _ _ _ _ + _ _ _ _

★★★ Vessels of Fame by Daniel R. Stark

ACROSS

1 Prepare the flour
5 Old keepsake
10 Seaweed derivative
14 Part of mph
15 Writer Jong
16 Relaxed gait
17 Italian menu word
18 Grill
19 Role for Ingrid
20 Henry Hudson vessel
22 Thataway
24 Surely he jests
25 Buying binge
26 Put up a fight
29 Lawyer's concern
30 Utmost degree
33 Meticulous
34 Performs alone
35 Loft filler
36 Pantry items
37 "Mazel __!"
38 Mispronounce "s"
39 German 101 verb
40 Slide on ice
42 Beatrice's admirer
43 Sweater letter
44 __ d'oeuvres
45 Hearth residue
46 Down East
48 Nudge forward
49 Found out
51 Robert Fulton vessel
55 Galley movers
56 Loafed around
58 Met highlight
59 Musical ensemble
60 Island near Oahu
61 Clothes holder
62 Wingspread
63 That is: Lat.
64 Toddler's perch

DOWN

1 Deposed Iranian ruler
2 Town in Kansas
3 Gas-tank status
4 Deals (in)
5 Start a computer again
6 *Captain Blood* name
7 Detroit gridder
8 Here, in Le Havre
9 Jacques Cousteau vessel
10 Flared skirt
11 Sir Francis Drake vessel
12 Church area
13 Trunk's locale
21 More than half
23 Assayers' samples
25 Ointment
26 Fix a cravat
27 Have a life
28 Christopher Columbus vessel
29 Stodgy ones
31 Common sense
32 Keyed up
34 It may be vacant
38 Tourist stop
40 Climb a rope
41 Thor Heyerdahl vessel
42 10 Down designer
45 Bank offering
47 Fire chief's suspicion
48 Tearful requests
49 Realty offerings
50 Tombstone lawman
51 Mystery board game
52 North African port
53 "Well done!"
54 Box-office total
57 Family member

★★ Find the Ships

Determine the position of the 10 ships listed to the right of the diagram. The ships may be oriented either horizontally or vertically. A square with wavy lines indicates water and will not contain a ship. The numbers at the edge of the diagram indicate how many squares in that row or column contain parts of ships. When all 10 ships are correctly placed in the diagram, no two of them will touch each other, not even diagonally.

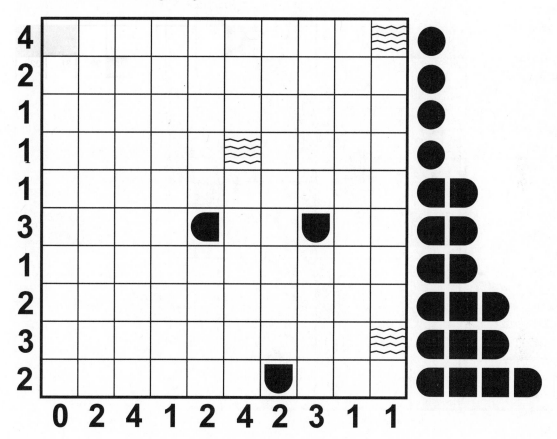

THREE AT A RHYME

Rearrange these letters to form three one-syllable words that rhyme.

E E M N N N O O P R R S T U W

_____   _____   _____

★★★ Hyper-Sudoku

Fill in the blank boxes so that every row, column, 3x3 box, *and* each of the four 3x3 gray regions contains all of the numbers 1 to 9.

	7	9	6		1			8
5		6				4		
		7	5					
2			4		3	6	9	
		5				9	1	
	8		1	9		2	4	
	2				4			

TONGUE TWISTER

From what language are all of these words derived:

EMBARRASS, MOLASSES, PAGODA, and PIRANHA?

A) Persian B) Chinese C) Czech D) Portuguese

★★★ Outside the Law by Robert H. Wolfe

ACROSS

1 RPM part
4 Where sparrows may sit
10 __ Le Pew
14 Libation station potation
15 Ideal spot
16 Moran of *Happy Days*
17 Kind of crook
19 Egg on
20 Be in accord
21 Felt regret
23 "Give me __!" (Columbus cheer start)
24 Frequent delivery
25 Kind of crook
28 Colony member
29 "I knew it!"
30 Ivy Leaguers, casually
31 Fr. holy woman
32 Ranch tyros
35 Area unit
36 Kind of crook
39 Fancy wheels
42 Minute quantity
43 HBO competitor
46 Becomes accustomed (to)
49 Tennis call
50 Word from the stands
51 Kind of crook
54 Horse hair
55 Extremity
56 Rights org.
57 Lesser part of a 45
58 Tale teller
60 Kind of crook
63 Volcanic mount
64 Mogul's home
65 Montreal summer
66 Changed color
67 Took five

68 Wine choice

DOWN

1 Night wear
2 Refined and tasteful
3 Script change
4 Exercise authority
5 Giant great
6 "Wow!"
7 Richard's veep
8 Bind
9 Free from risk
10 Get-up-and-go
11 Not consistent
12 Western settler
13 Get behind
18 Food fish
22 Circle line: Abbr.
25 Cast out
26 Attacked
27 Lacking bubbles
29 Bustle
33 Misplay the ball
34 Like old rye
36 Sort of stopper
37 Bakery finisher
38 Filming area
39 Defamed in print
40 Mindlessness
41 Quite ordinary

43 Tractor follower
44 Authorization to act
45 Rooted for
47 Important time
48 Suburban kids' sport
52 Nonchalantly unconcerned
53 Prank victims
54 Food additive initials
57 Raised, as horses
59 X-ray unit
61 Diamond wood
62 Sport __ (kind of vehicle)

★★★ Circular Reasoning

Connect all of the circles by drawing a single continuous line through every square of the diagram. All right-angle turns of your line must alternate between boxes containing a circle and boxes not containing a circle. You must make a right-angle turn out of every square that contains a circle. Your line must end in the same square that it begins, and it cannot enter any square more than once.

COUNTDOWN

Inserting plus signs and minus signs, as many as necessary, in between the digits from 9 to 1 below, create a series of additions and subtractions whose final answer is 150. Any digits without a sign between them are to be grouped together as a single number.

$$9 \quad 8 \quad 7 \quad 6 \quad 5 \quad 4 \quad 3 \quad 2 \quad 1 \quad = \quad 150$$

★★★ Looped Path

Draw a continuous, unbroken loop that passes through each of the red, blue, and white squares exactly once. Move from square to square in a straight line or by turning left or right, but never diagonally. You must alternate passing through red and blue squares, with any number of white squares in between.

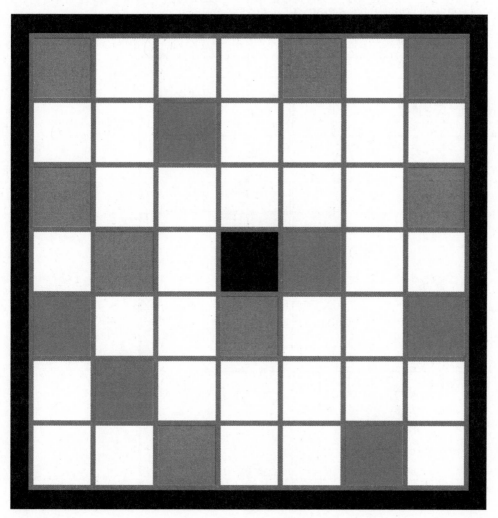

CITY SEARCH

Using the letters in VANCOUVER, we were able to form only three common uncapitalized six-letter words and one common uncapitalized seven-letter word. Can you find them all?

— — — — — —   — — — — — —

— — — — — —

— — — — — — —

★★ Islands

Shade in some of the white squares in the diagram with "water," so that each remaining white box is part of an island. Each island will contain exactly one numbered square, indicating how many squares that island contains. Each island is separated from the other islands by water but may touch other islands diagonally. All water is connected, but there are no 2x2 regions of water in the diagram.

6					
				3	
1					
		2			
				3	

COMMON SENSE

What five-letter word can be found in the dictionary definitions of all of these words:

SNAP, REVOLT, CRIME, and INTERRUPT?

_ _ _ _ _

★★★ That's a Wrap by Patrick Jordan

ACROSS

1 Toro competitor
6 Course ritual
10 Reduce to rubble
14 Intense eagerness
15 Austen novel
16 Victor's outburst
17 Playground shout
19 He works for M
20 Tongue suffix
21 *Wheel of Fortune* option
22 Waiter's stations
24 Find contemptible
26 Castor and Pollux sailed on it
27 Actress Gardner
28 Hive head
32 Locale for 32 Down
35 Protrudes
36 Cryptogram key
37 Publisher in a classic film
38 Loved ones
39 Sea adjoining Kazakhstan
40 Champagne chiller
41 Like moonless nights
42 Boris, to Bullwinkle
43 Flier with pontoons
45 Made a meal of
46 Tomato type
47 Revlon rival
51 Curly, e.g.
54 Medieval toiler
55 Cooking phrase
56 Bakery buy
57 Boom-box feature
60 Opposing
61 Polish a column
62 For all to hear
63 Horror film atmosphere
64 Turns rancid
65 Thorns in one's side

DOWN

1 Stepped out with
2 Clear, as a hard drive
3 Frontiers
4 Pop artist Lichtenstein
5 Causing disintegration
6 Reminiscent of Poe
7 Hugh Jackman film of 2000
8 "What __ saying?"
9 "The Princess and the Pea" prop
10 Sweet-shop selection
11 Mil. crime
12 Sector
13 Closes out
18 __-daisy
23 Leave in a wine cellar
25 Unrealized gain
26 "Here Comes Santa Claus" singer
28 Seismograph triggerer
29 Party pariah
30 Cheese in a rind
31 Prone to wriggling
32 Alberto Tomba gear
33 Valentine trim
34 Draftable
35 A First Daughter
38 Circle statistic
42 Winter-hat attachment
44 Skipper's record
45 47-stringed instrument
47 Is introduced to
48 Sends to the canvas
49 Alaska Peninsula dweller
50 Links units
51 Criticize harshly
52 Author Morrison
53 Granola grain
54 Narrow peninsula
58 __ Annie (*Oklahoma!* role)
59 Porter or stout

★★★ 123

Fill in the diagram so that each rectangular piece has one each of the numbers 1, 2, and 3, under these rules: 1) No two adjacent squares, horizontally or vertically, can have the same number. 2) Each completed row and column of the diagram will have an equal number of 1s, 2s, and 3s.

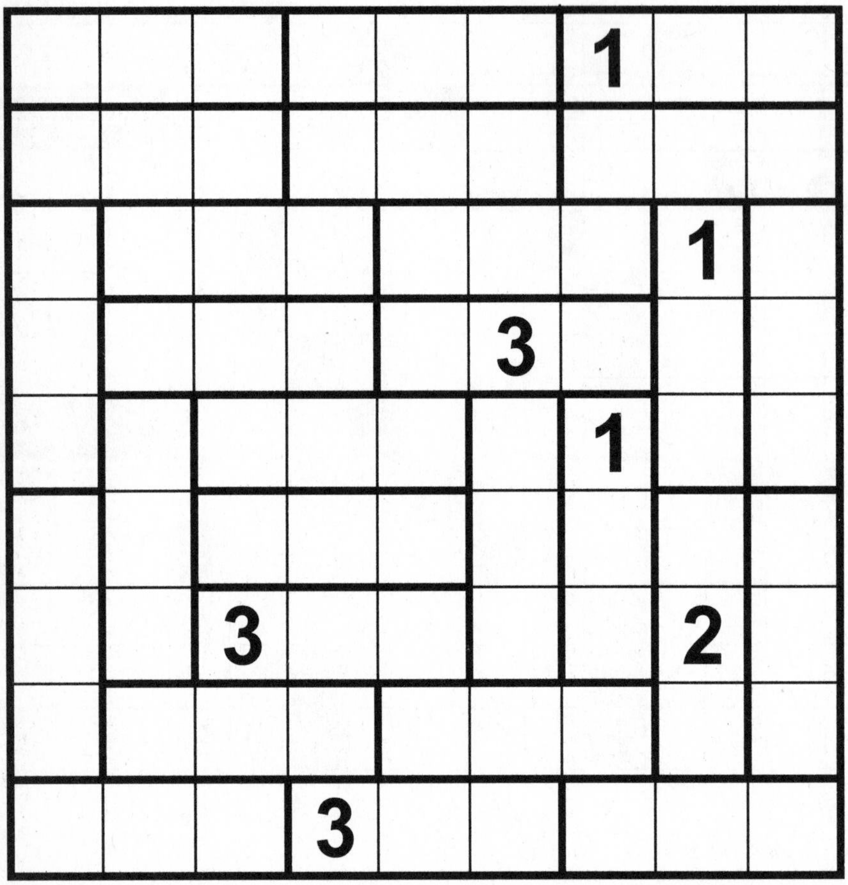

						1		
							1	
					3			
						1		
		3					2	
			3					

BETWEENER

What four-letter word belongs between the word at left and the word at right, so that the first and second word, and the second and third word, each form a common two-word phrase?

ANNUAL __ __ __ __ WAR

★★★ Find the Ships

Determine the position of the 10 ships listed to the right of the diagram. The ships may be oriented either horizontally or vertically. A square with wavy lines indicates water and will not contain a ship. The numbers at the edge of the diagram indicate how many squares in that row or column contain parts of ships. When all 10 ships are correctly placed in the diagram, no two of them will touch each other, not even diagonally.

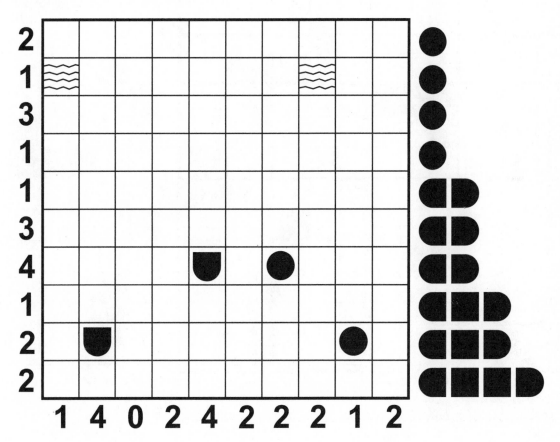

ADDITION SWITCH

Switch the positions of two of the digits in the incorrect sum at right, to get a correct sum.

```
  5 1 2
+ 3 9 8
-------
  8 0 0
```

★★★ Gotcha by Fred Piscop

ACROSS

1 Red Sox, on scoreboards
4 Fitness centers
8 Smoothly, in music
14 Eyebrow shape
15 *Vogue* competitor
16 Arthurian paradise
17 Resort, for short
18 *The Ghost and Mrs. __*
19 Israeli, e.g.
20 Basketball broadcaster's remark
23 Essayist's nom de plume
24 Board flaw
25 Abridge too far?
28 Sordid
30 Jerusalem's land: Abbr.
32 Novelist Deighton
33 Spearheaded
35 __ carte
36 Patchy in color
37 Sinatra film of '55
41 Uprising
42 Not as large as lge.
43 Sundial hour
44 Sushi fish
45 Little drink
46 Sub detector
50 French port
52 "Oh, woe!"
56 San __, Italy
57 E.B. White children's story
60 *Seinfeld* woman
62 Enjoy a novel
63 Yalie
64 To the point
65 Basilica's center
66 Go astray
67 Made soapy
68 "So be it!"

69 Street game

DOWN

1 Noble's partner
2 Black-and-orange bird
3 Nova __
4 Highway hauler
5 Coin-on-the-counter sound
6 Set straight
7 __-Croatian
8 Go the distance
9 More uniform
10 Video-arcade enthusiast
11 Carrier to Rome

12 Young'un
13 Latish lunchtime
21 Shakespearean prince
22 Of service
26 Trickle (out)
27 Phase out
29 Thus far
31 Delhi attire
34 Moore of film
35 Say further
36 Rap-sheet listings
37 Stadium level
38 Asset held in reserve
39 Katmandu's land
40 "__ the season ..."

41 CSA soldier
45 Batter's position
47 Most current
48 Aviator Earhart
49 Dressing after a bath, perhaps
51 Recoils, with "away"
53 Fictional Doone
54 First-stringers
55 Barrel strip
58 On Soc. Sec., perhaps
59 Genesis locale
60 Mag. staffers
61 Lucy of *Charlie's Angels*

★★ About Time

Find the 24 "timely" words that are hidden in the diagram either across, down, or diagonally. One of the words is TIME; the rest are for you to discover.

```
H E B R O H Q F I Q E T
E G A T S I C N L R W I
E T U N I M T T U A N M
C M D T T E A T E C S E
I S S U R I C M S R L H
R B H V R N C L A I T T
T H A V U A S K H Y N S
O L K J D I T W P I A F
T X E H N N V I O X C D
J N O P O S E P O Z D S
R U I K C T S P A N P F
R L Y T E A M O M E N T
K E E W S N G Z L K N J
J I F F Y T U L Y T I W
```

CLUELESS CROSSWORD

Complete the crossword with common uncapitalized seven-letter words, based entirely on the letters already filled in for you.

★★★ Word Maze

Starting in the center, find the continuous loop that passes through all the other words without retracing any paths, and ends in the center. Each word you visit must be exactly one letter different from the word you just visited.

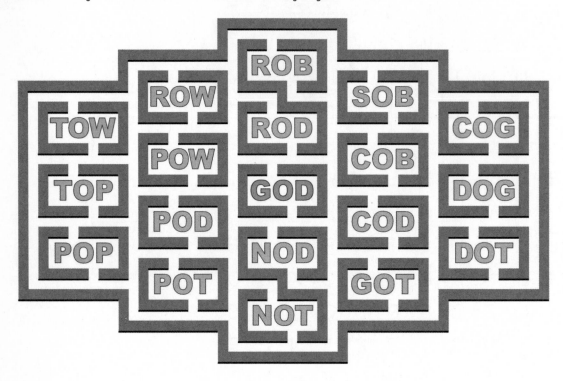

SOUND THINKING

We can think of seven common uncapitalized words whose only consonant sounds are V, R, and D, in that order. How many can you think of?

_____   _____   _____

_____   _____

_____   _____

★★★ Star Search

Find the stars that are hidden in some of the blank squares. The numbered squares indicate how many stars are hidden in the squares adjacent to them (including diagonally). There is never more than one star in any square.

		2		1				
				4				2
1		2	3					
1				5		6	3	
1			2					
1		2				2		1
			5					
			2			1		
				2				

TELEPHONE TRIOS

1	ABC 2	DEF 3
GHI 4	JKL 5	MNO 6
PRS 7	TUV 8	WXY 9
*	O	#

Using the numbers and letters on a standard telephone, what three seven-letter words from the same category can be formed from these telephone numbers?

222-4637 _ _ _ _ _ _ _

688-6626 _ _ _ _ _ _ _

444-4269 _ _ _ _ _ _ _

★★★ Temperature's Rising by Randall J. Hartman

ACROSS

1 Thompson and Samms
6 Patron saint of Norway
10 Hula-Hoop and pogo stick
14 Act like a sleepyhead
15 Capital of Latvia
16 Rap star
17 Ache soother
19 World's longest river
20 Completely
21 Memphis-to-Mobile dir.
22 Scan for errata
23 Abel's younger brother
25 Enjoys a mint julep
27 *Little Women* girl
30 Fire extinguisher ingredient
35 Porous gem
37 Feel peaked
38 Buenos __
39 Port for 6 Across
40 Faucet annoyances
43 Penpoints
44 Sorrow
46 "Boola Boola" boy
47 Clinton's veep
48 Incriminating evidence
51 Cole of song
52 Frankenstein's assistant
53 Read quickly
56 Ollie's associate
59 Run in
61 Stuck, perhaps
65 Flash Gordon foe
66 Buckley TV forum
68 Not fooled by
69 Once more
70 Tune of yore
71 Acquire
72 New hand
73 Takes out for a spin

DOWN

1 Pre-coll.
2 One's carriage
3 Substantive content
4 Assembly-line products
5 Rancor
6 Pt. of AFL-CIO
7 Chicken's lack
8 1999 U.S. Open champ
9 Film technique
10 Handling deftly
11 Citric, for instance
12 Neighborhood shop
13 Dele's opposite
18 Acceptable
24 "Aquarius" musical
26 Tiger Woods' grp.
27 Dispositions
28 British racetrack locale
29 Vintners' surname
31 __ light (film-set need)
32 "Belted" constellation
33 Winger or Paget
34 Balance-sheet plus
36 Watching
41 Arithmetic sign
42 Become understood
45 CBer's vehicle
49 Like some milk
50 Less than sharp, as a photo
54 Fort Knox bar
55 *Atlantic City* director
56 Unclean air
57 Fey of *30 Rock*
58 Not pro
60 __ Rabbit
62 Disencumbers
63 One of a set
64 Driving aids
67 __ Jima

★★★ Sudoku

Fill in the blank boxes so that every row, column, and 3x3 box contains all of the numbers 1 to 9.

		3	8					
1			6	9		8		7
				5		9		1
	2		5					3
						7		
		5		7	4	6		
	7	9		6				
8							2	9
5	4	2		8				

AND SO ON

Unscramble the letters in the phrase SHIP PILOTS, to form two words that are part of a common phrase that has the word AND between them.

_____ and _____

★★★ One-Way Streets

The diagram represents a pattern of streets. A and B are parking spaces, and the black squares are stores. Find the route that starts at A, passes through all stores exactly once, and ends at B. Arrows indicate one-way traffic for that block only. No block or intersection may be entered more than once.

COMMON SENSE

What five-letter adjective can be found in the dictionary definitions of all of these words:

SLAM, MAGPIE, SLURP, and RIOT?

_ _ _ _ _

★★★ ABC

Enter the letters A, B, and C into the diagram so that each row and column has exactly one A, one B, and one C. The letters outside the diagram indicate the first letter encountered, moving in the direction of the arrow. Keep in mind that after all the letters have been filled in, there will be two blank boxes in each row and column.

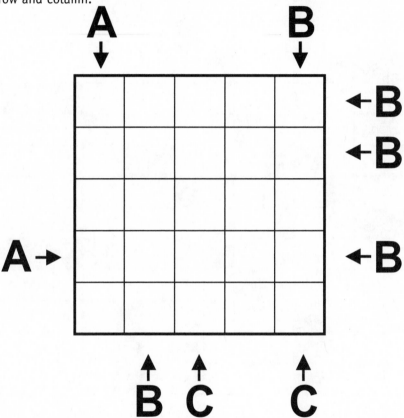

MIXAGRAMS

Each line contains a five-letter word and a four-letter word that have been mixed together (the order of the letters in each word has not been changed). Unmix the two words on each line and write them in the spaces provided. When you're done, find a two-word answer to the clue by reading down the letter columns in the answers.

CLUE: Stole, perhaps

N I M I B C U K E = _ _ _ _ _ + _ _ _ _

A C H I L O P E D = _ _ _ _ _ + _ _ _ _

V A N E G A L S T = _ _ _ _ _ + _ _ _ _

W I S K E T H I N = _ _ _ _ _ + _ _ _ _

★★★ Olympic Memories by Patrick Jordan

ACROSS

1 Mideast seaport
5 Meant to happen
10 Hydroelectric structures
14 "In your dreams!"
15 Be of one mind
16 Drop
17 Melodious Horne
18 *Little House on the Prairie* girl
19 Festive affair
20 Former Olympic event
22 *Wheel of Fortune* guess
24 Hi-___ computer graphics
25 Rogers' frequent partner
26 Former Olympic event
31 Phrase in an arrow
32 Forelimb feature
33 Smidgen
36 "Without a doubt!"
37 Downed
38 Dispatch from the boss
39 Seek, as a price
40 Made the scene
42 Operator, at times
44 Former Olympic event
46 Fine points
49 Floor covering
50 Burro or bronco
51 Former Olympic event
56 Ancient, to Burns
57 Come to ___ (begin bubbling)
59 Alarmed outburst
60 Honor a judge's entrance
61 *Marching Along* autobiographer
62 Actress Lollobrigida
63 Connect the banks of
64 Adds up, informally
65 Watch winder

DOWN

1 Impudence
2 On a whale watch, maybe
3 Multivitamin mineral
4 At a distance
5 In a spurious manner
6 Andre of tennis
7 Quiz answer
8 Eternally, in verse
9 Buys and sells
10 G.I.'s ID
11 Stradivarius alternative
12 Long-distance runner
13 Behold rudely
21 Seal-hunting swimmer
23 Europe's tallest volcano
25 Showing talent
26 One of California's Santas
27 Unpleasant task
28 Brighten (up)
29 Meadow bleater
30 Not as loud
33 Salami source
34 Grace ender
35 Jimmy Connors rival
37 "Famous" cookie guy
38 Doorstep covering
40 Bit of change
41 No fewer than
42 Lincoln debate opponent
43 Othello's ill-wisher
44 Damsel
45 Banana blemish
46 Beloved folk
47 Outfit
48 Garth Brooks' birthplace
51 Sing the praises of
52 Steams up
53 Smallest amount
54 Author Rice
55 Emulate buffaloes
58 Startling shout

★★★ Go With the Flow

Enter the maze at left, pass through all the starred circles, then exit at right.
You must go with the flow, making no sharp turns. Your path can cross itself, but
you may not retrace your path.

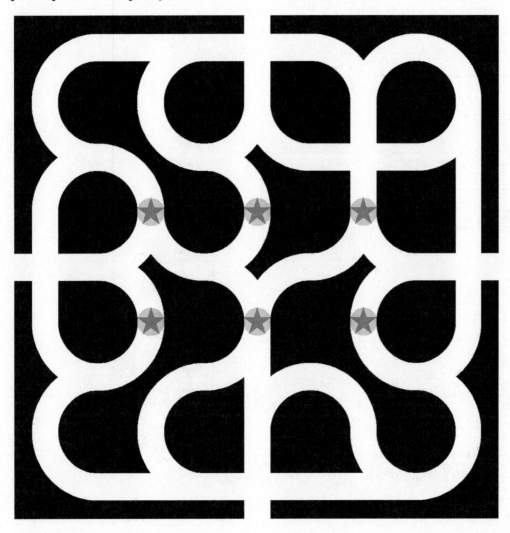

TWO-BY-FOUR

The eight letters in the word NUTRIENT can be rearranged to form a pair of common four-letter
words in three different ways, if no four-letter word is repeated. Can you find all three pairs of
words?

__ __ __ __　__ __ __ __

__ __ __ __　__ __ __ __

__ __ __ __　__ __ __ __

★★★ Find the Ships

Determine the position of the 10 ships listed to the right of the diagram. The ships may be oriented either horizontally or vertically. A square with wavy lines indicates water and will not contain a ship. The numbers at the edge of the diagram indicate how many squares in that row or column contain parts of ships. When all 10 ships are correctly placed in the diagram, no two of them will touch each other, not even diagonally.

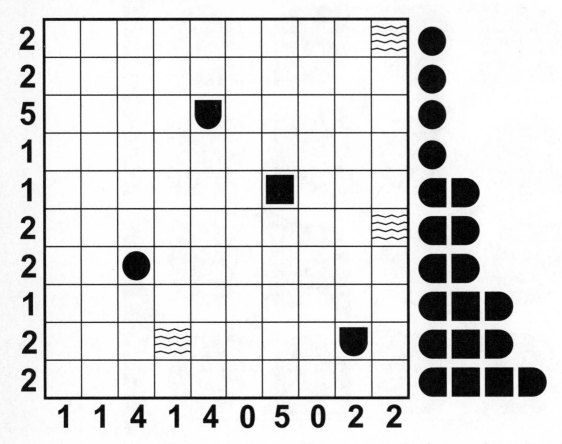

SUDOKU SUM

Without repeating any digits, complete the sum at right, by filling one digit in each of the five blanks.

$$
\begin{array}{r}
3\ \_\ 1 \\
+\ \_\ 6\ \_ \\
\hline
8\ \_\ \_
\end{array}
$$

★★★ 123

Fill in the diagram so that each rectangular piece has one each of the numbers 1, 2, and 3, under these rules: 1) No two adjacent squares, horizontally or vertically, can have the same number. 2) Each completed row and column of the diagram will have an equal number of 1s, 2s, and 3s.

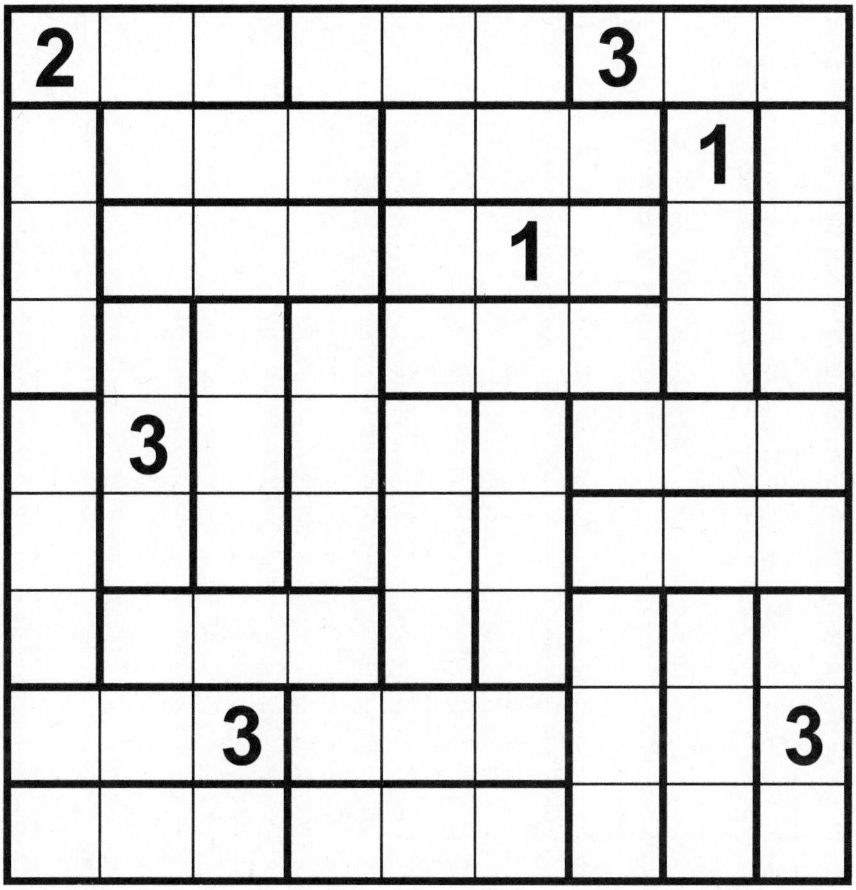

IN OTHER WORDS

There are four common uncapitalized words that contain the consecutive letters WPO. How many of them can you think of?

_____   _____

_____   _____

bRain BREAtHEr
AMAZING TIDBITS
ABOUT U.S. PRESIDENTS

History has taught us which president presided over America during this or that war, and which laws they passed and vetoed. But did you know that ...

President William Henry Harrison served just one month in office? He died of pneumonia not very long after taking the oath.

* * *

President Herbert Hoover and his wife, Lou, spoke Chinese when they wanted to speak privately in the presence of White House guests? Shortly after they married, the Hoovers had spent time in China while Herbert Hoover was a consultant to the Chinese director of the Ministry of Mines.

* * *

After President Woodrow Wilson suffered a stroke in 1919, his wife, Edith, barred everyone from visiting him, and reportedly made many state decisions in her husband's stead?

* * *

President William H. Taft (whose term was 1909–1913) was the only chief executive who later became chief justice of the Supreme Court?

* * *

George Washington created the Purple Heart award, for military enlistees wounded in action, in 1782. It lapsed into disuse for 150 years, and was reinstated to honor Washington's 200th birthday.

* * *

President Gerald Ford was a model before he went into politics? He was featured in a 1940 *Look* magazine article.

* * *

President Grover Cleveland was diagnosed with jaw cancer in 1893, during his second term in office. To avert public panic, he told no one—not even his pregnant wife—about his diagnosis. He secretly underwent surgery to remove the cancer aboard a friend's yacht that was moored in New York's East River. Because the cancer was so advanced, most of the president's upper left jaw was removed. He was later fitted with a prosthetic device that enabled him to speak. The truth was not revealed until 20 years after the surgery was done.

* * *

Here is out favorite and most remarkable tidbit: Abraham Lincoln's first vice president (1861-1865) was Hannibal Hamlin. Take a good look at Abra**HAM LIN**coln's name and you'll find HAMLIN hidden within it.

★★★★ Two Women by Richard Silvestri

ACROSS

1 Way of walking
5 Bard's Muse
10 Kid
14 Skin soother
15 Farmer, at times
16 Kal Kan rival
17 Minstrel's instrument
18 Pageant prize
19 Cause distress
20 Musical pair?
22 Put in the pot
23 Part of TGIF
24 Father goose
26 Emulate Sherlock
30 Tournament breaks
32 Surfaced
33 Self-righteous pair?
38 Polar drift
39 Conscience-stricken
40 Sufficient, once
41 Regional pair?
43 "Common Sense" author
44 A piece of cake
45 Got an apartment
46 Tie-up
50 Cal. column
51 Cookie favorite
52 Happy pair?
59 Tug
60 Nolan or Napoleon
61 Game with mallets
62 Play to ___ (draw)
63 Kitchen utensil
64 Party to
65 Look like Groucho
66 Castor and Pollux
67 Horn, for one

DOWN

1 Dressy event
2 Grad
3 Little bit
4 New driver, often
5 Probate matter
6 Stirs up
7 Absent
8 Arctic flier
9 Hothouse for fruit
10 Kobe's home
11 African antelope
12 Malice
13 Copier need
21 Atlantic City rollers
25 Simile center
26 Silly
27 Colleague of Agatha
28 It's shown to some
29 Person at a terminal
30 Opponent of Lyndon
31 Dr. Zhivago
33 Jersey sounds
34 Low-fat
35 "What's ___ for me?"
36 Region
37 Blown away
39 Speaks falteringly
42 Roll-call vote
43 Baker's implement
45 King and queen
46 Faithful
47 Make a speech
48 Bottled spirit
49 Extra card
50 Polk predecessor
53 Cloverleaf component
54 Costa ___
55 DeMille film
56 Hebrides island
57 Gooey stuff
58 Sharpen

★★★ Circular Reasoning

Connect all of the circles by drawing a single continuous line through every square of the diagram. All right-angle turns of your line must alternate between boxes containing a circle and boxes not containing a circle. You must make a right-angle turn out of every square that contains a circle. Your line must end in the same square that it begins, and it cannot enter any square more than once.

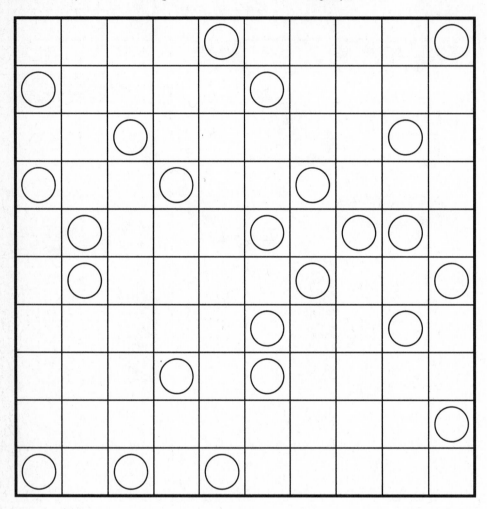

AND SO ON

Unscramble the letters in the phrase LOAD EGG RACK, to form two words that are part of a common phrase that has the word AND between them.

_____ and _____

★★★ Islands

Shade in some of the white squares in the diagram with "water," so that each remaining white box is part of an island. Each island will contain exactly one numbered square, indicating how many squares that island contains. Each island is separated from the other islands by water but may touch other islands diagonally. All water is connected, but there are no 2x2 regions of water in the diagram.

				1			
					2		
		4					
	3		4				
2					3		
		3					

THREE AT A RHYME

Rearrange these letters to form three one-syllable words that rhyme.

A A A C E K M P Q R R R S U

_____ _____ _____

★★★★ Average Addition by Doug Peterson

ACROSS

1 Triangular letter
6 "Over here!"
10 Footnote abbr.
14 Says with authority
15 Mongibello alias
16 Long skirt
17 *Vertigo* actress
18 "Agreed!"
19 Domino's dots
20 Dog groomer's business?
23 Status ___
24 Festive night
25 Yuletide
26 Turn away from
28 Flying off the shelves
31 "Jingle Bells" vehicle
33 From the heart
37 Geometry calculation
38 Sound from O'Leary's chicken?
42 Pigpen plaint
43 Make believe
44 Spy of fiction
46 Supernatural
50 Birds, to Brutus
51 Insightful one
54 ___ Dhabi
55 Tad's dad
56 Duplicate a forestry pro?
60 Griffin of TV
62 Toaster waffle brand
63 Lothario's looks
64 Flatten
65 Mellowed, perhaps
66 Bert's pal
67 Snake eyes
68 Private Gomer
69 Musical postscripts

DOWN

1 Music video extra
2 Develop over time
3 Imposed, as a tax
4 Golfer's bane
5 Sets, as a price
6 Martinez of baseball
7 Martin or Martini
8 Symbol of slowness
9 Bath powder
10 Little rascal
11 Bar order
12 Strikes out
13 Japanese soup flavoring

21 Concept in thermodynamics
22 U.S. immigrant's subj.
27 Trump, at times
29 Razz from the stands
30 Flooring material
31 Type of clam
32 "Take that!"
34 Grid org.
35 LAX info
36 Just short
38 NYSE listings
39 Succotash ingredient

40 Cosmos
41 More than aloof
45 PC key
47 Last part
48 Albéniz suite
49 Villain's outburst
51 Too wet
52 Play backer
53 Crystalline rock
55 Firearm filler
57 Hurdle
58 Obi-Wan portrayer
59 Galba predecessor
61 Tape letters

★★★ Color Squares

Enter the maze at bottom left, pass through all the color squares once and then exit at top right, all without retracing your path. You must pass through the color squares in this order: red, blue, yellow, red, blue, yellow, etc.

BETWEENER

What five-letter word belongs between the word at left and the word at right, so that the first and second word, and the second and third word, each form a common two-word phrase?

RABBIT _ _ _ _ _ BOWL

★★★ Hyper-Sudoku

Fill in the blank boxes so that every row, column, 3x3 box, *and* each of the four
3x3 gray regions contains all of the numbers 1 to 9.

		1		2		9		
		3	1		4	2		
					9		3	
	7							
3		8			1		2	9
5		9						
		4	6					
						1		
6					5	4	7	

TELEPHONE TRIOS

1	ABC **2**	DEF **3**
GHI **4**	JKL **5**	MNO **6**
PRS **7**	TUV **8**	WXY **9**
*	**0**	**#**

Using the numbers and letters on a standard telephone, what
three seven-letter words from the same category can be formed
from these telephone numbers?

226-8282   _ _ _ _ _ _ _

585-5229   _ _ _ _ _ _ _

724-8463   _ _ _ _ _ _ _

★★ Three-for-One Word Search

Find the seven hidden words in each of the three diagrams, either across, down, or diagonally. A hint to each group of words is found above each diagram.

DIAMOND

```
D  Z  Q  H  D  Y  C
B  L  U  X  Y  N  O
M  G  A  R  N  E  T
I  L  R  R  U  S  A
J  A  T  L  E  B  U
N  P  Z  V  X  M  Y
T  O  P  A  Z  O  E
```

CLUB

```
W  P  J  H  R  T  Y
E  G  U  S  R  T  O
R  A  U  O  E  P  X
C  U  U  I  R  D  E
G  P  C  N  L  G  K
E  O  B  A  N  D  Z
S  E  L  C  R  I  C
```

SPADE

```
L  M  N  E  S  F  M
F  E  O  O  R  O  J
X  H  V  W  A  R  Q
V  Z  S  O  E  K  W
E  K  A  R  H  R  G
U  I  B  R  S  S  A
T  R  O  W  E  L  H
```

ADDITION SWITCH

Switch the positions of two of the digits in the incorrect sum at right, to get a correct sum.

```
   3 9 1
 + 2 4 4
 ───────
   4 3 7
```

★★★★ New-Wave Composers by Daniel R. Stark

ACROSS

1 Free pass
5 Seize, as power
10 Fronts of overalls
14 Buffalo's lake
15 Madame Curie
16 Modern Persia
17 Composer's fee?
19 Rigatoni kin
20 Building site
21 Outfits
22 Coffeemaker switch
24 Not aboard ship
26 "Say __?"
27 Stein filler
28 Feet
32 Emerald or aquamarine
35 Motel amenity
36 Just a bit
37 Writer Bagnold
38 Goody-goody
39 Grab hold of, with "onto"
40 Footballer Swann
41 Tholes' contents
42 Preposterous
43 Dilly-dalliers
45 Harem room
46 Dog in *Beetle Bailey*
47 "The flower of my heart"
51 California peak
54 Befuddled
55 *The Confessions of __ Turner*
56 Angler's device
57 Composer's meal?
60 Tommie of baseball
61 Margarita ingredients
62 *Quo Vadis?* role
63 Crest
64 Actress Verdugo
65 Natural resources

DOWN

1 String quartet member
2 Rigel's constellation
3 Drizzles lightly
4 Dispenser candy
5 Ballpark official
6 NCO nickname
7 *Topaz* author
8 Ocasek of rock
9 Door feature
10 Composer's cue?
11 Tall flower
12 Diminish
13 Grumpy mood
18 Billy Goats Gruff foe
23 Lab denizen
25 Composer's game?
26 Tiger with trophies
28 Travel agent offerings
29 Kansas town
30 Ian Fleming alma mater
31 Identical
32 Saved by the __
33 Gaelic pop star
34 Circus stage
35 Madrid art gallery
38 Easy to carry
42 Just right
44 Bar mem.
45 Forsyth's *The __ File*
47 Scared-looking
48 Hidden
49 Conch lining
50 Social mores
51 Challenge to a duel
52 Gargantuan
53 Linoleum measurement
54 Summit
58 Have a cold
59 Numero __

★★ Triad Split Decisions

In this clueless crossword puzzle, each answer consists of two words whose spellings are the same, except for the consecutive letters given. All answers are common words; no phrases or hyphenated or capitalized words are used. Some of the clues may have more than one solution, but there is only one word pair that will correctly link up with all the other word pairs.

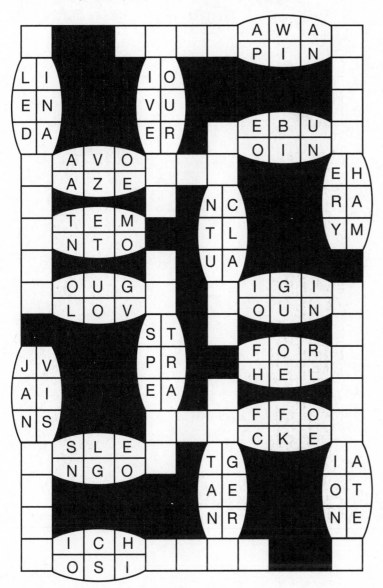

TRANSDELETION

Delete one letter from the word HIGHWAYMEN and rearrange the rest, to get the last name of an American author.

_____

★★★ One-Way Streets

The diagram represents a pattern of streets. A and B are parking spaces, and the black squares are stores. Find the route that starts at A, passes through all stores exactly once, and ends at B. Arrows indicate one-way traffic for that block only. No block or intersection may be entered more than once.

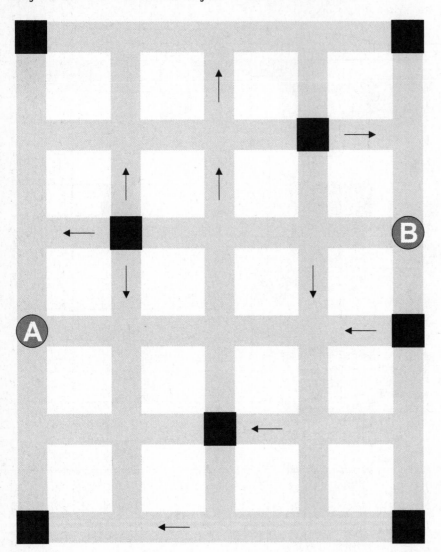

SOUND THINKING

We can think of four common uncapitalized words whose only consonants sounds are K, R, T, and L, in that order. How many can you think of?

_____ _____

_____ _____

★★★★ Soil Bank by Merle Baker

ACROSS

 1 Frequency range
 5 Take exception
10 Don on the radio
14 From a distance
15 Wipe away
16 Spanish surrealist
17 Started
20 Defeat, in a way
21 Showy flowers
22 Test run
23 11 Down souvenir
24 Less than ideal
29 Sky blue
33 One or more
36 River termini
38 Part of QED
39 Pulls off a double cross
42 Solemn declaration
43 Wall Street index
44 Red, for one
45 Hobbits' home, with "The"
47 Accelerate
49 Press agent's quest
51 It comes from the heart
55 Conspicuously fine
59 Living room pieces
61 Get real
63 Open slightly
64 Embarked on
65 Gross weight deduction
66 Little League transporters
67 Pretentious ones
68 __ even keel

DOWN

 1 __ tricks
 2 In conflict with, with "of"
 3 Cooper character
 4 Large numbers
 5 Skillful
 6 *Harper's Bazaar* illustrator
 7 __-jongg
 8 Hand-me-down
 9 Fit for a king
10 Like an icon
11 Molokai neighbor
12 Arm bone
13 Caesar et al.
18 Public meetings
19 Ostrich kin
25 Blessing
26 Big cats
27 "This is only __"
28 __ Island
30 *Trinity* author
31 Few and far between
32 Singer James
33 Fusses
34 Daniel Webster cousin
35 Hairy Himalayan
37 Break
40 Children's hospital benefactors
41 Consider the same
46 Sooner State city
48 Picnic salad ingredient
50 Radio controls
52 Put on again
53 Aquarium fish
54 Wan
55 Defraud
56 IHOP alternative
57 Muslim prayer leader
58 Actress Verdon
59 Pencil throwaway
60 Seemingly forever
62 __ Dinh Diem

★★★ Dicey

Draw a continuous, unbroken loop that passes through every die exactly once. Move from die to die in a straight line or by turning left or right, but never diagonally. You may not pass through two consecutive dice that add up to seven.

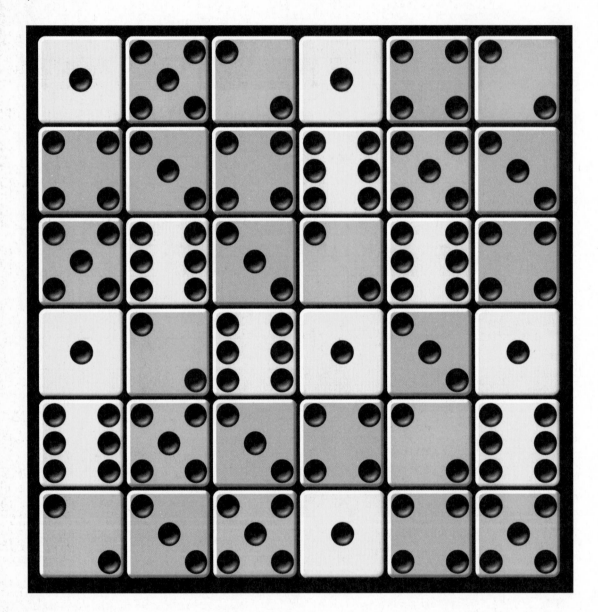

TRANSDELETION

Delete one letter from the word CERTAINLY and rearrange the rest, to get a musical instrument.

★★★ Star Search

Find the stars that are hidden in some of the blank squares. The numbered squares indicate how many stars are hidden in the squares adjacent to them (including diagonally). There is never more than one star in any square.

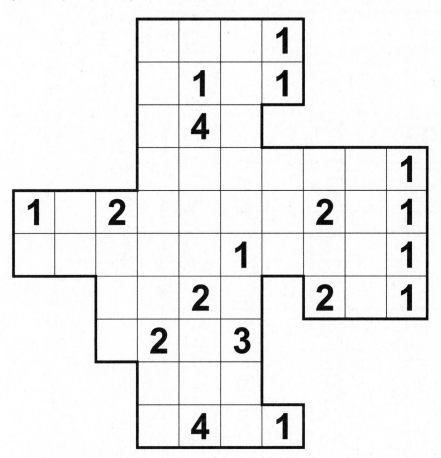

MIXAGRAMS

Each line contains a five-letter word and a four-letter word that have been mixed together (the order of the letters in each word has not been changed). Unmix the two words on each line and write them in the spaces provided. When you're done, find a two-word answer to the clue by reading down the letter columns in the answers.

CLUE: Armor?

S H Y R E W E D S = _ _ _ _ _ + _ _ _ _

S O L A K E D E N = _ _ _ _ _ + _ _ _ _

B E E R A R T O R = _ _ _ _ _ + _ _ _ _

H I D E L E R O D = _ _ _ _ _ + _ _ _ _

★★★★ Sudoku

Fill in the blank boxes so that every row, column, and 3x3 box contains all of the numbers 1 to 9.

	8		5					9
				3	1			5
		4	9		6	8	7	
			4		7		6	
		9			5			8
7						3		
5	1							
9			6	1	8		4	
	4							

THREE OF A KIND

Find the three hidden words in the sentence that, read in order, go together in some way.

Agnes photographed the Grand Canyon's scenic old ruins.

★★★★ Fault Line by Patrick Jordan

ACROSS

1 "Anything __?"
5 Composer Philip
10 Fuse
14 Computer input
15 Lake of *Hairspray*
16 Brainchild
17 Start of a Cervantes quote
20 Catch a few winks
21 Inning's six
22 '50s Dodger star
23 Inferior
25 Susan B. Anthony colleague
27 Eau __, WI
29 Hunting dog
33 Auto pioneer
34 More underhanded
35 Educators' org.
36 Middle of quote
40 French Mrs.
41 Out of kilter
42 Moon of Jupiter
43 Dictionary's first animal
45 African menace
47 Chessboard row
48 Jazz legend Washington
49 Passive protest
52 Don Corleone
53 Bolt down
56 End of quote
60 Attendee
61 Kick out of the country
62 Small dam
63 Torah storers
64 Mythical king of Crete
65 Dutch cheese

DOWN

1 Shangri-la
2 Kilauea product
3 Roofer's need
4 Din detector
5 Be crabby
6 Like some suits
7 Deck foursome
8 Item for a biathlon
9 Marie, to Donny
10 Aware of
11 Competitive superiority
12 Late-July babies
13 Miami-__ County
18 Possessive pronoun
19 Word form for "joint"
24 It joins the Seine
25 Wishing-well deposits
26 Plied a hatchet
27 Pause mark
28 Camel cousin
29 Hooch holder
30 Not tied up
31 Cries out for
32 Mother of Perseus
34 The Joker's expression
37 Gloria Estefan's birthplace
38 Somalian supermodel
39 Beagle botherer
44 Laundromat lineup
45 Bookstore inventory
46 Frosty's composition
48 One way to get information
49 Multi-generational novel
50 *M*A*S*H* cook
51 Arduous journey
52 Ore layer
54 __ Minor
55 What to call it
57 President pro __
58 511, in the Forum
59 Have yet to repay

★★★ ABC

Enter the letters A, B, and C into the diagram so that each row and column has exactly one A, one B, and one C. The letters outside the diagram indicate the first letter encountered, moving in the direction of the arrow. Keep in mind that after all the letters have been filled in, there will be two blank boxes in each row and column.

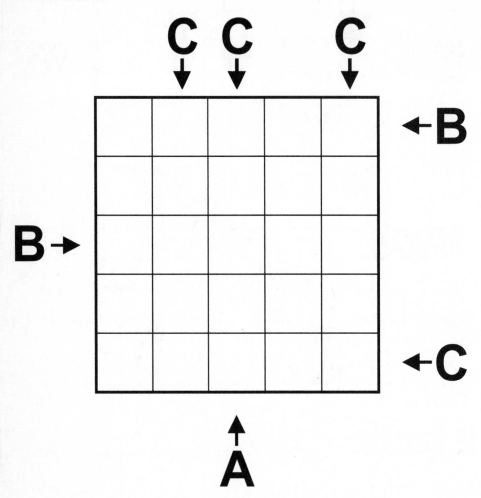

SUDOKU SUM

Without repeating any digits, complete the sum at right, by filling one digit in each of the five blanks.

```
    _  4  5
+   7  _  _
    _  _  3
```

★★★ Find the Ships

Determine the position of the 10 ships listed to the right of the diagram. The ships may be oriented either horizontally or vertically. A square with wavy lines indicates water and will not contain a ship. The numbers at the edge of the diagram indicate how many squares in that row or column contain parts of ships. When all 10 ships are correctly placed in the diagram, no two of them will touch each other, not even diagonally.

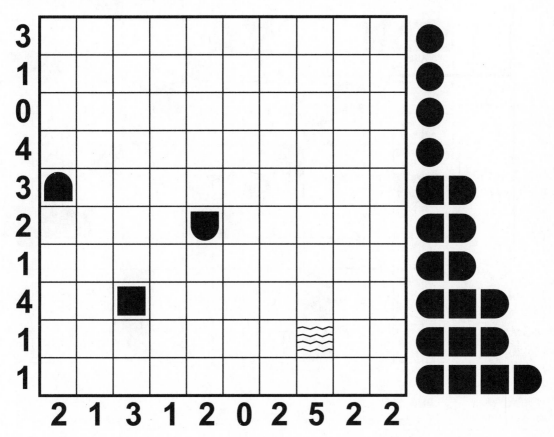

TWO-BY-FOUR

The eight letters in the word GRUMBLED can be rearranged to form a pair of common four-letter words in two different ways, if no four-letter word is repeated. Can you find both pairs of words?

_ _ _ _   _ _ _ _

_ _ _ _   _ _ _ _

★★★★ Drinks All Around by Merle Baker

ACROSS

1 Whole lot
5 Antlered animals
10 Baby 'roo
14 13th-century explorer
15 Lofty nest
16 Church section
17 Golden or new finish
18 Have a fancy (for)
19 Software development stage
20 Polishing mechanism
23 Squealer
24 Spigoted server
25 Ancient Egyptian amulets
27 They may be paid
32 Take down __
33 "Delicious!"
34 Inept person
36 Assuage
39 Zodiac animal
41 Flub on the field
43 Speaker's platform
44 Santa's helpers
46 Penalizes, in a way
48 Letters on some race cars
49 Necessary nutrient
51 Jazz pianist Oscar
53 Crestfallen
56 Ethan Allen's brother
57 Mork's spaceship
58 Yachting prize
64 Lawn chemical
66 Make amends
67 Reactor part
68 Favorable mention
69 Affleck associate
70 Pond growth
71 Utah's state flower
72 Hit the trail
73 Onion kin

DOWN

1 Practice boxing
2 Letterhead design
3 A util.
4 Prepare, as a proposal
5 Give in
6 Abound
7 Speedy steed
8 Misses
9 New York lake
10 Zinger
11 Lorgnette
12 Business sign abbr.
13 "Sailing to Byzantium" poet

21 Arduous journey
22 Emulates Eminem
26 Pore over
27 Run like heck
28 James __ Carter
29 Tonsorial need
30 Neighborhood, so to speak
31 Comic __
35 Region
37 Don Corleone
38 Armchair quarterback's network
40 Arctic Ocean hazard
42 Balky

45 Soft drink
47 Antitoxins
50 Bedouins, e.g.
52 Scalawag
53 Pitches in
54 Like acrobats
55 Suggest
59 "Arrivederci __"
60 "Are you __ out? "
61 Colleague of Irving and George
62 Push for
63 Reach a maximum
65 I: Lat.

★★★ Switch Track

Which two adjacent tiles (tiles sharing a common side) can be switched so that a single track visits all tiles at least once? A track follows the flow straight at intersections, turning neither right nor left.

TELEPHONE TRIOS

1	ABC **2**	DEF **3**
GHI **4**	JKL **5**	MNO **6**
PRS **7**	TUV **8**	WXY **9**
✱	**0**	#

Using the numbers and letters on a standard telephone, what three seven-letter words from the same category can be formed from these telephone numbers?

423-5263   _ _ _ _ _ _ _

267-7422   _ _ _ _ _ _ _

786-2872   _ _ _ _ _ _ _

★★★ **123**

Fill in the diagram so that each rectangular piece has one each of the numbers 1, 2, and 3, under these rules: 1) No two adjacent squares, horizontally or vertically, can have the same number. 2) Each completed row and column of the diagram will have an equal number of 1s, 2s, and 3s.

COMMON SENSE

What five-letter word can be found in the dictionary definitions of all of these words:

TENANT, WEATHERIZE, TABERNACLE, and CONGRESS?

— — — — —

★★★ Circular Reasoning

Connect all of the circles by drawing a single continuous line through every square of the diagram. All right-angle turns of your line must alternate between boxes containing a circle and boxes not containing a circle. You must make a right-angle turn out of every square that contains a circle. Your line must end in the same square that it begins, and it cannot enter any square more than once.

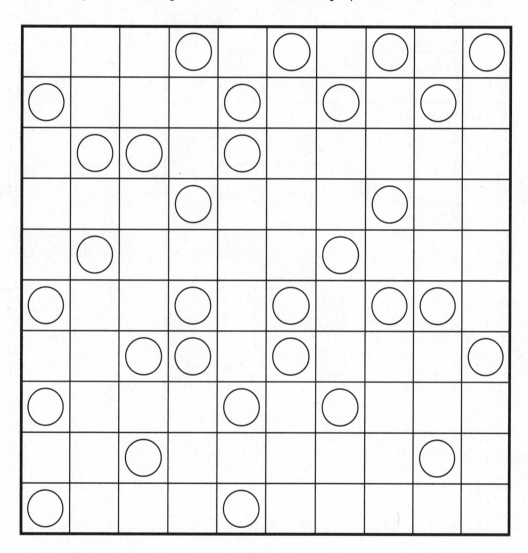

THREE AT A RHYME

Rearrange these letters to form three one-syllable words that rhyme.

B B M M M M O O O P R

_____ _____ _____

★★★★ Embedded Businesses by Fred Piscop

ACROSS

1 Mexican munchies
6 Ponderosa son
10 *Lucky Jim* writer
14 Was awful
15 Zoo home
16 In the cellar
17 Sewing-kit item
19 Oscar winner Kedrova
20 Some marbles
21 Stanford-__ IQ test
22 This puzzle's key-word, in the U.K.
23 Picks out
25 At first, maybe
29 Words of optimism
30 Skillet medium
31 Singer Twain
33 NATO member
36 Visibly shocked
38 Actor Wallach
39 Weight allowances
41 Memo letters
42 Cause's partner
45 "Quick!"
46 Fine point
48 Ballpark workers
50 Pie-chart parts
52 __-Cat (winter vehicle)
53 Vampire repeller
54 Eau de __
59 Steak order
60 Minnesota metro area
62 List ender
63 Port or pad starter
64 Mr. Chips portrayer
65 Eat in a hurry
66 Netsters' org.
67 Bergen dummy

DOWN

1 Cough syrup amts.
2 Working hard
3 Chaplin prop
4 Give the __-over
5 Crossbones' partners
6 Felt sore
7 Roaster's spot
8 In years past
9 Playing pieces
10 Axis foes
11 Lobster or steak
12 Dot in the sea
13 Data
18 Web spots
21 Sheep sound
23 SST part
24 Prefix with log
25 Norwegian saint
26 '50s leader of Hungary
27 Reef-building creature
28 Internet pop-ups, e.g.
29 Comets leader
32 Tests the weight of
34 Burn slightly
35 Nile slitherers
37 Texas river
40 "What a relief!"
43 Not "agin"
44 Forum garb
47 "... is fear __"
49 3-D objects
50 Nail alternative
51 Poet's Muse
52 Actress Braga
54 Pinball flub
55 School on the Thames
56 Fork prong
57 Go like the wind
58 Business sign abbr.
60 Day of the wk.
61 Director Craven

★★★ Hyper-Sudoku

Fill in the blank boxes so that every row, column, 3x3 box, *and* each of the four 3x3 gray regions contains all of the numbers 1 to 9.

	9		1	8			4	6
		8	9		2			
	6						5	
			3		6			5
	2							
			5	1				
				3				
	4	9						3
			4	7	8	9		

ADDITION SWITCH

Switch the positions of two of the digits in the incorrect sum at right, to get a correct sum.

$$
\begin{array}{r}
2\,8\,0 \\
+\,3\,1\,4 \\
\hline
5\,8\,5
\end{array}
$$

★★★ Split Decisions

In this clueless crossword puzzle, each answer consists of two words whose spellings are the same, except for the consecutive letters given. All answers are common words; no phrases or hyphenated or capitalized words are used. Some of the clues may have more than one solution, but there is only one word pair that will correctly link up with all the other word pairs.

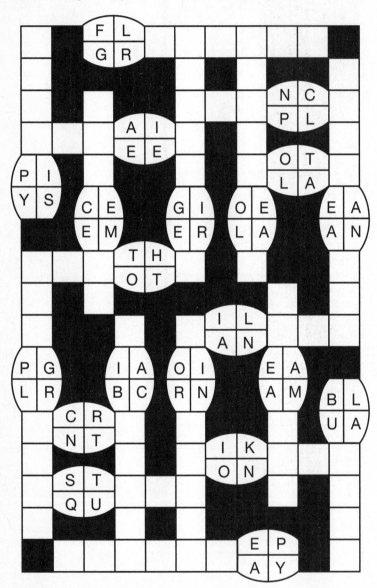

TONGUE TWISTER

The only common English word derived from the Finnish language is a five-letter word for an amenity often found in health clubs. What's that word?

_ _ _ _ _

★★★★ That Follows by Richard Silvestri

ACROSS

1 Shower bar
5 Forearm bones
10 Stereo's short-lived successor
14 Kind of cabbage
15 Show the way
16 Sicilian resort
17 Playing-fields place
18 Shire of films
19 Airhead
20 Start of a quote
23 Water tester
24 One or more
25 Mean
27 G.I. Joe maker
31 Cruise ship
33 __ close to schedule
34 Part 2 of quote
39 Best and Everage
41 Capt. Spaulding explored there
42 Orchestra section
43 Part 3 of quote
46 Slow time
47 Like some mouthwashes
48 Still
50 Trig function
53 REO center
54 Menu words
55 End of quote, and its speaker
62 Primer girl
64 Choose
65 Words of understanding
66 Basic building block
67 Free-for-all
68 Cat o' no tails?
69 Smallville surname
70 Filled to capacity
71 Go on the green

DOWN

1 Distort
2 Testimony preceder
3 Cosmetic additive
4 Friend of distinction
5 So far
6 Like rich soil
7 Site of a Nelson victory
8 Have __ with (be connected to)
9 Putting on a show
10 Proof initials
11 Join forces
12 Bruckner or Chekhov
13 __ and Confused (1993 film)
21 No-skill card game
22 "__ Time" (Queen Latifah tune)
26 High range
27 Tilling toiler
28 The Egg __
29 Porter product
30 Hindu "Creator"
31 Towering
32 Bit of legalese
35 Huge amount
36 Mad Libs fill-in
37 Stylist's stock
38 Christiania, today
40 Be frugal
44 Pre-game renditions
45 Told
49 Compete
50 Wheel man
51 Fill with glee
52 Author's total output
53 Run the show
56 Zeno's place
57 Go all gooey
58 Non-macho type
59 Son of Isaac
60 Put in the mail
61 Prepared remarks
63 CPR specialist

★★★ Möbius Maze

If the four ants are following each other in a continuous loop, mark the path they are following. Draw a dark line to represent the side that is visible, and a lighter line to represent the unseen side.

BETWEENER

What six-letter word belongs between the word at left and the word at right, so that the first and second word, and the second and third word, each form a common two-word phrase?

COMMON _ _ _ _ _ _ CREW

★★★ Islands

Shade in some of the white squares in the diagram with "water," so that each remaining white box is part of an island. Each island will contain exactly one numbered square, indicating how many squares that island contains. Each island is separated from the other islands by water but may touch other islands diagonally. All water is connected, but there are no 2x2 regions of water in the diagram.

	4				4		4
			3				
4							
							5
1							
		3					

MIXAGRAMS

Each line contains a five-letter word and a four-letter word that have been mixed together (the order of the letters in each word has not been changed). Unmix the two words on each line and write them in the spaces provided. When you're done, find a two-word answer to the clue by reading down the letter columns in the answers.

CLUE: Shotmakers of a sort

E G A R O C U P H = _ _ _ _ _ + _ _ _ _

S A D L O V U R O = _ _ _ _ _ + _ _ _ _

C A V I E M E D O = _ _ _ _ _ + _ _ _ _

M A U V A S H I L = _ _ _ _ _ + _ _ _ _

★★★ One-Way Streets

The diagram represents a pattern of streets. Ps are parking spaces, and the black squares are stores. Find the route that starts at a parking space, passes through all stores exactly once, and ends at the other parking space. Arrows indicate one-way traffic for that block only. No block or intersection may be entered more than once.

AND SO ON

Unscramble the letters in the phrase ROOMERS SMIRK, to form two words that are part of a common phrase that has the word AND between them.

_____ and _____

★★★★ Pet Peeve by Bob Frank

ACROSS

1 Successful, as in *Variety*
6 Complaint
10 Where a mark is taken
14 Mork or Superman
15 *Camino __* (Williams play)
16 Seep like sap
17 Saw again
18 Pretentious
19 Boot adjunct
20 Start of an observation
23 PC key
24 Seek damages
25 Assume, as a character
27 Every last bit
30 Yanks' opponents
33 Orlando's backup
34 Stumblebum
36 New Zealand bird
38 Plugs away
41 Part 2 of observation
44 Saunter
45 Divider's word
46 Trumpet insert
47 Shade trees
49 Greek sandwich
51 Do needlework
52 Car-window sign
55 Whiskey grain
57 Unspecific amount
58 End of observation
64 Predisposition
66 Church calendar
67 House style
68 Actress Loughlin
69 Her work may be measured by the foot
70 Money or Murphy
71 Football linemen
72 1040 entries
73 Bowling-lane button

DOWN

1 S.F. train system
2 Bread spread
3 Paycheck acronym
4 They might lead to war
5 Traveling and playing
6 Behave like an ass
7 Architect Saarinen
8 Consume wholly
9 Angling tool
10 Distress signal
11 Prominent lunar crater
12 City near Los Angeles
13 Compassion
21 Like a dweeb
22 Poet's Muse
26 Baby-feeding time
27 __ Romeo
28 Potting soil
29 Builder's supplier
31 Netanyahu's nickname
32 Took a cut (at)
35 Money drawers
37 __-bitty
39 After the bell
40 Do a slow burn
42 '60s Air Force chief of staff
43 Yankees manager
48 Single-masted vessels
50 Shade of white
52 Moralistic tale
53 Fragrant bulb
54 Continental currency
56 Practice piece
59 Yemeni city
60 Goes bad
61 Tacks on
62 Liver, in Lille
63 Guitar neck part
65 Family member

★★★★ Sudoku

Fill in the blank boxes so that every row, column, and 3x3 box contains all of the numbers 1 to 9.

4				2				
			5	7	8			
	8			1				3
						7		
				8		1		9
		7	4	9	5			
	5		6					1
8						2		6
	7			5	1		9	

TRANSDELETION

Delete one letter from the word HISTORIC and rearrange the rest, to get something with wings.

_____

★★★★ Star Search

Find the stars that are hidden in some of the blank squares. The numbered squares indicate how many stars are hidden in the squares adjacent to them (including diagonally). There is never more than one star in any square.

				4			1	
2		2						
				3		4		1
	2	5		6				1
						3		1
	2	2		3				
						2		
	1			2				

SUDOKU SUM

Without repeating any digits, complete the sum at right, by filling one digit in each of the five blanks.

```
    4 _ 1
+   _ 6 _
  ─────────
    _ 5 _
```

★★★★ Take Monday Off by Richard Silvestri

ACROSS

1 Make lawn repairs
4 Winter Palace resident
8 Tousle
14 Dam org.
15 Cartoonist Goldberg
16 Kind of watch
17 Cartoon Chihuahua
18 Pub round
19 *Charmed* star
20 Crafty insect?
23 Think-tank product
24 Elation
25 Famous pharaoh
28 Usual
31 Took charge
32 Passport stamp
33 Spells and such
35 Brought into line
36 Caviar credo?
39 Seafood morsel
41 Stage platform
42 Adjutant
43 Theater area
44 Aquanauts' habitat
49 Stat for A-Rod
50 Master of the macabre
51 Director Clair
52 Locksmith's idea of fun?
58 Comeback
60 Arp art
61 Hogwash
62 Fire up
63 The gamut
64 Rock producer Brian
65 __ snake
66 Simple
67 Drops in the grass

DOWN

1 Exertion
2 Go to extremes with
3 One of the reindeer
4 Chesapeake Bay catch
5 Communications code ender
6 Aid in crime
7 Sit a spell
8 Symbol of straightness
9 Make one
10 Shopping site
11 Recess, for schoolkids
12 Quasimodo portrayer
13 Swelled head
21 Sandwich filler
22 Bounces
26 Put to work
27 Wee distance
29 Expression of assent
30 Young fellow
31 Constitutional
32 It may move you
34 More sensational, as details
35 Get pooped
36 Heating device
37 Run up a tab
38 Scale notes
39 Something to shoot for
40 Barbecue bit
43 Pullman attendant
45 Boat of refuge
46 Looked impolitely
47 Whoever
48 Confer, as an award
50 Do a grammar chore
53 Ring happening
54 Dutch export
55 Past one's bedtime
56 What the nose knows
57 Throw for a loop
58 Joplin tune
59 Period of note

★★★★ Alternating Tiles

Start somewhere along the left column of tiles and, alternating between yellow and red tiles, end somewhere along the right column. You may move horizontally or vertically from tile to tile, but never diagonally.

SOUND THINKING

We can think of three common uncapitalized words whose only consonant sounds are R, P, R, and T, in that order. How many can you think of?

_____   _____   _____

★★★ Tracking Game

Starting with JAGUAR, then moving up, down, left, or right, one letter at a time, track all 23 animals that are hidden in the diagram. Animal names include two two-word phrases. All the letters in the diagram will be used.

J A G U A R T A H W A L
R E G I T C E E H C A L
W O L A R O U G A E N A
P P F E B A L A R Y H B
O I H H E R K O C A L Y
P O T T N N O I L M E B
U M A P A K N T E S F U
S G O O N A A M O U F A
R I R A G P H R E C O L
A R D E L E S O N O P O
F A E L R E O H I E B L
F P O T H T T R R A R A
E S L O A A R D V A R K

MIXAGRAMS

Each line contains a five-letter word and a four-letter word that have been mixed together (the order of the letters in each word has not been changed). Unmix the two words on each line and write them in the spaces provided. When you're done, find a two-word answer to the clue by reading down the letter columns in the answers.

CLUE: Cold-war weapon

T H A U S B E T Y = _ _ _ _ _ + _ _ _ _

T U B N I R C A Y = _ _ _ _ _ + _ _ _ _

W I S P O L O K T = _ _ _ _ _ + _ _ _ _

B O W H E L E R M = _ _ _ _ _ + _ _ _ _

★★★ ABC

Enter the letters A, B, and C into the diagram so that each row and column has exactly one A, one B, and one C. The letters outside the diagram indicate the first letter encountered, moving in the direction of the arrow. Keep in mind that after all the letters have been filled in, there will be two blank boxes in each row and column.

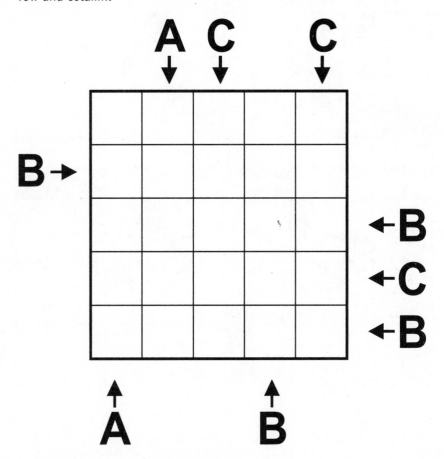

CLUELESS CROSSWORD

Complete the crossword with common uncapitalized seven-letter words, based entirely on the letters already filled in for you.

★★★★★ Themeless Toughie by Daniel R. Stark

ACROSS

1 Do away with
8 Elegant
15 Hoodlum
16 *Green Acres* cow
17 Great joy
18 Velocipede
19 Court need
20 Lemnos' sea
22 Brake part
23 Mill starter
25 Palm locales
27 Actress Harding
28 Lays down turf
29 Crafty move
30 Brit's bread spread
32 Messenger's wear, maybe
34 More roomy
35 __ and goings
38 Curator's concern
39 Far point
40 Smudged
41 Fishing device
42 Bangalore attire
43 Laird's daughter
47 Paycheck abbr.
48 Scottish topography
50 Ancient storyteller
51 Picture borders
53 Horse's lead
55 Soil turner
56 Ceaseless
58 Spring flower
60 Work with antiques
61 Shrugged off
62 Gated acreage
63 Window covering

DOWN

1 Moles, maybe
2 Short jacket
3 Held forth
4 Not dark
5 High schooler's reading
6 Purple fruit
7 Popular places
8 Cheapen
9 Skirt style
10 Jiffy
11 Onetime film censor
12 Boss
13 Opposite of currently
14 Shrubs and such
21 Leisure
24 Post
26 Feel a sting
29 Height of fashion
31 Hose pattern
33 Lower oneself
34 Actress Singer
35 Fine fabric
36 Runs
37 Most humid
38 Kit's purpose
40 *You Only Live Twice* screenwriter
42 Piano practice
44 On the ground
45 First
46 Efficient
49 CTA Blue Line terminus
50 Boxing venue
52 Tijuana Ms.
54 Bridge bldr.
57 Teen's denial
59 Unruly hair

bRain BREatHER
CONTAIN YOUR CLUTTER

Stowing everyday clutter out from sight is the surest way to bring order to a chaotic home. Here are a few ways to tame the junk piles and keep your home in tiptop shape!

Employ the basket trick.

Place a decorative basket or crate in or near the most cluttered room of your house. Place items that belong in other rooms in the basket. Anytime you exit the room, grab items out of the basket and return them to their rightful places.

Sort, then store, loose items.

Random little items such as batteries, buttons, light bulbs, and matches often end up scattered in junk drawers. You'll never find them when you need them! Keep these items at hand by grouping them by type or by room ("light bulbs," or "spare computer wires," etc.) and stowing them in labeled containers.

Use decorative baskets and boxes to hide frequently used items.

Your coffee table is probably cluttered with remote controls, nail files, notepads, pens, and bills. Keep a lidded, pretty box on the table and the mess magically disappears! Similarly, put a small dish on top of your dresser to collect loose change and earrings. Situate an old mug on top of your desk to hold pens, pencils, and scissors. All of your home's surfaces will be neater.

Know the best options for short-term and long-term storage.

Cardboard boxes are great for moving and for short-term storage, but they collapse when stacked. They also absorb moisture and attract insects, such as silverfish, that feed on paper. Plastic containers, on the other hand, are great for long-term storage, with a few caveats: Make sure stored items are dry before putting the lid on because plastic can trap moisture inside, promoting mold and mildew growth. And if you're going to use plastic, use small containers. There's no point in buying huge plastic boxes, filling them to the brim, and then not be able to move them!

Label laundry baskets.

Save time by presorting your laundry. Label bags or baskets: "Whites," "colors," "permanent press," and "dry cleaning." You will always know when it's time to do a particular load—the one with the full basket!

★★★★ Find the Ships

Determine the position of the 10 ships listed to the right of the diagram. The ships may be oriented either horizontally or vertically. A square with wavy lines indicates water and will not contain a ship. The numbers at the edge of the diagram indicate how many squares in that row or column contain parts of ships. When all 10 ships are correctly placed in the diagram, no two of them will touch each other, not even diagonally.

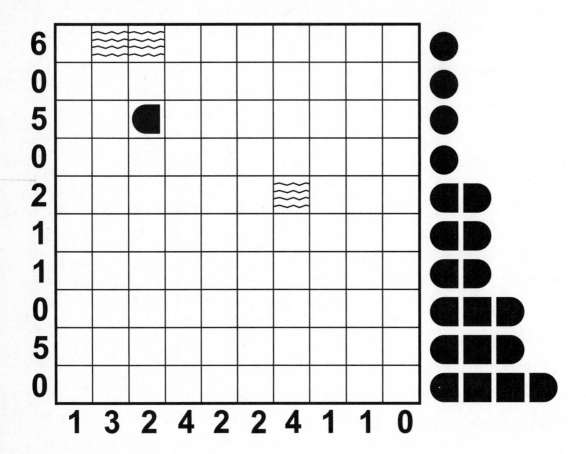

TWO-BY-FOUR

The eight letters in the word EUPHORIC can be rearranged to form a pair of common four-letter words in three different ways, if no four-letter word is repeated. Can you find all three pairs of words?

_ _ _ _   _ _ _ _

_ _ _ _   _ _ _ _

_ _ _ _   _ _ _ _

★★★★ Hyper-Sudoku

Fill in the blank boxes so that every row, column, 3x3 box, *and* each of the four 3x3 gray regions contains all of the numbers 1 to 9.

		5			1			
	6				8	7		
		4	3					
	5				6		4	1
		6					2	
7		2						9
					3			
				8	4		9	
						6		4

CITY SEARCH

Using the letters in ANN ARBOR, we were able to form only one common uncapitalized five-letter word besides ARBOR. Can you find it?

— — — — —

★★★★★ Themeless Toughie by Merle Baker

ACROSS

1 Puffery
9 Sales promoter
15 Plant pigment
16 *The Dark Angel* Oscar nominee
17 Memorable sitcom couple
18 Bath, e.g.
19 Coat cut
20 Swedish scientist
22 __ corde (piano music marking)
23 Drafts
24 One of the Monkees
25 Come __ agreement
26 Bit of work
27 Ottoman title
28 Sanctioned
29 Reduced severely
31 More welcome
34 Roman officials
35 Acceptable diplomat
37 Refuge for Robert the Bruce
38 Words to follow
39 Union adversary: Abbr.
42 Nurture
43 Revue feature
44 Jazz fans
45 Do wrong
46 Reflective one
47 Durango dwellings
48 Pas de deux section
50 Look up to
52 Scylla/Charybdis separator
53 Hoop sites
54 They're trifling
55 War of the Roses battle site

DOWN

1 Plight
2 Roofer's tool
3 Electrical problem
4 Sources of Zen enlightenment
5 French 101 verb
6 Multivolume ref.
7 On the spot
8 Mountainous kingdom
9 More sensitive
10 Onetime steel-workers' leader
11 Word form for "middle"
12 Diplomat's concern
13 Metz's region
14 Accords
21 Scram
24 Sacramental server
25 Knee neighbor
27 Feigned
28 Precipitated
29 Hotelier Ritz
30 Superintends
31 Least abundant
32 Enjoyed doing
33 Adventures of old
36 Makes unhappy
39 Yellow-skinned fruit
40 __ Island, NY
41 Size up
43 Cooking fats
44 Health-food store buy
46 Dayan contemporary
47 Solar __
49 Explorer of the Canadian Arctic
51 Depression-era program

★★★★ Arrow Routes

Start in the center, pass over all the arrows in the direction they point, then exit at bottom. You may not retrace your path.

THREE AT A RHYME

Rearrange these letters to form three one-syllable words that rhyme.

B C D I L R R R T T T U U

_____   _____   _____

★★★★ Circular Reasoning

Connect all of the circles by drawing a single continuous line through every square of the diagram. All right-angle turns of your line must alternate between boxes containing a circle and boxes not containing a circle. You must make a right-angle turn out of every square that contains a circle. Your line must end in the same square that it begins, and it cannot enter any square more than once.

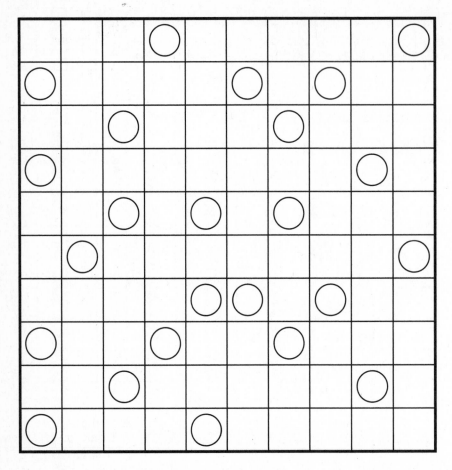

TELEPHONE TRIOS

Using the numbers and letters on a standard telephone, what three seven-letter words from the same category can be formed from these telephone numbers?

236-8287   _ _ _ _ _ _ _

746-3649   _ _ _ _ _ _ _

864-2676   _ _ _ _ _ _ _

★★★★★ Themeless Toughie by Anna Stiga

ACROSS

1 *The Man Who Came to Dinner* cowriter
9 Lab animal
15 Well-off
16 Most sound
17 Battleground of 1777
18 Plum relative
19 Modicum
20 Carrying on
22 Theater abbr.
23 Day starter
25 *Madre*'s boy
26 *Slate*, for one
27 Kind of bookmark
29 *Ottawa Morning* network
30 __ cooler
31 Clavicle connector
33 Turns away
35 Numerical prefix
36 Age
37 Bank offering
41 Unavailing response
46 On maneuvers, maybe
47 *Évangile* writer
49 Attached, in a way
50 Admissions Dept. concern
51 Hindmost
53 Something to insure
54 Uris character
55 Fair
57 Moore poem beginning
58 Agency
60 Heist helpers
62 Orioles' group
63 Louis Joliet discovery
64 Boil
65 Make no changes

DOWN

1 Is totally wrong?
2 Painting the town
3 Marley's partner
4 Joint
5 Overwrought
6 Stand behind
7 Shakespearean daughter
8 Melancholy
9 Ionesco play
10 Knack
11 *Ragtime* monogram
12 Earth-shaking
13 Johnson successor
14 *Loco Boy Makes Good* trio
21 Constitutional
24 Start of many Spanish place names
26 One in a fold
28 Sparse mail area
32 *Surprise Symphony* movement
34 Tony ex
37 Winter fruits
38 Typically
39 Former staffer
40 Start of many Spanish place names
42 Made fun of
43 Rubens' home
44 Glass-walled rooms
45 Unicameral legislature
48 Plots
52 African capital
55 *A Beautiful Mind* subject
56 Metric prefix
59 Pack away
61 What 56 Down means

★★★★ 123

Fill in the diagram so that each rectangular piece has one each of the numbers 1, 2, and 3, under these rules: 1) No two adjacent squares, horizontally or vertically, can have the same number. 2) Each completed row and column of the diagram will have an equal number of 1s, 2s, and 3s.

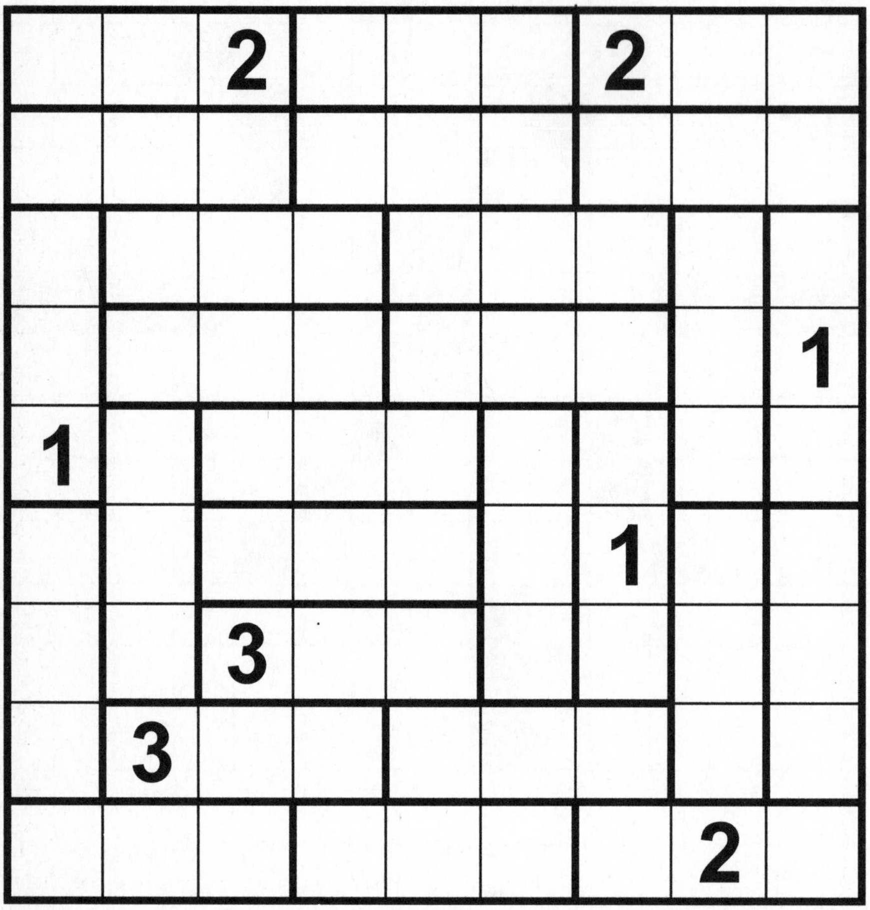

BETWEENER

What five-letter word belongs between the word at left and the word at right, so that the first and second word, and the second and third word, each form a common two-word phrase?

RAIN __ __ __ __ __ HALL

★★★ Islands

Shade in some of the white squares in the diagram with "water," so that each remaining white box is part of an island. Each island will contain exactly one numbered square, indicating how many squares that island contains. Each island is separated from the other islands by water but may touch other islands diagonally. All water is connected, but there are no 2x2 regions of water in the diagram.

				4			3
							3
4		3					
					6		
	6						1

IN OTHER WORDS

There is only one common uncapitalized word that contains the consecutive letters RYD. What is that word?

_____

★★★★★ Themeless Toughie by Daniel R. Stark

ACROSS

1 Town in oaters
7 *Dante's Dream* painter
15 Confounded
16 Covalent bond particle
17 Got the wrinkles out
18 First grade topic
19 __ Mahal
20 Soul
22 Piedmont city
23 Comets, to ancients
25 *My Friend Flicka* author
27 __ ear
28 *Miami Vice* cop
29 Recital offering
30 Informal usage
32 Homesteaders
34 Distinctive accents
35 Needs healing
36 Hog's domain
37 Thinly populated
40 Bit of water
44 Sahara nation
45 Follow
46 Large kangaroo
47 S&L offering
48 Avoids
50 Warble
51 Camera moves
53 At a discount
55 Vote against
56 Phone cable site
58 Activating
60 Like some alphabets
61 Two-Oscar winner
62 Shoal
63 Battleground of 1968

DOWN

1 Whom reporters report to
2 Town in oaters
3 Jut out
4 Richards of Texas
5 Oozes
6 Chance quote
7 Gets to
8 Behind the times
9 Exodus feast
10 Part of M.S.
11 Katharine Ross role
12 Wagner tenor
13 Street noise
14 Scoreboard columns
21 Letter ender
24 Deed authenticator
26 Lake Nasser's dam
29 Expunge
31 Library device
33 Simpson et al.
34 Labor
36 Former Russian first lady
37 Mistakes
38 Amazon menace
39 Forsake
40 Comb through
41 Totaling
42 *As You Like It* hero
43 Geometric figure
45 Listen to the news, perhaps
49 Shade-loving plant
50 Livy's land
52 Ship
54 Popular dogs
57 Gettysburg soldier
59 *Avril* follower

★★★ Pathfinder

Starting with TRAIN, then moving up, down, left, or right, one letter at a time, trace a path of 20 words that are all forms of transportation. All the letters in the diagram will be used.

```
L I R D I N G B A L L
G D E A L P H Y C R O
T P I N E T F A R E O
H Y H S J A L H O V N
C A R T Y P O M A R T
Y C A K O T R A I S C
C L E R G R E B N N O
R K C I T A N U L I O
O S H A W X I S E P T
T D E M A I L Z E P E
O M P O L O D N O G R
```

COMMON SENSE

What six-letter word can be found in the dictionary definitions of all of these words:

WEAKLING, TIDAL WAVE, MAGNETIC, and HUNGER?

_ _ _ _ _ _

★★★★ Bead Maze

Enter the maze at right center, pass through all beads exactly once, and then exit somewhere at left. You may not pass through three consecutive beads of the same color.

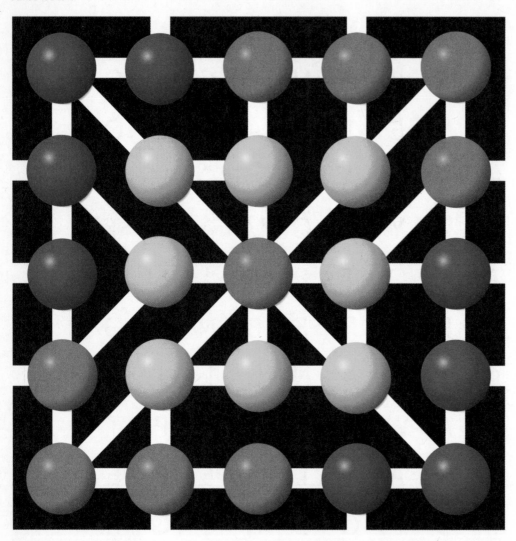

COUNTDOWN

Inserting plus signs and minus signs, as many as necessary, in between the digits from 9 to 1 below, create a series of additions and subtractions whose final answer is 12. Any digits without a sign between them are to be grouped together as a single number.

$$9 \quad 8 \quad 7 \quad 6 \quad 5 \quad 4 \quad 3 \quad 2 \quad 1 \quad = \quad 12$$

★★★★★ **Themeless Toughie** by S.N.

ACROSS

1 Makes, with "to"
8 Totalitarian belief
15 *1984* setting
16 South American predator
17 Golf official
18 Alarm, often
19 Protective material
20 Of sights or sounds
21 Broadcasting
22 Wire measure
23 Most glamorous
26 Large hall
30 Julius Caesar, once
32 Gershwin tune of 1927
37 Cover too well
38 Sum things
39 Artistic technique
45 Diner offering
46 Wiz
47 Not on the level
52 Din creator
54 Fighting words
55 Cut off
56 Have nothing left
57 Former Chrysler products
58 Hair
59 Least trivial

DOWN

1 Sagan series
2 Pump stat
3 No delicate instrument
4 Sequel indicator
5 Gross
6 Debt securer
7 Bil Baird mentor
8 Hot spots
9 Flag
10 *East of Eden* character
11 Sweater letters
12 Stephen King novel
13 *School for Scandal* writer
14 Laurel's locale
24 While away
25 Tie tightly
26 Grade starter
27 Different
28 Water tester
29 Metropolitan area
31 *Simpsons* clerk
32 Most slippery, perhaps
33 Supermarket debut of '54
34 Star of Buffalo Bill's Wild West Show
35 Burn up
36 Family member
40 Ask too much
41 Shake a leg
42 Go up
43 Altoids alternative
44 Partake of
48 Dutch master
49 Son of Chaos
50 Both, in music
51 Kennel clientele
52 *Adventure Galley* skipper
53 Noncommittal response

★★★★ ABCD

Enter the letters A, B, C, and D into the diagram so that each row and column has exactly one A, one B, one C, and one D. The letters outside the diagram indicate the first letter encountered, moving in the direction of the arrow. Keep in mind that after all the letters have been filled in, there will be two blank boxes in each row and column.

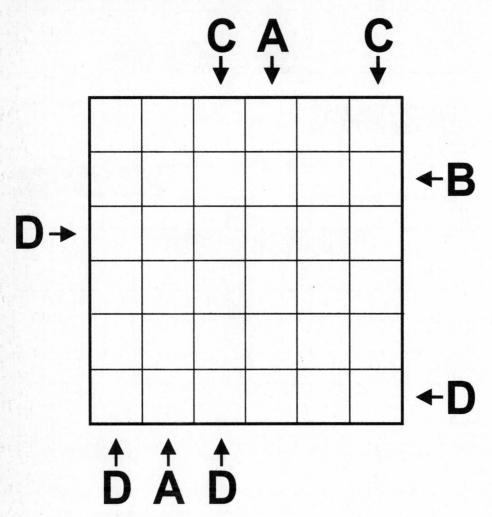

SOUND THINKING

We can think of three common uncapitalized words whose only consonant sounds are M, L, and N, in that order. How many can you think of?

_____   _____   _____

★★★★ Sudoku

Fill in the blank boxes so that every row, column, and 3x3 box contains all of the numbers 1 to 9.

			2			6		
2			4			1		8
				3				4
					8			
4							9	
7	3			6				
3				7				
		9			3	8		6
			1	2		5		

ADDITION SWITCH

Switch the positions of two of the digits in the incorrect sum at right, to get a correct sum.

$$\begin{array}{r} 705 \\ +186 \\ \hline 911 \end{array}$$

★★★★★ Themeless Toughie by Daniel R. Stark

ACROSS

1 Ultimate
9 Wenceslas Square locale
15 Lower Peninsula city
16 Dustups
17 Become one
18 Inedible oranges
19 Fire __
20 Tacks on
22 Slaw and fries
28 Cutting remarks
33 Top
34 Bugs Bunny animator
35 Go slow
37 Id product
38 Masked crime fighter
39 Nol of Cambodia
40 Propeller shape
41 Double
42 "__ chance!"
43 Tea partner
44 Longer of limb
46 Shrugged off
48 Wine source
50 Ancient African kingdom
51 View
57 *Moonraker* locale
61 Handel genre
63 Mrs. Ivanhoe
64 High-tech collection
65 Fail to deliver
66 Makeup device

DOWN

1 Blouse trim
2 Erelong
3 Disadvantage
4 Ankle bones
5 Nest builder
6 Haunt
7 Sinbad's transport
8 Don't look forward to
9 Encouraged
10 Chagall's homeland
11 Literary compilation
12 Band booking
13 French article
14 Hairpin curve
21 Suave
23 Pleads with
24 Molding material
25 Novel category
26 City near Willamette National Forest
27 Cooked, in a way
28 Friend of de Beauvoir
29 Frank admission
30 Mend, as a book
31 Shrink away
32 Literary pseudonym
36 Ground parcel
40 Worker's ID
42 Distant clouds
45 Ticking off
47 Whirl
49 __ Island
52 Footnote abbr.
53 Region traversed by Marco Polo
54 Galway Bay islands
55 Ascendancy
56 Mover and shaker
57 Wintry cry
58 Soirée spread
59 Beard on barley
60 Omega counterpart
62 Moonbeam

★★★★ One-Way Streets

The diagram represents a pattern of streets. Ps are parking spaces, and the black squares are stores. Find the route that starts at a parking space, passes through all stores exactly once, and ends at the other parking space. Arrows indicate one-way traffic for that block only. No block or intersection may be entered more than once.

AND SO ON

Unscramble the letters in the phrase OVERDID QUINCE, to form two words that are part of a common phrase that has the word AND between them.

_____ and _____

★★★ Split Decisions

In this clueless crossword puzzle, each answer consists of two words whose spellings are the same, except for the consecutive letters given. All answers are common words; no phrases or hyphenated or capitalized words are used. Some of the clues may have more than one solution, but there is only one word pair that will correctly link up with all the other word pairs.

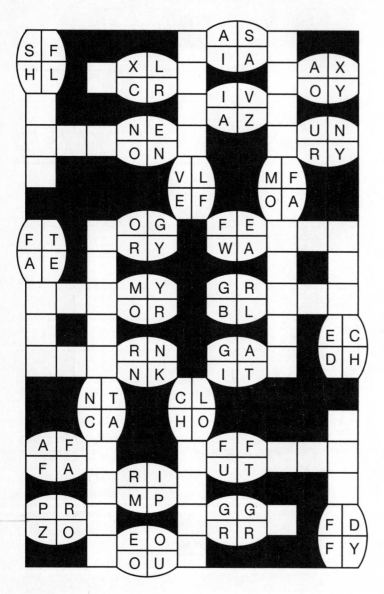

TRANSDELETION

Delete one letter from the word ALDERMEN and rearrange the rest, to get something that can be bought in a jewelry store.

★★★★★ Themeless Toughie by Anna Stiga

ACROSS

1 No fun at all
8 Clinical-trial need
15 Act badly
16 Hosts
17 Follow closely
18 Like many a 36 Across
19 Mercury, for one
20 Ashy
22 Milne marsupial
23 Crunchy lunches
24 Word on a nickel
26 eBay photo, often
27 Falsification
28 Mixed
30 Jodie Foster, while in college
31 Evokes affection in, with "to"
33 George Gershwin nickname
35 "Rumble in the Jungle" winner
36 Buff
37 Is inevitable
41 Quick look
45 Parabola part
46 Go camping, for example
48 For
49 Shot in the dark
51 WWI vessel
52 *Friendship 7* org.
53 Trunk attachment
55 Loan-document stat.
56 Funnel-like
57 Leave the Limited
59 Continental, e.g.
61 Witt milieu
62 Misbehaving, and then some
63 '20s transportation
64 *Time After Time* hero

DOWN

1 Sewer accessory
2 Piper's place
3 Sent out
4 Street vendor offerings
5 EEC member
6 14th-century B.C. ruler
7 Volcanoes, e.g.
8 Mirage
9 Whippersnapper
10 Dilbert coworker
11 Mrs. Dithers et al.
12 Displays
13 Language of India
14 Carbon-based
21 Crossword cuckoo
24 Reindeer relative
25 Overabundance
28 Grit
29 Quick-thinking
32 Polish off
34 First premier of Burma
37 Sect founded in Poland
38 Chrysler Building style
39 Sang like Ella
40 *Newlywed Game* host
41 Title for 6 Down
42 Droopy-eared pet
43 Bag of tricks
44 Shutterbugs, often
47 NYC conveners in '04
50 Ballet practice need
52 *Affliction* star
54 Author Sheehy
56 Animal stomach
58 Acct. addition
60 "Minuet __"

★★★★ Think Straight

Enter the grid at the rightmost white square at bottom, pass through the 16 yellow squares, then leave the grid somewhere at right. You may travel only horizontally or vertically in a straight line, and may turn only to avoid passing through a black square. It is okay to pass through a square more than once.

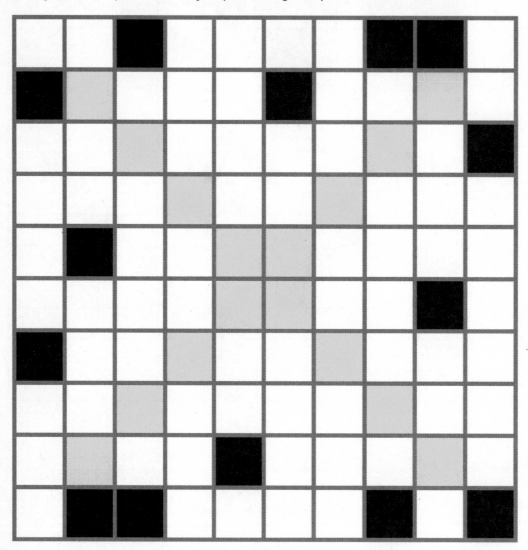

THREE OF A KIND

Find the three hidden words in the sentence that, read in order, go together in some way.

Intermediate Math is, to me, answers to a stack of way-out examples.

★★★ Star Search

Find the stars that are hidden in some of the blank squares. The numbered squares indicate how many stars are hidden in the squares adjacent to them (including diagonally). There is never more than one star in any square.

	2		5		6		
							1
	4		4		4		4
			2	3	3	3	3	3
2	2	2	2	2	2	2	2
	1	1	1	1	1	1	

MIXAGRAMS

Each line contains a five-letter word and a four-letter word that have been mixed together (the order of the letters in each word has not been changed). Unmix the two words on each line and write them in the spaces provided. When you're done, find a two-word answer to the clue by reading down the letter columns in the answers.

CLUE: Kind of play

C A B H A I D E T = _ _ _ _ _ + _ _ _ _

G O R O S E N E T = _ _ _ _ _ + _ _ _ _

P A I N F I D E R = _ _ _ _ _ + _ _ _ _

D I E D T O L E R = _ _ _ _ _ + _ _ _ _

★★★★★ Themeless Toughie by Merle Baker

ACROSS

1 Dye source
7 It's ingenious
15 Reagan speechwriter
16 Out, in a way
17 Conclude, as a debate
18 Restaurant freebie
19 Ancient city of Mesopotamia
20 It means "minerals"
21 Game winner
22 One of like mind
23 World's largest professional org.
24 "Rats!"
25 Emperor's answer to a petition
27 Isocrates, for one
29 Reacts to goodies
31 Previn's *A Streetcar Named Desire*, e.g.
32 Venting
38 Rouse, with "up"
39 Hockey great's nickname
40 Bull riding et al.
42 Dewey, notably
48 Uncool sort
49 Sound of impact
51 Rostand character
52 Washout
53 Mythical craft
54 Pitchers' partners
55 More sporadic
57 Spill the beans
58 Dwelled on
59 *Garfield* cat
60 Prying
61 Imparted nurture

DOWN

1 Engaged
2 Pest
3 Charitable organizations
4 Very soon
5 Guffaw provoker
6 Alex Trebek or Shania Twain
7 Another way, say
8 Like Mom's sister
9 Come to light
10 Shooters
11 1040 deduction
12 Perform perfectly
13 Title lady of a Poe tale
14 Overseas letter
24 Agr. or HUD
26 Index number
28 Bk. after Daniel
30 Dirty Harry's org.
32 Adds and stirs
33 Fulfill
34 Produces a surplus
35 Go
36 Mortgage fig.
37 Very positive
41 Puck, for instance
43 Be consistent
44 Scapula neighbor
45 More improbable
46 Like some reference sources
47 Fresh
50 Architectural moldings
53 __ advantage
56 Section starter

★★★ Islands

Shade in some of the white squares in the diagram with "water," so that each remaining white box is part of an island. Each island will contain exactly one numbered square, indicating how many squares that island contains. Each island is separated from the other islands by water but may touch other islands diagonally. All water is connected, but there are no 2x2 regions of water in the diagram.

				1					
5									
				2					4
4						3			
				4					
	3								
					8				
						2			
			4						
		3							

INITIAL REACTION

The "equation" below contains the initials of words that will make it correct, forming a numerical fact. Solve the equation by supplying the missing words.

25 = C. in a Q. _____

★★ Line Drawing

Draw two straight lines, each from one edge of the square to another edge, so that the five words in each of the three regions go together in some way.

BEAUTIFUL

GREAT   TERRIBLE

FAIR

CERTAINLY

NO

PERHAPS

ALWAYS

VILE

MAYBE

UH-UH

SO-SO   YES

SOMETIMES   NEVER

TWO-BY-FOUR

The eight letters in the word MATURITY can be rearranged to form a pair of common four-letter words in only one way. Can you find the two words?

— — — —   — — — —

★★★★★ Themeless Toughie by S.N.

ACROSS

1 Fed
10 Feeling
15 *Lady in the Shower* artist
16 Works
17 Sincerely
18 Anthony Hopkins' birthplace
19 Device used by pilots
20 Sub-Saharan fliers
22 At heart
23 Sign of peace
24 Get going
25 Semiconductor giant
26 Added up
28 Highly regarded
29 Hostile
30 *Middlemarch* character
31 Ends
32 Truck part
35 On the lam
36 Prop preceder
37 Detective author's pen name
40 Colleague of Peter and Davy
41 Speed
42 Take a course
43 Reggae players, perhaps
44 Trap
46 Turn to
47 Obtrusive
48 Oscar role of '56
50 Storage unit
51 Loathsome
52 Red deer
53 Source of Chickamauga Creek

DOWN

1 Of hives, honey, etc.
2 Softness
3 Harped on
4 German __
5 First name in jazz piano
6 Walker or Wilson
7 Migrate slowly
8 One-striper: Abbr.
9 It may mean "under construction"
10 Victor at Bunker Hill
11 Stuck
12 Dillinger gang member
13 Where catches are kept
14 Pain
21 Inasmuch (as)
23 Bugs, to Yosemite Sam
26 Sensei's teaching
27 __ rack
29 Type of hard-hat
31 Profusion
32 Organ-pipe and rat-tail
33 Basic
34 Emily Dickinson's home
35 Abstract painter Newman
36 Opposite of *buona*
37 Foul quality
38 *Dama*
39 Jackie Kennedy alma mater
40 *61** subject
43 Frankfurt flowers
45 Pro group
46 Bo's'n boss
49 Born

★★ Triad Split Decisions

In this clueless crossword puzzle, each answer consists of two words whose spellings are the same, except for the consecutive letters given. All answers are common words; no phrases or hyphenated or capitalized words are used. Some of the clues may have more than one solution, but there is only one word pair that will correctly link up with all the other word pairs.

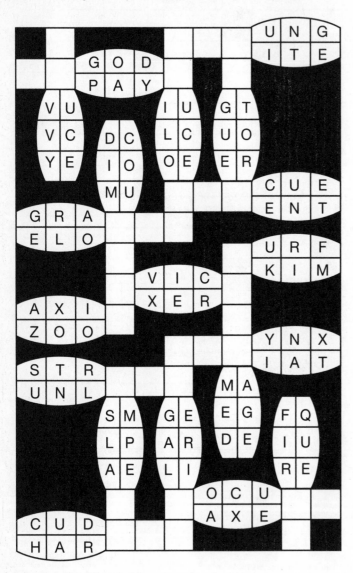

SUDOKU SUM

Without repeating any digits, complete the sum at right, by filling one digit in each of the five blanks.

```
    _ 5 _
  + 3 _ 1
  _ 2 _
```

★★★★ Color Paths

Find the shortest path through the maze, entering at the bottom and exiting at
the top, by using paths in this color order: red, blue, yellow, red, blue, etc.
Change path colors through the white squares. It is okay to retrace your path.

THREE AT A RHYME

Rearrange these letters to form three one-syllable words that rhyme.

B C F H H M M M O R T U U

_____　_____　_____

★★★★★ Themeless Toughie by Daniel R. Stark

ACROSS

1 Spa offerings
9 Not overwhelming
15 Song of praise
16 Albéniz subject
17 Combining chemically
18 Nice neighbor
19 Persisted with
20 Yours, on the Seine
22 Evaluation
28 Lady from Madrid
32 Cape waver
33 Dwelt
34 They make lots of calls
36 Jackknife, for one
37 Tony group
38 It's out on a limb
39 Dishes (out)
40 Cooped (up)
41 Open materials
42 Statues of goddesses
43 Fuzzy
45 Teaching assistants
47 Unshakable resolve
49 Say firmly
50 For some time
56 Spiteful one
60 Got back
62 Impassioned
63 Wearing, perhaps
64 Pint-size
65 Feedback

DOWN

1 Annotate
2 On the sheltered side
3 Insult, so to speak
4 Faction
5 Banff's loc.
6 Segovia's specialty
7 German article
8 Lengthy narratives
9 Brunch beverages
10 Orchestra member
11 Thieves' place
12 Time
13 Often-bracketed word
14 Lao-Tzu's creative force
21 Stormy weather
23 White wine
24 Coped
25 Harold Ross, e.g.
26 Beach reading
27 Hair sample
28 Like some auctions
29 Show clearly
30 Prickly plant
31 Work by Keats
33 Hare constellation
35 Clever turn of phrase
39 Caltech rival
41 Lack of experience
44 Lancelot's mother
46 Applications
48 Goof
51 Lumber flaw
52 City near Mauna Loa
53 Barge __
54 Camera part
55 Margin
56 Almanac page
57 It sounds like "air"
58 Citrus cooler
59 Just hired
61 Festive night

PAGE 17

Beddy-Bye

M	O	P	U	P		E	G	R	E	T		W	A	N
T	U	L	S	A		T	O	I	L	E		E	L	I
G	R	O	U	N	D	C	O	V	E	R		T	L	C
	S	P	A	C	E		D	A	V	E		B	E	E
		L	A	L	A		L	A	S	T	L	Y		
S	O	S		K	I	L	T		T	A	R	A		
W	H	O	L	E		E	U	R	O		A	N	T	E
I	N	F	O		R	U	L	E	R		S	K	I	T
T	O	T	S		A	T	I	P		S	H	E	E	N
	S	E	M	I		P	E	R	U		T	R	A	
	S	P	R	I	N	G		L	O	I	N			
S	I	R		N	C	O	S		S	T	O	R	K	
A	R	E		C	O	O	K	I	E	S	H	E	E	T
T	E	A		E	A	S	E	D		M	I	N	E	D
E	N	D		S	T	E	W	S		E	T	O	N	S

PAGE 18

Color Paths

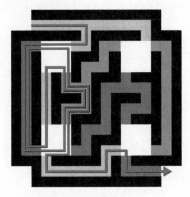

ADDITION SWITCH
7 0 5 + 1 5 7 = 8 6 2

PAGE 19

United Nations

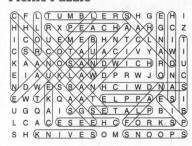

COMMON SENSE
TEN

PAGE 20

Sudoku

8	4	5	2	6	9	1	7	3
6	9	3	1	5	7	2	4	8
7	1	2	4	3	8	6	9	5
1	3	6	7	8	5	9	2	4
2	8	7	3	9	4	5	6	1
4	5	9	6	1	2	8	3	7
5	2	8	9	7	3	4	1	6
3	6	4	5	2	1	7	8	9
9	7	1	8	4	6	3	5	2

MIXAGRAMS
WAIST MOLE
MUSHY OPAL
BARON MICA
INNER FLED

PAGE 21

Hot Day

S	C	O	W		A	M	A	S	S		O	R	A	L
U	R	G	E		L	U	C	C	I		N	O	N	O
D	O	L	L		T	I	T	A	N		A	L	T	O
S	W	E	L	T	E	R	I	N	G		S	E	E	M
Y	E	S	S	I	R			S	E	T				
			C	E	N	T	S		B	R	E	A	K	
M	I	N	I		G	A	R	P		B	E	L	L	E
U	S	E	R		O	D	O	R	S		A	S	A	P
T	E	A	R	S		E	V	I	L		K	E	N	T
E	E	R	I	E		R	E	G	I	S				
			T	A	R			T	H	A	M	E	S	
S	O	F	A		A	L	L	T	H	E	R	A	G	E
A	H	A	B		M	O	O	R	E		E	Y	R	E
P	I	L	L		P	R	I	O	R		N	E	E	D
S	O	L	E		S	E	N	D	S		A	R	T	S

PAGE 22

Circular Reasoning

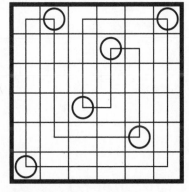

COUNTDOWN
98+7-6-5-4-3-21 = 66

PAGE 23

Line Drawing

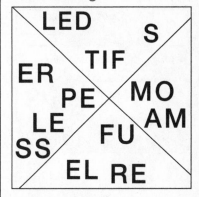

AMMO, PEERLESS,
REFUEL, STIFLED

INITIAL REACTION
8 = SIDES ON A STOP SIGN

PAGE 24

Picnic Puzzle

[word search grid with TUMBLER, PEACH, SANDWICH, FORKS, KNIVES, SNOOPS, PLATES, CUPS circled]

TONGUE TWISTER
ARABIC

PAGE 25

Squeeze Play

W	E	D	G	E		I	D	O	L		S	T	U	B
I	D	E	A	L		N	O	N	O		T	A	R	A
G	A	L	L	S		C	O	L	A		O	L	G	A
	M	I	L	I	T	A	R	Y	F	O	R	C	E	
			O	E	R			E	N	E				
S	P	A	N		U	G	H		R	I	D	G	E	S
O	L	D		E	R	I	E			C	U	L	P	A
L	E	A	D	E	R	O	F	T	H	E	P	A	C	K
E	A	G	E	R		W	I	N	E			R	O	E
S	T	E	P	I	N		S	A	W		P	E	T	S
			A	C	E			E	T	A				
	S	T	R	A	W	B	E	R	R	Y	J	A	M	
B	O	A	T		C	A	R	E		P	A	L	E	R
E	R	L	E		A	L	A	N		E	M	O	T	E
D	E	E	D		R	E	S	T		D	A	T	E	D

PAGE 26

Islands

AND SO ON
ROD and REEL

PAGE 27

Shades of Meaning

SUDOKU SUM
503 + 179 = 682

PAGE 28

Canine Clothing

PAGE 29

One-Way Streets

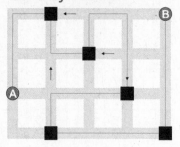

THREE AT A RHYME
FIR, MYRRH, WERE

PAGE 30

Split Decisions

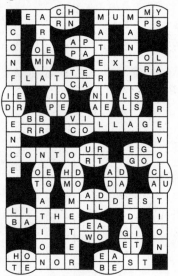

TWO-BY-FOUR
CHEF, RULE (or LURE)

PAGE 31

Star Search

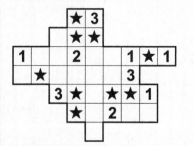

MIXAGRAMS
COURT TALC
OPTIC MAMA
LEMON THUS
DOUSE MASH

PAGE 32

Building Blocks

TELEPHONE TRIOS
BALLOON, BIPLANE, AIRSHIP

PAGE 33

Cut to the Chase

A	R	O	S	E		A	D	D	S		S	H	O	W

(Cut to the Chase crossword grid)

```
A R O S E   A D D S   S H O W
C A P O N   W R A P   N O N O
T H E F T   A N T E   A M E R
  R A I L R O A D T R A C K
A B E   R O E   A L G A E
N O T Y E T   S U I T   E R R
A S T A   B A R T A B
  C A M P A I G N T R A I L
    S H I N E S   S N I P
M E T   O D D S   M E E K E R
A S H E N   C P R   S N O
S C A V E N G E R H U N T
C A M E   A N T I   P E A C H
O P E N   P A N S   T R I T E
T E S T   S W A P   S O N N Y
```

PAGE 34

Hyper-Sudoku

5	6	3	7	9	2	1	8	4
8	7	1	6	3	4	5	2	9
2	4	9	5	1	8	6	3	7
4	3	8	2	5	1	9	7	6
7	2	5	9	8	6	3	4	1
9	1	6	4	7	3	2	5	8
6	5	7	8	2	9	4	1	3
1	9	2	3	4	7	8	6	5
3	8	4	1	6	5	7	9	2

TRANSDELETION
COSTA RICA

PAGE 35

Loops

BETWEENER
ORDER

PAGE 36

123

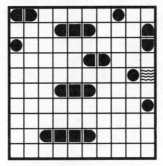

2	1	3	1	2	3
3	2	1	2	3	1
1	3	2	3	1	2
2	1	3	1	2	3
1	3	2	3	1	2
3	2	1	2	3	1

THREE OF A KIND
Many students are
<u>mad</u>—English Literature
exam <u>is tak</u>en on Thursday.

PAGE 37

Auto-Graph

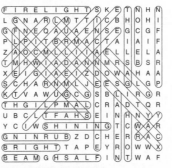

PAGE 38

ABC

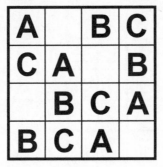

CLUELESS CROSSWORD

S	M	E	A	R	E	D
P		X		A		I
I	M	P	E	D	E	S
G		R		I		T
O	R	E	G	A	N	O
T		S		T		R
S	U	S	P	E	C	T

PAGE 39

Find the Ships

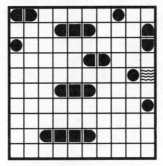

SOUND THINKING
DESPOIL, DISCIPLE, DISPEL,
DISPLAY

PAGE 40

Light Reading

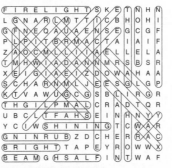

IN OTHER WORDS
PLAYGROUND, POLYGRAPH,
CANDYGRAM

PAGE 41

Fruity Remarks

PAGE 42

Go With the Flow

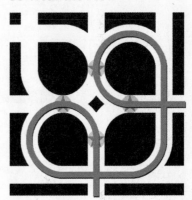

TWO-BY-FOUR
TORN, VEIN (or VINE); VENT,
IRON

PAGE 43

Circular Reasoning

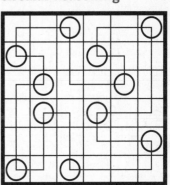

ADDITION SWITCH
438 + 109 = 547

PAGE 44

Beastly

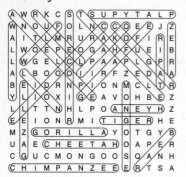

CITY SEARCH
ASPEN, PANDA, SEDAN, SPADE, SPEND

PAGE 45

Three Headed Relatives

O R A L		T A D S		O N E P M
N A N A		A C R E		N O S E D
T U T U		K E N T		T S A R S
	L E G G E D O U T A H I T	
	H I P		P A R	
A F T		L A V A		I G E T I T
D E E P		R I C O		E L E N A
A R M E D T O T H E T E E T H		
M A P L E		L O I S		E U R O
S L E E P S		R O T S		P O E
	U S A		E O N	
	F O O T E D T H E B I L L	
P A T T I		L O A M		C O O P
A R T I E		I D L E		H A V E
C R O S S		B O L D		E D E N

PAGE 46

Sudoku

4	3	8	7	9	2	5	6	1
7	6	2	5	1	8	3	9	4
5	9	1	6	3	4	8	7	2
1	4	7	9	8	5	6	2	3
8	2	6	1	4	3	7	5	9
3	5	9	2	7	6	1	4	8
9	7	4	3	6	1	2	8	5
6	1	5	8	2	9	4	3	7
2	8	3	4	5	7	9	1	6

SUDOKU SUM
3 1 9 + 5 0 7 = 8 2 6

PAGE 47

123

2	3	2	1	3	1
3	1	3	2	1	2
1	2	1	3	2	3
2	3	2	1	3	1
3	1	3	2	1	2
1	2	1	3	2	3

AND SO ON
FUN and GAMES

PAGE 48

In Place

P E N S		B A B A		S H I N E
A L O T		U S E S		T O N E R
T I R E		L E N S		O U T E R
H O M E P L A T E		P R O D S
S T A P L E		T W I G	
	O T I S		A T L A S T
S A P P Y		C A L L		A U T O
A L A I		D E V I L		S N A G
K E P T		I D E S		A S T R O
E X A C T A		S T I R	
	H A Z E		R O O S T S
R E E F S		L O V I N G C U P
A L L O T		O D E S		D A N E
F L A R E		P O R E		E L I A
T A L K S		E R A S		N E C K

PAGE 49

One-Way Streets

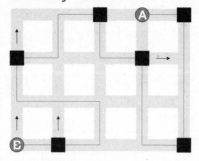

MIXAGRAMS
D U C A T   E L S E
O B O E S   S I L T
I N L E T   S P A R
E V E N T   K I W I

PAGE 50

Star Maze

COMMON SENSE
FAR

PAGE 51

Star Search

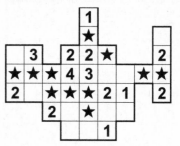

TELEPHONE TRIOS
CHEETAH, LEOPARD, PANTHER

PAGE 52

Noble Names

L A T T E		E P E E		A L A I
O R R I N		R O L L		L A R D
C O U N T B A S I E		O R E O
H M M		R O S E		P L U R A L
	A P I E C E		S H A D Y
	H E A D G E A R		K O S
A L T O S		R A N K		I D O
S E E P		S L A N T		E N I D
T A D		E K E S		M A G N A
A S K		D I S P L A Y S	
	N A I L S		I N S E C T
C H I S E L		B E E T		A W E
L O G S		E A R L W A R R E N
A S H E		T R I O		R A G E D
M E T S		S T E W		S P O T S

PAGE 53
Three-for-One Word Search

BETWEENER
HOME

PAGE 55
Line Drawing

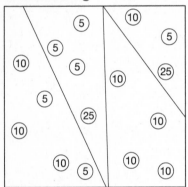

THREE AT A RHYME
BURN, FERN, YEARN

PAGE 56
ABC

C	B		A
A	B	C	
B	C	A	
A		C	B

SOUND THINKING
FAIL-SAFE, FALSIFY, PHILOSOPHY

PAGE 57
Basic Beverages

PAGE 58
Looped Path

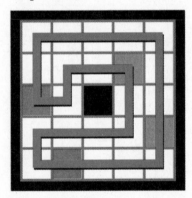

TWO-BY-FOUR
CRAM, NIGH; GRAM, INCH (or CHIN)

PAGE 59
Presidential Jigsaw

TRANSDELETION
NOTRE DAME

PAGE 60
Find the Ships

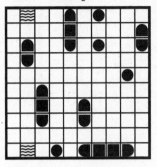

TONGUE TWISTER
CHINESE

PAGE 61
Sudoku

1	4	5	2	7	9	3	8	6
8	2	6	4	1	3	7	9	5
9	7	3	5	8	6	4	1	2
3	6	1	9	4	5	8	2	7
5	8	4	3	2	7	1	6	9
2	9	7	8	6	1	5	3	4
7	3	2	1	9	4	6	5	8
4	1	8	6	5	2	9	7	3
6	5	9	7	3	8	2	4	1

MIXAGRAMS
DOUBT ICES
PEKOE DAUB
BELOW AMID
SLATE UPON

PAGE 62
Just Kidding

PAGE 63
Circular Reasoning

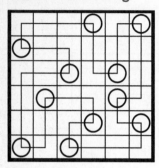

COUNTDOWN
9+8+7-6-5-4+32-1 = 40

PAGE 64
Triad Split Decisions

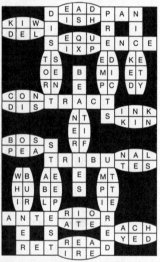

ADDITION SWITCH
3 7 5 + 2 6 8 = 6 4 3

PAGE 65
123

2	1	3	2	3	1
1	3	2	1	2	3
3	2	1	3	1	2
2	1	3	2	3	1
1	3	2	1	2	3
3	2	1	3	1	2

BETWEENER
CLUB

PAGE 66
In the Jungle

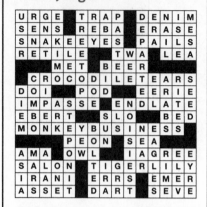

PAGE 67
Islands

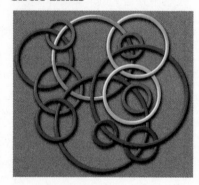

SOUND THINKING
OUTDOOR, TAWDRY

PAGE 68
Circle Links

INITIAL REACTION
9 = JUSTICES of the SUPREME COURT

PAGE 69
Elementary

COMMON SENSE
JOB

PAGE 70
Handyman Special

A	C	I	D		A	T	B	A	T		L	O	L	A
D	U	D	E		T	H	E	R	E		E	P	I	C
D	R	I	L	L	T	E	A	M	S		V	E	N	T
L	E	O		I	O	N	S		S	P	E	C	K	S
E	S	T	H	E	R		T	R	I	L	L			
			A	N	N	A		H	E	E	H	A	W	S
B	E	A	M		E	R	G	O		D	E	B	I	T
A	L	U	M		Y	A	R	D	S		A	L	M	A
R	I	D	E	R		B	R	E	W		D	E	P	T
N	A	I	R	O	B	I		S	A	M	E			
			S	P	A	C	E		T	O	D	A	T	E
S	T	A	T	E	S		D	E	C	O		M	I	T
W	I	R	E		S	A	W	T	H	R	O	U	G	H
A	L	L	I		E	L	I	T	E		A	S	E	A
N	E	O	N		T	I	N	E	S		K	E	R	N

PAGE 71
One-Way Streets

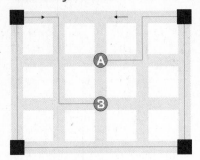

TWO-BY-FOUR
MICA, GAIN

PAGE 72
Hyper-Sudoku

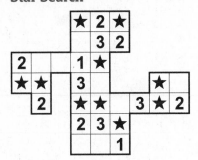

1	2	6	5	7	4	8	9	3
4	8	3	1	9	2	5	6	7
5	9	7	6	3	8	4	1	2
6	5	2	4	8	7	9	3	1
8	7	1	9	5	3	6	2	4
9	3	4	2	1	6	7	5	8
3	1	5	7	4	9	2	8	6
7	6	9	8	2	1	3	4	5
2	4	8	3	6	5	1	7	9

TELEPHONE TRIOS
STADIUM, COTTAGE, MANSION

PAGE 73
Star Search

SUDOKU SUM
3 7 8 + 2 1 6 = 5 9 4

PAGE 74
Clothes to You

C	A	M	E	L		S	A	S	S		C	L	A	M
O	R	A	T	E		A	R	C	H		Z	O	N	E
W	E	A	R	I	N	G	T	H	E	P	A	N	T	S
S	A	M	E		E	A	S	E		U	R	G	E	S
			H	I	S			D	A	N				
C	H	A	P	E	L		J	U	N	K	M	A	I	L
O	A	T	E	R		P	O	L	K		E	L	S	A
D	R	E	S	S	R	E	H	E	A	R	S	A	L	S
E	D	I	T		I	N	N	S		T	A	M	E	S
S	Y	N	O	P	S	I	S		D	E	S	O	T	O
			L	E	N		W	A	S					
A	C	H	O	O		S	P	A	S		E	U	R	O
K	E	E	P	Y	O	U	R	S	H	I	R	T	O	N
I	D	E	A		A	L	O	T		D	R	A	P	E
N	E	L	L		F	A	M	E		A	S	H	E	S

PAGE 75
ABC

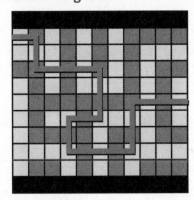

AND SO ON
CAT and MOUSE

PAGE 76
Alternating Tiles

BETWEENER
ROLL

PAGE 77
Sudoku

6	3	4	1	7	9	8	2	5
2	7	9	6	5	8	4	1	3
5	1	8	3	4	2	7	6	9
8	5	2	4	1	3	9	7	6
3	6	7	8	9	5	1	4	2
9	4	1	7	2	6	5	3	8
7	2	5	9	6	1	3	8	4
1	9	3	2	8	4	6	5	7
4	8	6	5	3	7	2	9	1

MIXAGRAMS
BRIBE SEAM
COULD VETO
STRUM POLO
ABLER ROAN

PAGE 78
Put on the Dog

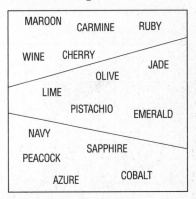

C	A	R	E		B	E	S	T		P	H	O	N	E
A	L	A	S		O	A	H	U		O	I	L	E	R
R	I	N	T	I	N	T	I	N		S	E	D	E	R
A	C	C	E	D	E		P	E	L	T		Y	D	S
T	E	H	E	E			S	A	U	C	E			
			M	A	L	T	S		D	R	I	L	L	S
S	A	Y		S	O	S	A		D	E	A	L	I	N
E	M	U		B	E	N	J	I			E	V	A	
A	S	K	E	R	S		T	R	E	E		R	E	P
L	O	O	K	A	T		A	S	S	E	T			
		N	E	V	E	R		R	U	S	S	O		
O	A	K		I	R	A	S		S	I	F	T	E	R
A	S	I	A	N		W	H	I	T	E	F	A	N	G
F	E	N	C	E		L	O	R	E		E	L	S	A
S	A	G	E	S		S	E	E	P		T	E	E	N

PAGE 79
Line Drawing

MAROON CARMINE RUBY
WINE CHERRY
OLIVE JADE
LIME
PISTACHIO EMERALD
NAVY
SAPPHIRE
PEACOCK
AZURE COBALT

THREE AT A RHYME
BEEF, GRIEF, LEAF

PAGE 80
Find the Ships
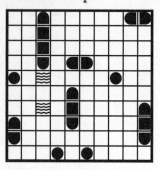

CLUELESS CROSSWORD

B	R	O	W	N	E	D
O		V		E		O
U	N	E	Q	U	A	L
Q		R		T		L
U	N	D	E	R	G	O
E		U		A		P
T	R	E	L	L	I	S

PAGE 81
Circular Reasoning
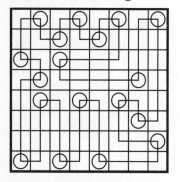

SOUND THINKING
BAGEL, BEAGLE, BEGUILE, BOGGLE, BUGLE

PAGE 82
At the Beach

B	E	R	E	T		A	C	E	S		S	W	A	P
O	C	H	E	R		T	H	A	I		T	A	M	E
S	H	O	R	E	L	E	A	V	E		A	T	O	P
C	O	S	I	N	E		R	E	S	T	L	E	S	S
		E	D	G	E			T	I	E	R			
A	L	F		S	A	N	D	M	A	N		S	K	I
S	A	L	T		L	I	R	A		T	U	D	O	R
P	R	O	O	F		G	I	N		S	P	O	R	E
I	V	A	N	A		M	E	E	T		S	W	A	N
C	A	T		C	O	A	S	T	E	D		N	N	E
		A	W	E	D			S	N	I	T			
P	O	L	I	T	E	S	T		E	T	H	I	C	S
S	L	O	T		S	U	R	F	T	H	E	N	E	T
S	E	A	T		S	N	O	B		E	R	O	D	E
T	O	N	Y		A	S	T	I		R	E	N	E	W

PAGE 83
Sets of Three

CITY SEARCH
CORSET, ESCORT, ESCROW, RECTOR, RESORT, ROSTER, SECRET, SECTOR, STEREO

PAGE 84
123

2	1	3	2	3	1	2	3	1
1	3	2	1	2	3	1	2	3
3	2	1	3	1	2	3	1	2
1	3	2	1	2	3	1	2	3
2	1	3	2	3	1	2	3	1
3	2	1	3	1	2	3	1	2
1	3	2	1	2	3	1	2	3
3	2	1	3	1	2	3	1	2
2	1	3	2	3	1	2	3	1

TRANSDELETION
NITROGEN

PAGE 85
Islands

TWO-BY-FOUR
ARMY, CHAP; ACHY, RAMP

PAGE 86
Feeling Blue

PAGE 87
Color Squares
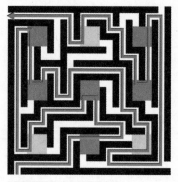

ADDITION SWITCH
1 1 9 + 2 6 4 = 3 8 3

PAGE 88
Split Decisions
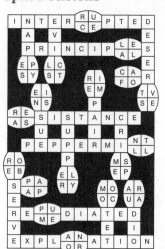

COMMON SENSE
CALL

PAGE 89
Hyper-Sudoku

4	2	6	3	7	8	5	9	1
1	7	9	6	2	5	3	4	8
5	3	8	1	4	9	2	7	6
3	4	5	2	9	1	6	8	7
9	8	7	5	6	4	1	3	2
2	6	1	7	8	3	4	5	9
7	5	3	8	1	2	9	6	4
6	9	2	4	5	7	8	1	3
8	1	4	9	3	6	7	2	5

MIXAGRAMS
CHEER DUMB
RIFLE CODA
AGREE BOWL
THREE OPAL

PAGE 90
Lion Around

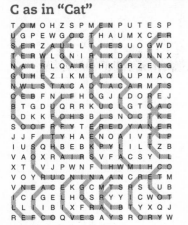

PAGE 91
C as in "Cat"

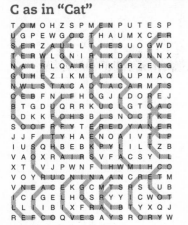

TONGUE TWISTER
DUTCH

PAGE 93
One-Way Streets

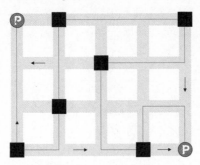

TRANSDELETION
GERSHWIN

PAGE 94
Materialization

H	A	M	S		E	L	M	S		M	A	J	O	R
E	L	I	E		N	O	A	H		O	P	E	R	A
N	O	N	E		D	A	R	E		D	E	R	B	Y
C	H	I	F	F	O	N	C	A	K	E		S	S	E
E	A	S	I	E	R			E	R	L	E			
		T	E	S	S		A	N	N	O	Y	E	D	
S	S	N		D	E	T	E	S	T		A	C	R	E
O	L	E	G			O	O	H			D	O	M	E
R	A	T	E		H	O	N	E	S	T		W	A	R
T	W	I	N	B	E	D		S	L	A	P			
	N	E	A	R			A	L	L	S	E	T		
T	I	C		C	O	T	T	O	N	C	A	N	D	Y
A	R	O	M	A		B	E	N	T		T	A	S	K
C	A	M	E	L		S	A	T	E		T	R	E	E
K	N	E	L	L		P	R	O	D		E	E	L	S

PAGE 95
Think Straight

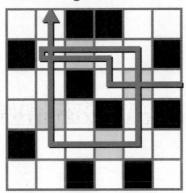

THREE OF A KIND
A toxic, horrid ether ails one of the ward's patients.

PAGE 96
Star Search

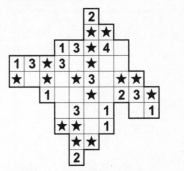

TELEPHONE TRIOS
REVENUE, CAPITAL, DOLLARS

PAGE 97
Triad Split Decisions

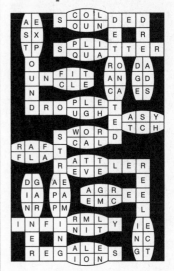

IN OTHER WORDS
HIGHCHAIR

PAGE 98
Gnawing Issue

S	A	C	H	S		P	A	D	R	E		G	P	S
A	L	L	A	H		A	N	N	U	L		O	A	T
B	E	A	V	E	R	S	T	A	T	E		P	E	I
E	X	P	E	D	I	T	E		M	A	H	A	L	
			D	A	Y		P	R	E	V	E	N	T	
C	A	R	T	E	L		L	E	A	N	E	R		
O	N	A	I	R		M	E	A	N	T		B	B	S
D	O	T	S		H	E	A	R	T		V	A	I	L
A	N	A		T	A	R	R	Y		L	I	L	L	E
		T	U	R	N	I	N		B	A	I	L	E	D
S	T	A	T	I	S	T		S	E	X				
T	O	T	E	M		A	L	A	N	A	L	D	A	
A	N	T		M	O	U	S	E	K	E	T	E	E	R
L	E	A		E	L	S	I	E		S	T	O	A	T
E	S	T		R	E	C	A	P		S	U	N	N	Y

PAGE 99

ABC

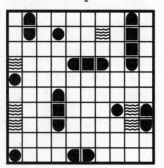

SUDOKU SUM

1 2 3 + 4 6 7 = 5 9 0

PAGE 100

Find the Ships

AND SO ON

ROOM and BOARD

PAGE 101

Brake Job

A	S	H		L	I	L	A	C		P	O	S	E	R
C	H	I		A	M	E	B	A		O	L	L	I	E
H	O	L	D	U	P	M	A	N		L	I	O	N	S
E	N	D	E	D			A	L	L	O	W		
S	E	A	S		A	B	I	D	E		S	P	A	R
		P	O	P	U	L	A	T	E		I	R	E
L	A	B	O	R	E	R	S			B	U	T	T	E
E	G	O	T	I	S	T		S	T	E	N	C	I	L
G	O	O	S	E		S	E	A	R	C	H	E	S
A	R	K		L	I	B	R	E	T	T	O	
L	A	S	T		L	E	O	N	E		U	V	E	A
	T	W	E	E	T			I	T	E	M	S
S	T	A	I	N		R	A	I	N	C	H	E	C	K
H	E	L	L	O		A	G	R	E	E		R	E	E
Y	E	L	L	S		Y	E	A	T	S		S	E	W

PAGE 102

Twelve-Letter Word

BETWEENER

TALK

PAGE 103

Sudoku

6	7	2	4	9	1	3	8	5
9	8	1	5	3	2	6	7	4
4	5	3	7	6	8	1	2	9
5	4	9	8	1	6	7	3	2
7	3	6	2	5	9	8	4	1
2	1	8	3	4	7	5	9	6
8	6	7	1	2	4	9	5	3
3	9	4	6	8	5	2	1	7
1	2	5	9	7	3	4	6	8

MIXAGRAMS

EKING JADE
SNARE EMIT
WEIRD ROTE
NEWLY KALE

PAGE 104

Circular Reasoning

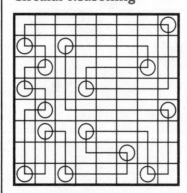

THREE AT A RHYME

CRATE, STRAIT, WEIGHT

PAGE 105

At the Bank

C	R	A	W		S	A	W	S		S	O	F	A	R
R	A	S	H		E	L	E	E		W	E	A	V	E
I	N	C	A		T	O	L	L		A	R	C	E	D
S	T	O	R	Y	T	E	L	L	E	R		E	S	S
P	O	T	F	U	L			S	M	O	G		
			L	E	A	D	U	P		R	U	I	N
M	A	P	L	E		T	O	N	Y		D	A	N	E
O	B	O	E	S		E	L	I		S	E	R	T	A
B	E	L	A		D	I	E	T		A	R	D	O	R
S	T	E	S		E	N	D	E	A	R		
	V	E	A	L				G	A	S	K	E	T
A	L	A		C	L	O	T	H	E	S	L	I	N	E
C	O	U	R	T		O	R	E	O		I	O	T	A
I	G	L	O	O		P	U	R	L		E	W	E	S
D	E	T	E	R		S	E	E	D		R	A	R	E

PAGE 106

Islands

COMMON SENSE

COLD

PAGE 107

Hyper-Sudoku

7	5	2	9	6	8	1	4	3
3	9	1	2	4	7	5	6	8
6	8	4	5	1	3	9	2	7
5	3	7	6	2	1	4	8	9
2	4	8	7	9	5	6	3	1
1	6	9	8	3	4	7	5	2
8	2	5	1	7	6	3	9	4
9	7	3	4	5	2	8	1	6
4	1	6	3	8	9	2	7	5

TRANSDELETION

LAVENDER

PAGE 108
From A to B

P	T	A	S		O	P	A	L		B	A	T	O	N
L	E	N	T		N	O	D	E		A	D	O	R	E
E	N	D	O		L	O	O	N		B	O	N	E	R
A	E	R	O	S	O	L	B	O	M	B		G	O	D
S	T	E	L	L	A		E	X	A	L	T			
			I	N	T			V	E	R	B	A	L	
C	O	H	A	N		Y	O	R	E		I	O	T	A
A	L	A	S	K	A	N	K	I	N	G	C	R	A	B
R	E	U	P		B	E	S	T		R	E	E	D	S
L	O	L	I	T	A			A	S	A				
			C	O	S	T	A		A	C	T	I	V	E
A	G	E		A	H	A	B	T	H	E	A	R	A	B
L	A	V	E	S		M	O	M	A		T	I	L	E
A	G	E	N	T		E	V	E	R		U	S	S	R
S	A	N	D	Y		R	O	N	A		M	E	E	T

PAGE 109
AND Enders

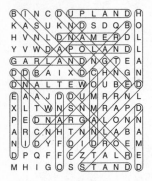

INITIAL REACTION
30 = DAYS in SEPTEMBER, APRIL, JUNE, and NOVEMBER

PAGE 110
Four-Letter Word Routes

AND SO ON
LOST and FOUND

PAGE 111
Starting Line

H	I	T	O	N		H	O	P	S		V	E	G	A
A	D	E	L	A		O	R	A	L		A	X	E	L
R	E	A	D	Y	A	N	D	W	I	L	L	I	N	G
M	A	K	E	S	D	O		S	T	E	E	L	I	E
				A	R	P			F	R	E	E	R	
R	E	F	O	R	M		E	V	I	T	A			
A	K	I	T	A		A	N	O	N		T	A	U	
S	E	T	T	H	E	C	L	O	C	K	B	A	C	K
P	S	S			S	H	I	M		O	A	K	I	E
			A	G	L	E	T		S	H	R	E	D	S
B	A	S	R	A		E	S	E						
A	N	T	I	W	A	R		P	A	N	A	C	H	E
G	O	A	S	K	Y	O	U	R	M	O	T	H	E	R
E	D	G	E		E	L	S	A		D	O	A	L	L
L	E	G	S		S	E	A	T		S	N	I	D	E

PAGE 112
One-Way Streets

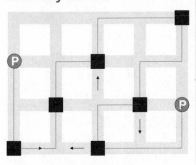

ADDITION SWITCH
771 + 179 = 950

PAGE 113
123

3	1	3	2	1	2	1	2	3
2	3	2	1	3	1	3	1	2
1	2	1	3	2	3	2	3	1
3	1	2	1	3	2	1	2	3
2	3	1	3	2	1	3	1	2
1	2	3	2	1	3	2	3	1
3	1	2	1	3	2	1	2	3
1	2	3	2	1	3	2	3	1
2	3	1	3	2	1	3	1	2

TELEPHONE TRIOS
SILICON, BROMINE, CALCIUM

PAGE 114
Line Drawing

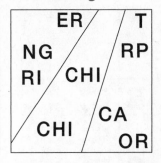

CARPORT, CHICHI, RINGER

SOUND THINKING
ADULATE, AGILITY, GELATI, JILT, JOLLITY, JOLT

PAGE 115
Cleanup Crew

F	A	V	E	S		L	A	H		S	T	E	T
O	N	A	L	L		S	U	M	O		E	A	V	E
U	N	C	L	E		A	L	I	T		A	R	E	A
L	O	U	I	E		D	U	S	T	S	T	O	R	M
	U	P	T	O			S	U	E	T				
A	D	M	S		T	H	U		B	A	L	S	A	M
P	E	T	E		T	O	T	S		M	E	C	C	A
I	C	U		M	O	P	T	O	P	S		R	U	T
N	O	B	L	E		S	E	M	I		C	U	T	E
G	R	E	A	T	S		R	E	L		O	B	E	Y
			B	U	C	S			L	Y	O	N		
S	W	E	E	P	H	A	N	D		E	L	U	D	E
H	A	L	L		E	L	I	A		T	A	R	E	S
E	R	I	E		M	E	L	D		I	N	S	E	T
S	P	E	D		E	S	E			S	T	E	P	S

PAGE 116
Star Search

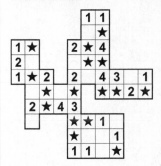

MIXAGRAMS
TRIPE PITY
SCRAP EARN
BURLY LEEK
KARMA NEED

PAGE 117

Bead Maze

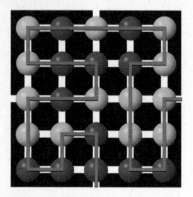

SUDOKU SUM
5 8 1 + 3 2 6 = 9 0 7

PAGE 118

Imitative

C	O	M	B		S	P	E	C	K		O	N	U	S
E	L	I	A		T	I	A	R	A		R	E	N	T
R	I	L	L		O	C	C	U	R		D	E	M	O
F	O	L	L	O	W	T	H	E	L	E	A	D	E	R
			Y	V	E	S			M	I	S	T	Y	
O	M	A	H	A			H	A	V	E	N			
K	A	T	O		C	H	O	S	E	N		G	E	L
A	U	T	O	G	R	A	P	H	E	D	C	O	P	Y
Y	I	N		E	E	R	I	E	R		O	W	E	N
		D	E	E	D	S			A	N	N	E	X	
O	N	I	O	N			B	E	L	T				
T	A	R	Z	A	N	T	H	E	A	P	E	M	A	N
H	I	K	E		A	R	E	A	S		M	I	K	E
E	V	E	N		P	U	R	S	E		P	R	I	X
R	E	D	S		S	E	A	T	S		T	E	N	T

PAGE 119

Hyper-Sudoku

9	5	6	4	1	3	2	8	7
4	1	8	6	2	7	9	3	5
7	3	2	5	9	8	4	6	1
6	7	4	9	3	1	5	2	8
8	9	3	2	5	4	7	1	6
5	2	1	8	7	6	3	4	9
1	4	5	3	6	9	8	7	2
3	6	9	7	8	2	1	5	4
2	8	7	1	4	5	6	9	3

COUNTDOWN
98-7+6+5+4-3-2-1 = 100

PAGE 120

ABC

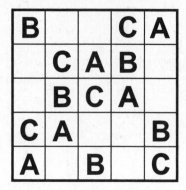

IN OTHER WORDS
BLACKJACK, LOCKJAW, REYKJAVIK

PAGE 121

On Top

G	A	L	E		A	B	A	L	L		C	E	N	T
A	B	E	L		T	A	L	I	A		L	I	E	U
S	U	M	M	I	T	T	A	L	K		I	R	A	N
U	S	O		V	I	E	S		E	F	F	E	T	E
P	E	N	C	I	L	S		R	E	E	F			
			R	N	A		H	A	R	D	H	A	T	S
R	O	P	E	S		F	I	F	I		A	M	I	E
A	M	O	S		F	O	R	T	E		N	O	D	E
S	A	L	T		E	X	E	S		O	G	R	E	S
P	R	O	F	I	L	E	S		A	R	E			
			A	D	D	S		B	L	A	R	I	N	G
D	A	L	L	A	S		L	I	L	T		S	O	U
O	R	A	L		P	E	A	K	S	E	A	S	O	N
N	I	C	E		A	G	R	E	E		R	U	N	G
E	D	E	N		R	O	A	S	T		M	E	S	A

PAGE 122

Pencil Pile

CITY SEARCH
ABRIDGE, BRIGADE, GRIMACE, CARBIDE

PAGE 123

Find the Ships

CLUELESS CROSSWORD

A	C	Q	U	I	R	E		R	
C		U		S		Y			
E	P	I	S	O	D	E			
R		N		B		L			
B	R	I	G	A	D	E			
I		N		R		T			
C	H	E	E	S	E	S			

PAGE 124

Triad Split Decisions

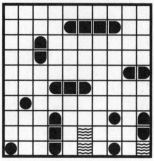

THREE AT A RHYME
FEIGN, GAIN, VEIN

PAGE 125
Meal Time

C	A	R	A		A	D	J	O	I	N		S	R	A
O	M	E	N		L	E	A	N	T	O		T	O	N
B	E	D	A	N	D	B	R	E	A	K	F	A	S	T
A	L	A		O	O	O			L	I	O	N	E	L
L	I	C	K	S		N	A	E		A	N	D	R	E
T	A	T	A		B	E	N	C	H		T	I	E	R
			T	I	E		T	O	O	T		S	D	S
	L	E	T	S	D	O	L	U	N	C	H			
S	A	O		S	E	E	N		R	N	A			
O	D	O	R		T	A	I	L	S		S	P	I	N
D	U	K	E	D		R	O	E		V	E	R	N	E
A	L	I	C	E	S		T	E	M		A	T	A	
C	A	N	D	L	E	L	I	T	D	I	N	N	E	R
A	T	T		L	E	A	D	E	D		A	C	R	E
N	E	O		A	R	M	O	R	Y		B	E	N	D

PAGE 126
123

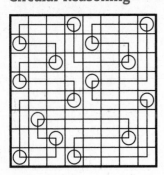

```
3 1 2 3 2 1 3 1 2
1 2 3 1 3 2 1 2 3
2 3 1 2 1 3 2 3 1
3 1 2 3 2 1 3 1 2
1 2 3 1 3 2 1 2 3
2 3 1 2 1 3 2 3 1
3 1 2 3 2 1 3 1 2
1 2 3 1 3 2 1 2 3
2 3 1 2 1 3 2 3 1
```

TWO-BY-FOUR
TRAY, HIDE (or HIED); THEY,
RIDE (or DIRE); TIDY, HERE

PAGE 127
Circular Reasoning

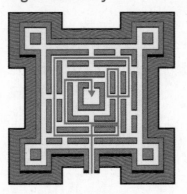

COMMON SENSE
WISH

PAGE 128
Means of Support

D	E	E	R	E		A	L	E	S		M	A	L	L
A	L	L	E	N		K	E	P	T		E	D	I	E
S	E	M	I	S		I	C	E	R		X	I	N	G
	C	O	L	U	M	N	H	E	A	D	I	N	G	
		L	E	A			S	P	E	C				
R	U	B	Y		T	W	I		S	T	A	R	E	D
I	T	E		L	E	O	N	E		E	L	E	N	A
P	I	L	L	A	R	O	F	S	O	C	I	E	T	Y
E	L	I	O	T		L	E	A	P	T		S	R	A
R	E	E	V	E	S		R	U	T		T	E	E	N
	E	N	T	O			I	R	A					
	P	O	S	T	O	F	F	I	C	E	B	O	X	
M	I	D	I		L	A	I	N		G	A	P	E	D
E	P	I	C		E	G	A	N		I	R	E	N	E
L	E	E	K		N	E	T	S		A	D	L	A	I

PAGE 129
Right Turn Only

THREE OF A KIND
Trash or treasure? The drab
bronze relic: a showpiece to a
dealer.

PAGE 131
Anatomical

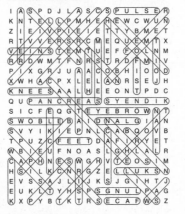

TRANSDELETION
TEASPOON

PAGE 132
Hyper-Sudoku

5	7	1	9	3	8	2	6	4
8	9	3	2	6	4	5	7	1
2	4	6	5	7	1	8	9	3
4	1	8	7	9	3	6	2	5
6	3	2	8	1	5	7	4	9
9	5	7	6	4	2	1	3	8
1	2	9	3	5	7	4	8	6
3	8	4	1	2	6	9	5	7
7	6	5	4	8	9	3	1	2

BETWEENER
ART

PAGE 133
Off the Ground

L	I	D	S		T	H	A	N	E		M	A	S	C
U	N	I	T		H	E	L	E	N		A	S	E	A
G	D	A	Y		R	E	A	C	T		P	S	A	T
O	I	L		M	U	D	S	K	I	P	P	E	R	S
S	A	U	C	Y			S	C	I	E	N	C	E	
I	N	P	U	B	L	I	C		E	A	R	T	H	Y
		R	A	I	L	A	T			E	E	E		
	P	U	D	D	L	E	J	U	M	P	E	R	S	
E	E	N			S	U	B	D	U	E				
A	N	I	M	A	L		N	E	S	T	L	I	N	G
T	E	R	E	S	A	S			T	Y	R	O	S	
C	L	O	D	H	O	P	P	E	R	S		O	S	U
R	O	N	I		T	I	A	R	A		B	N	A	I
O	P	E	C		S	E	R	I	F		S	I	L	T
W	E	D	S		E	L	E	C	T		A	C	E	S

PAGE 134
One-Way Streets

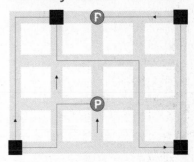

ADDITION SWITCH
4 2 5 + 1 7 6 = 6 0 1

PAGE 135
Star Search

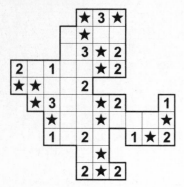

MIXAGRAMS
COMIC VISE
FLESH ROUT
FOLIO BRED
TULIP KEYS

PAGE 136
Sound-Alike Celebs

A	L	O	U	D		S	W	E	A	T		C	O	S
S	E	G	A	R		T	A	M	P	A		A	L	I
C	A	R	R	Y	N	A	T	I	O	N		R	E	G
A	S	E		N	O	G	S		S	T	A	Y	O	N
P	E	S	T	E	R	S		S	T	A	N	G		
		A	S	A		S	T	A	R	T	R	E	K	
J	U	J	U	S		P	L	A	T	A		A	D	A
I	R	I	S		C	A	I	N	E		K	N	I	T
V	I	M		C	H	U	C	K		D	I	T	T	Y
E	S	C	A	R	O	L	E		P	E	W			
	A	V	E	R	Y		C	O	D	I	C	I	L	
S	P	R	E	A	D		T	H	O	U		A	R	A
A	I	R		M	A	R	I	A	H	C	A	R	E	Y
L	E	E		E	T	O	N	S		T	H	I	N	E
T	R	Y		D	E	N	S	E		S	A	B	E	R

PAGE 137
Candy Corn

AND SO ON
PROFIT and LOSS

PAGE 138
Sudoku

2	1	9	6	8	5	7	4	3
4	8	7	2	3	1	6	5	9
6	3	5	7	9	4	2	8	1
5	2	8	4	1	9	3	7	6
3	7	4	5	6	2	1	9	8
9	6	1	8	7	3	4	2	5
8	5	6	1	4	7	9	3	2
7	9	2	3	5	6	8	1	4
1	4	3	9	2	8	5	6	7

SUDOKU SUM
$169 + 205 = 374$

PAGE 139
Saintliness

C	E	S	T	A		P	A	R	D		S	P	C	A
D	R	E	A	M		I	D	E	A		T	R	I	P
S	A	N	T	A		L	A	D	Y		R	I	T	A
	S	T	A	N	L	E	Y	S	T	E	A	M	E	R
			D	U	D	S		O	L	D	E	S	T	
T	A	R	M	A	C		A	N	I					
E	L	I	A		C	O	U	P		H	O	I	S	T
S	T	O	C	K	I	N	G	S	T	U	F	F	E	R
T	I	T	H	E		C	H	O	O		F	A	R	E
			V	I	E			G	A	S	T	A	X	
A	S	K	S	I	N		I	M	A	N				
S	T	A	I	N	L	E	S	S	S	T	E	E	L	
S	O	R	T		A	R	I	D		H	A	D	I	T
E	L	E	E		N	O	N	O		E	V	I	T	A
T	E	N	S		D	O	G	S		M	E	T	E	D

PAGE 140
Split Decisions

SOUND THINKING
APOSTLE, EPISTLE, PASSEL, PESTLE

PAGE 141
Islands

TELEPHONE TRIOS
SHERBET, PUDDING, GELATIN

PAGE 142
Best Friends

C	A	S	S		D	A	M	E		S	H	A	F	T
A	R	A	T		A	M	E	N		L	O	V	I	N
R	E	V	E	A	L	I	N	G		I	N	E	R	T
P	O	I	N	T	E	R	S	I	S	T	E	R	S	
A	L	L	O	W		A	R	E			S	T	E	
L	E	E		I	T	S		D	A	R	T	E	R	S
			A	T	E	I	N		B	E	A	T	U	P
	M	A	L	T	E	S	E	F	A	L	C	O	N	
M	A	R	T	E	N		V	I	S	I	T			
A	R	T	E	R	I	O		G	S	A		A	B	C
E	L	L		E	B	B			B	E	R	R	A	
	B	O	X	E	R	R	E	B	E	L	L	I	O	N
H	O	V	E	L		I	N	A	S	E	C	O	N	D
A	R	E	N	A		A	N	T	S			I	S	T	O
M	O	R	A	L		N	Y	S	E		D	E	E	R

PAGE 143
ABC

B	A		C	
		C	A	B
A	C	B		
	B	A		C
C			B	A

TWO-BY-FOUR
LACK, THEY

PAGE 144
Card Maze

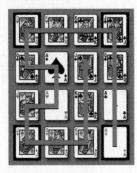

INITIAL REACTION
3 = BEATS per MEASURE in WALTZ TIME

PAGE 145
Line Drawing

ANTIC, CACTI, KHAKI, RADII, VALVE

MIXAGRAMS
ASIDE FLAW
ROBOT ARIA
SILLY CURE
FAULT EGGS

PAGE 146
Vessels of Fame

S	I	F	T		R	E	L	I	C		A	G	A	R
H	O	U	R		E	R	I	C	A		L	O	P	E
A	L	L	A		B	R	O	I	L		I	L	S	A
H	A	L	F	M	O	O	N		Y	O	N	D	E	R
			F	O	O	L		S	P	R	E	E		
R	E	S	I	S	T		C	A	S	E		N	T	H
E	X	A	C	T		S	O	L	O	S		H	A	Y
T	I	N	S		T	O	V		L	I	S	P		
I	S	T		S	K	A	T	E		D	A	N	T	E
E	T	A		H	O	R	S		C	I	N	D	E	R
		M	A	I	N	E		P	R	O	D			
L	E	A	R	N	T		C	L	E	R	M	O	N	T
O	A	R	S		I	D	L	E	D		A	R	I	A
T	R	I	O		K	A	U	A	I		R	A	C	K
S	P	A	N		I	D	E	S	T		K	N	E	E

PAGE 147
Find the Ships

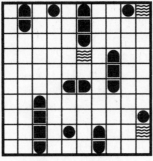

THREE AT A RHYME
MOON, PRUNE, STREWN

PAGE 148
Hyper-Sudoku

3	7	9	6	4	1	5	2	8
5	1	6	8	7	2	4	3	9
8	4	2	9	3	5	7	6	1
6	3	7	5	2	9	1	8	4
2	5	8	4	1	3	6	9	7
1	9	4	7	6	8	3	5	2
4	6	5	2	8	7	9	1	3
7	8	3	1	9	6	2	4	5
9	2	1	3	5	4	8	7	6

TONGUE TWISTER
PORTUGUESE

PAGE 149
Outside the Law

P	E	R		R	O	O	S	T	S		P	E	P	E
A	L	E		U	T	O	P	I	A		E	R	I	N
J	E	W	E	L	T	H	I	E	F		P	R	O	D
A	G	R	E	E			R	U	E	D		A	N	O
M	A	I	L		S	H	O	P	L	I	F	T	E	R
A	N	T		A	H	A			Y	A	L	I	E	S
S	T	E		D	U	D	E	S		A	C	R	E	
			C	O	N	A	R	T	I	S	T			
L	I	M	O			T	R	A	C	E		T	M	C
I	N	U	R	E	S		L	E	T		R	A	H	
B	A	N	K	R	O	B	B	E	R		M	A	N	E
E	N	D		A	C	L	U		B	S	I	D	E	
L	I	A	R		C	A	T	B	U	R	G	L	A	R
E	T	N	A		E	S	T	A	T	E		E	T	E
D	Y	E	D		R	E	S	T	E	D		R	E	D

PAGE 150
Circular Reasoning

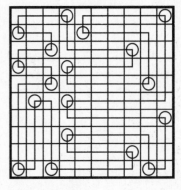

COUNTDOWN
9+87-6+54+3+2+1 = 150

PAGE 151
Looped Path

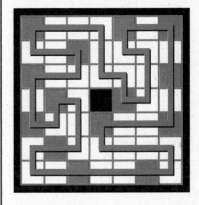

CITY SEARCH
CAVERN, CORNEA, CRAVEN, UNCOVER

PAGE 152
Islands

COMMON SENSE
BREAK

PAGE 153

That's a Wrap

D	E	E	R	E	■	E	X	A	M	■	R	A	Z	E
A	R	D	O	R	■	E	M	M	A	■	I	W	O	N
T	A	G	Y	O	U	R	E	I	T	■	B	O	N	D
E	S	E	■	S	P	I	N	■	T	A	B	L	E	S
D	E	S	P	I	S	E	■	A	R	G	O	■	■	■
■	■	■	A	V	A	■	Q	U	E	E	N	B	E	E
S	L	O	P	E	■	J	U	T	S	■	C	O	D	E
K	A	N	E	■	D	E	A	R	S	■	A	R	A	L
I	C	E	R	■	I	N	K	Y	■	E	N	E	M	Y
S	E	A	P	L	A	N	E	■	H	A	D	■	■	■
■	■	■	R	O	M	A	■	M	A	R	Y	K	A	Y
S	T	O	O	G	E	■	S	E	R	F	■	A	L	A
L	O	A	F	■	T	A	P	E	P	L	A	Y	E	R
A	N	T	I	■	E	D	I	T	■	A	L	O	U	D
M	I	S	T	■	R	O	T	S	■	P	E	S	T	S

PAGE 154

123

1	2	3	1	3	2	1	2	3
2	3	1	2	1	3	2	3	1
3	2	3	1	2	1	3	1	2
2	1	2	3	1	3	2	3	1
1	3	1	2	3	2	1	2	3
3	1	2	3	1	3	2	1	2
1	2	3	1	2	1	3	2	3
2	3	1	2	3	2	1	3	1
3	1	2	3	2	1	3	1	2

BETWEENER
WAGE

PAGE 155

Find the Ships

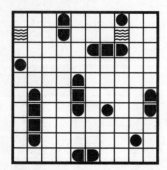

ADDITION SWITCH
5 1 2 + 3 8 8 = 9 0 0

PAGE 156

Gotcha

B	O	S	■	S	P	A	S	■	L	E	G	A	T	O
A	R	C	■	E	L	L	E	■	A	V	A	L	O	N
R	I	O	■	M	U	I	R	■	S	E	M	I	T	E
N	O	T	H	I	N	G	B	U	T	N	E	T	■	■
E	L	I	A	■	K	N	O	T	■	E	R	A	S	E
S	E	A	M	Y	■	■	I	S	R	■	L	E	N	■
■	■	L	E	D	■	A	L	A	■	P	I	E	D	■
■	T	H	E	T	E	N	D	E	R	T	R	A	P	■
R	I	O	T	■	M	E	D	■	I	I	I	■	■	■
E	E	L	■	S	I	P	■	■	S	O	N	A	R	■
B	R	E	S	T	■	A	L	A	S	■	R	E	M	O
■	■	C	H	A	R	L	O	T	T	E	S	W	E	B
E	L	A	I	N	E	■	R	E	A	D	■	E	L	I
D	I	R	E	C	T	■	N	A	V	E	■	S	I	N
S	U	D	S	E	D	■	A	M	E	N	■	T	A	G

PAGE 157

About Time

CLUELESS CROSSWORD

L	A	N	T	E	R	N
A	■	E	■	C	■	U
B	U	C	O	L	I	C
O	■	T	■	A	■	L
R	E	A	L	I	Z	E
E	■	R	■	R	■	U
R	E	S	I	S	T	S

PAGE 158

Word Maze

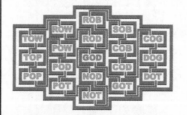

SOUND THINKING
AVERRED, EVERYDAY, OVERDO,
OVERDUE, OVERRIDE, VARIED,
VEERED

PAGE 159

Star Search

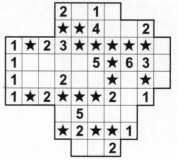

TELEPHONE TRIOS
CABINET, OTTOMAN, HIGHBOY

PAGE 160

Temperature's Rising

E	M	M	A	S	■	O	L	A	F	■	F	A	D	S
L	I	E	U	P	■	R	I	G	A	■	I	C	E	T
H	E	A	T	I	N	G	P	A	D	■	N	I	L	E
I	N	T	O	T	O	■	S	S	E	■	E	D	I	T
■	■	■	S	E	T	H	■	S	I	P	S	■	■	■
M	E	G	■	B	A	K	I	N	G	S	O	D	A	■
O	P	A	L	■	A	I	L	■	■	A	I	R	E	S
O	S	L	O	■	D	R	I	P	S	■	N	I	B	S
D	O	L	O	R	■	■	E	L	I	■	G	O	R	E
S	M	O	K	I	N	G	G	U	N	■	N	A	T	■
■	■	■	I	G	O	R	■	S	K	I	M	■	■	■
S	T	A	N	■	N	A	B	■	I	N	A	R	U	T
M	I	N	G	■	F	I	R	I	N	G	L	I	N	E
O	N	T	O	■	A	N	E	W	■	O	L	D	I	E
G	A	I	N	■	T	Y	R	O	■	T	E	S	T	S

PAGE 161

Sudoku

7	9	3	8	4	1	2	6	5
1	5	4	6	9	2	8	3	7
2	6	8	7	5	3	9	4	1
6	2	7	5	1	8	4	9	3
4	3	1	9	2	6	7	5	8
9	8	5	3	7	4	6	1	2
3	7	9	2	6	5	1	8	4
8	1	6	4	3	7	5	2	9
5	4	2	1	8	9	3	7	6

AND SO ON
SPIT and POLISH

PAGE 162
One-Way Streets

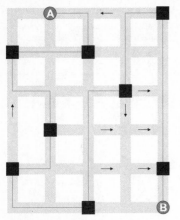

COMMON SENSE
NOISY

PAGE 163
ABC

A	C	B		
C		A		B
B			C	A
	A	C	B	
	B		A	C

MIXAGRAMS
IMBUE NICK
AILED CHOP
ANGST VEAL
SKEIN WITH

PAGE 164
Olympic Memories

G	A	Z	A		F	A	T	E	D		D	A	M	S
A	S	I	F		A	G	R	E	E		O	M	I	T
L	E	N	A		L	A	U	R	A		G	A	L	A
L	A	C	R	O	S	S	E		L	E	T	T	E	R
			R	E	S		A	S	T	A	I	R	E	
R	O	P	E	C	L	I	M	B	I	N	G			
O	N	E	W	A	Y		U	L	N	A		D	A	B
S	U	R	E			A	T	E			M	E	M	O
A	S	K		C	A	M	E		D	I	A	L	E	R
		M	O	T	O	R	B	O	A	T	I	N	G	
D	E	T	A	I	L	S		R	U	G				
E	Q	U	I	N	E		T	U	G	O	F	W	A	R
A	U	L	D		A	B	O	I	L		O	H	N	O
R	I	S	E		S	O	U	S	A		G	I	N	A
S	P	A	N		T	O	T	E	S		S	T	E	M

PAGE 165
Go With the Flow

TWO-BY-FOUR
TINE, TURN (or RUNT);
RENT, UNIT; TENT, RUIN

PAGE 166
Find the Ships

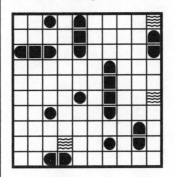

SUDOKU SUM
3 5 1 + 4 6 9 = 8 2 0

PAGE 167
123

2	3	1	3	2	1	3	2	1
3	1	3	2	1	3	2	1	2
1	2	1	3	2	1	3	2	3
2	1	3	2	3	2	1	3	1
1	3	2	1	2	3	2	1	3
3	2	1	3	1	2	1	3	2
2	3	2	1	3	1	3	2	1
1	2	3	2	1	3	2	1	3
3	1	2	1	3	2	1	3	2

IN OTHER WORDS
COWPOKE, SLOWPOKE,
STEWPOT, VIEWPOINT

PAGE 169
Two Women

G	A	I	T		E	R	A	T	O		J	E	S	T
A	L	O	E		S	O	W	E	R		A	L	P	O
L	U	T	E		T	I	A	R	A		P	A	I	N
A	M	A	N	D	A	L	Y	N	N		A	N	T	E
		I	T	S			G	A	N	D	E	R		
D	E	D	U	C	E		B	Y	E	S				
A	R	O	S	E		M	A	U	R	A	L	I	Z	A
F	L	O	E		S	O	R	R	Y		E	N	O	W
T	E	R	R	Y	T	O	R	I		P	A	I	N	E
				E	A	S	Y		R	E	N	T	E	D
L	O	G	J	A	M			T	U	E				
O	R	E	O		M	E	R	Y	L	L	E	I	G	H
Y	A	N	K		E	X	I	L	E		P	O	L	O
A	T	I	E		R	I	C	E	R		I	N	O	N
L	E	E	R		S	T	A	R	S		C	A	P	E

PAGE 170
Circular Reasoning

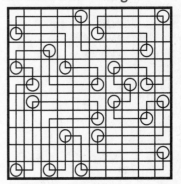

AND SO ON
CLOAK and DAGGER

PAGE 171
Islands

THREE AT A RHYME
ARC, MARQUE, SPARK

PAGE 172
Average Addition

D	E	L	T	A		P	S	S	T		I	D	E	M
A	V	E	R	S		E	T	N	A		M	A	X	I
N	O	V	A	K		D	E	A	L		P	I	P	S
C	L	I	P	S	E	R	V	I	C	E		Q	U	O
E	V	E			N	O	E	L		S	H	U	N	
R	E	D	H	O	T				S	L	E	I	G	H
		E	A	R	N	E	S	T		A	R	E	A	
C	L	U	C	K	O	F	T	H	E	I	R	I	S	H
O	I	N	K		P	L	A	Y	A	C	T			
S	M	I	L	E	Y			M	Y	S	T	I	C	
	A	V	E	S		S	A	G	E			A	B	U
A	B	E		C	L	O	N	E	R	A	N	G	E	R
M	E	R	V		E	G	G	O		L	E	E	R	S
M	A	S	H		A	G	E	D		E	R	N	I	E
O	N	E	S		P	Y	L	E		C	O	D	A	S

PAGE 173
Color Squares

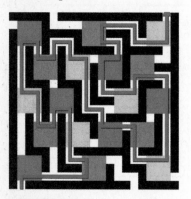

BETWEENER
PUNCH

PAGE 174
Hyper-Sudoku

7	6	1	5	2	3	9	8	4
8	9	3	1	7	4	2	6	5
4	2	5	8	6	9	7	3	1
2	7	6	4	9	8	5	1	3
3	4	8	7	5	1	6	2	9
5	1	9	2	3	6	8	4	7
1	5	4	6	8	7	3	9	2
9	8	7	3	4	2	1	5	6
6	3	2	9	1	5	4	7	8

TELEPHONE TRIOS
CANTATA, LULLABY, RAGTIME

PAGE 175
Three-for-One Word Search

ADDITION SWITCH
1 9 3 + 2 4 4 = 4 3 7

PAGE 176
New-Wave Composers

C	O	M	P		U	S	U	R	P		B	I	B	S
E	R	I	E		M	A	R	I	E		I	R	A	N
L	I	S	Z	T	P	R	I	C	E		Z	I	T	I
L	O	T		R	I	G	S		P	R	E	S	E	T
O	N	S	H	O	R	E		W	H	A	T			
		A	L	E		T	O	O	T	S	I	E	S	
B	E	R	Y	L		P	O	O	L		I	O	T	A
E	N	I	D		P	R	U	D	E		G	L	O	M
L	Y	N	N		O	A	R	S		I	N	A	N	E
L	A	G	G	A	R	D	S		O	D	A			
		O	T	T	O		A	D	E	L	I	N	E	
S	H	A	S	T	A		A	S	E	A		N	A	T
L	U	R	E		B	A	C	H	S	L	U	N	C	H
A	G	E	E		L	I	M	E	S		N	E	R	O
P	E	A	K		E	L	E	N	A		O	R	E	S

PAGE 177
Triad Split Decisions

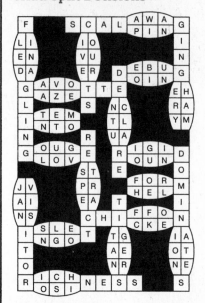

TRANSDELETION
HEMINGWAY

PAGE 178
One-Way Streets

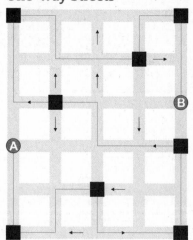

SOUND THINKING
CARTEL, COURTLY, CURTAIL, CURTLY

PAGE 179
Soil Bank

B	A	N	D		D	E	M	U	R		I	M	U	S
A	F	A	R		E	R	A	S	E		D	A	L	I
G	O	T	O	F	F	T	H	E	G	R	O	U	N	D
O	U	T	V	O	T	E		D	A	H	L	I	A	S
F	L	Y	E	R				L	E	I				
			S	U	B	P	A	R		A	Z	U	R	E
A	N	Y		M	O	U	T	H	S		E	R	A	T
D	O	E	S	S	O	M	E	O	N	E	D	I	R	T
O	A	T	H		N	A	S	D	A	Q		S	E	A
S	H	I	R	E		S	T	E	P	U	P			
			I	N	K					A	O	R	T	A
S	H	I	N	I	N	G		S	E	T	T	E	E	S
C	O	M	E	D	O	W	N	T	O	E	A	R	T	H
A	J	A	R		B	E	G	U	N		T	A	R	E
M	O	M	S		S	N	O	B	S		O	N	A	N

PAGE 180
Dicey

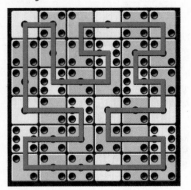

TRANSDELETION
CLARINET

PAGE 181
Star Search

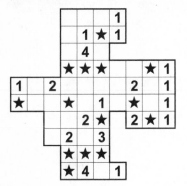

MIXAGRAMS
SHRED YEWS
OAKEN SLED
ERROR BEAT
IDLED HERO

PAGE 182
Sudoku

2	8	1	5	7	4	6	3	9
6	9	7	8	3	1	4	2	5
3	5	4	9	2	6	8	7	1
1	3	5	4	8	7	9	6	2
4	2	9	3	6	5	7	1	8
7	6	8	1	9	2	3	5	4
5	1	3	7	4	9	2	8	6
9	7	2	6	1	8	5	4	3
8	4	6	2	5	3	1	9	7

THREE OF A KIND
Agnes <u>photograph</u>ed the Gr<u>and</u>
Canyon's sceni<u>c old</u> ruins.

PAGE 183
Fault Line

E	L	S	E		G	L	A	S	S		W	E	L	D
D	A	T	A		R	I	C	K	I		I	D	E	A
E	V	E	R	Y	O	N	E	I	S	A	S	G	O	D
N	A	P		O	U	T	S			R	E	E	S	E
		L	O	U	S	Y		C	A	T	T			
C	L	A	I	R	E		F	O	X	H	O	U	N	D
O	L	D	S			S	L	I	E	R		N	E	A
M	A	D	E	H	I	M	A	N	D	O	F	T	E	N
M	M	E		A	M	I	S	S			L	E	D	A
A	A	R	D	V	A	R	K		T	S	E	T	S	E
		R	A	N	K		D	I	N	A	H			
S	I	T	I	N		V	I	T	O		E	A	T	
A	G	R	E	A	T	D	E	A	L	W	O	R	S	E
G	O	E	R		E	X	I	L	E		W	E	I	R
A	R	K	S		M	I	N	O	S		E	D	A	M

PAGE 184
ABC

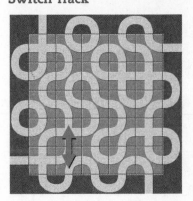

A		C	B
		B	A	C
B	C			A
C	A			B
	B	A	C	

SUDOKU SUM
2 4 5 + 7 1 8 = 9 6 3

PAGE 185
Find the Ships

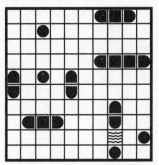

TWO-BY-FOUR
BRED, GLUM; MELD,
GRUB (or BURG)

PAGE 186
Drinks All Around

S	L	E	W		S	T	A	G	S		J	O	E	Y
P	O	L	O		A	E	R	I	E		A	P	S	E
A	G	E	R		Y	E	A	R	N		B	E	T	A
R	O	C	K	T	U	M	B	L	E	R		R	A	T
		U	R	N			S	C	A	R	A	B	S	
R	E	S	P	E	C	T	S		A	P	E	G		
A	A	H		K	L	U	T	Z		S	A	L	V	E
C	R	A	B		E	R	R	O	R		D	A	I	S
E	L	V	E	S		F	I	N	E	S		S	T	P
		I	R	O	N		P	E	T	E	R	S	O	N
H	A	N	G	D	O	G		I	R	A				
E	G	G		A	M	E	R	I	C	A	S	C	U	P
L	I	M	E		A	T	O	N	E		C	O	R	E
P	L	U	G		D	A	M	O	N		A	L	G	A
S	E	G	O		S	T	A	R	T		L	E	E	K

PAGE 187
Switch Track

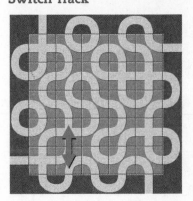

TELEPHONE TRIOS
ICELAND, CORSICA, SUMATRA

PAGE 188

123

2	1	3	2	3	1	2	1	3
3	2	1	3	1	2	3	2	1
1	3	2	1	2	3	3	1	2
2	1	3	2	3	1	2	1	3
3	2	1	3	1	2	3	2	1
1	3	2	1	2	3	3	1	2
2	1	3	2	3	1	2	1	3
1	3	2	1	2	3	3	1	2
3	2	1	3	1	2	3	2	1

COMMON SENSE
HOUSE

PAGE 189

Circular Reasoning

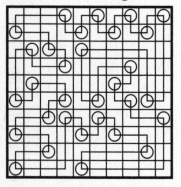

THREE AT A RHYME
BOMB, MOM, PROM

PAGE 190

Embedded Businesses

T	A	C	O	S		A	D	A	M		A	M	I	S
S	T	A	N	K			C	A	G	E		L	A	S	T
P	I	N	C	U	S	H	I	O	N		L	I	L	A
S	T	E	E	L	I	E	S			B	I	N	E	T
			L	T	D		S	E	L	E	C	T	S
O	N	B	A	S	E		H	O	P	E	S	O
L	A	R	D		S	H	A	N	I	A		U	S	A
A	G	A	S	P		E	L	I		T	A	R	E	S
F	Y	I		E	F	F	E	C	T		A	S	A	P
	N	I	C	E	T	Y		U	S	H	E	R	S
S	E	C	T	O	R	S		S	N	O
C	R	O	S	S			T	O	I	L	E	T	T	E
R	A	R	E		T	W	I	N	C	I	T	I	E	S
E	T	A	L		H	E	L	I		D	O	N	A	T
W	O	L	F		U	S	T	A		S	N	E	R	D

PAGE 191

Hyper-Sudoku

3	9	7	1	8	5	2	4	6
4	5	8	9	6	2	1	3	7
1	6	2	7	3	4	8	5	9
8	1	4	3	2	6	7	9	5
9	2	5	8	4	7	3	6	1
6	7	3	5	1	9	4	2	8
2	8	1	6	9	3	5	7	4
7	4	9	2	5	1	6	8	3
5	3	6	4	7	8	9	1	2

ADDITION SWITCH
2 8 1 + 3 0 4 = 5 8 5

PAGE 192

Split Decisions

TONGUE TWISTER
SAUNA

PAGE 193

That Follows

S	O	A	P		U	L	N	A	S		Q	U	A	D
K	A	L	E		P	O	I	N	T		E	N	N	A
E	T	O	N		T	A	L	I	A		D	I	T	Z
W	H	E	N	W	O	M	E	N	G	O		T	O	E
			A	N	Y			I	N	T	E	N	D
H	A	S	B	R	O		L	I	N	E	R
O	N	O	R		W	R	O	N	G	M	E	N	G	O
E	D	N	A	S		A	F	R		O	B	O	E	S
R	I	G	H	T	A	F	T	E	R		L	U	L	L
		M	I	N	T	Y		E	V	E	N	S	O
S	E	C	A	N	T		E	L	I
A	L	A		T	H	E	M	M	A	E	W	E	S	T
J	A	N	E		E	L	E	C	T		I	S	E	E
A	T	O	M		M	E	L	E	E		M	A	N	X
K	E	N	T		S	A	T	E	D		P	U	T	T

PAGE 194

Möbius Maze

BETWEENER
GROUND

PAGE 195

Islands

MIXAGRAMS
GROUP EACH
SALVO DOUR
CAMEO VIED
AVAIL MUSH

PAGE 196

One-Way Streets

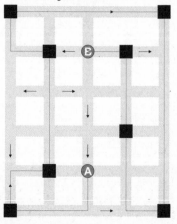

AND SO ON
SMOKE and MIRRORS

PAGE 197
Pet Peeve

B	O	F	F	O		B	E	E	F		S	C	A	M
A	L	I	E	N		R	E	A	L		O	O	Z	E
R	E	C	U	T		A	R	T	Y		S	P	U	R
T	O	A	D	O	G	Y	O	U	R	E		E	S	C
		S	U	E		P	O	R	T	R	A	Y		
A	L	L		R	E	B	S		D	A	W	N		
L	O	U	T		K	I	W	I		T	O	I	L	S
F	A	M	I	L	Y	B	U	T	T	O	A	C	A	T
A	M	B	L	E		I	N	T	O		M	U	T	E
	E	L	M	S		G	Y	R	O		S	E	W	
F	O	R	S	A	L	E		R	Y	E				
A	N	Y		Y	O	U	A	R	E	S	T	A	F	F
B	I	A	S		O	R	D	O		T	U	D	O	R
L	O	R	I		P	O	E	T		E	D	D	I	E
E	N	D	S		S	S	N	S		R	E	S	E	T

PAGE 198
Sudoku

4	1	5	3	2	6	9	8	7
6	9	3	5	7	8	4	1	2
7	8	2	9	1	4	5	6	3
9	2	8	1	6	3	7	4	5
5	6	4	2	8	7	1	3	9
1	3	7	4	9	5	6	2	8
3	5	9	6	4	2	8	7	1
8	4	1	7	3	9	2	5	6
2	7	6	8	5	1	3	9	4

TRANSDELETION
OSTRICH

PAGE 199
Star Search

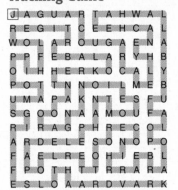

SUDOKU SUM
481 + 269 = 750

PAGE 200
Take Monday Off

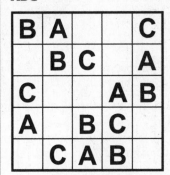

S	O	D		C	Z	A	R		R	U	M	P	L	E
T	V	A		R	U	B	E		A	N	A	L	O	G
R	E	N		A	L	E	S		M	I	L	A	N	O
A	R	C	H	B	U	T	T	E	R	F	L	Y		
I	D	E	A				J	O	Y		T	U	T	
N	O	R	M	A	L		L	E	D		V	I	S	A
		M	A	G	I	C		T	A	M	E	D		
	R	O	E	D	O	C	T	R	I	N	E			
P	R	A	W	N		R	I	S	E	R				
A	I	D	E		P	I	T		S	E	A	L	A	B
R	B	I		P	O	E				R	E	N	E	
	A	B	A	R	R	E	L	O	F	K	E	Y	S	
R	E	T	O	R	T		D	A	D	A		R	O	T
A	R	O	U	S	E		A	T	O	Z		E	N	O
G	A	R	T	E	R		M	E	R	E		D	E	W

PAGE 201
Alternating Tiles

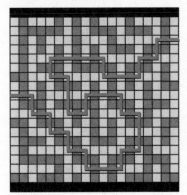

SOUND THINKING
AIRPORT, REPARTEE, REPORT

PAGE 202
Tracking Game

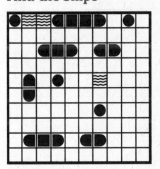

MIXAGRAMS
HASTY TUBE
TUNIC BRAY
SPOOK WILT
BOWER HELM

PAGE 203
ABC

B	A				C
	B	C			A
C				A	B
A		B	C		
C	A	B			

CLUELESS CROSSWORD

S	U	B	L	E	T	S		S
A		A		D		I		I
V	E	R	S	I	O	N		N
V		B		F		C		C
I	T	E	M	I	Z	E		E
E		L		C		L		R
R	E	L	I	E	V	E		

PAGE 204
Themeless Toughie

A	B	O	L	I	S	H		D	A	S	H	I	N	G
G	O	R	I	L	L	A		E	L	E	A	N	O	R
E	L	A	T	I	O	N		B	I	C	Y	C	L	E
N	E	T		A	E	G	E	A	N		S	H	O	E
T	R	E	A	D		O	A	S	E	S		A	N	N
S	O	D	S		R	U	S	E		M	A	R	G	E
		S	K	A	T	E		L	A	R	G	E	R	
C	O	M	I	N	G	S		F	O	R	G	E	R	Y
A	P	O	G	E	E		D	I	R	T	Y			
S	E	I	N	E		S	A	R	I		L	A	S	S
H	R	S		L	O	C	H	S		A	E	S	O	P
M	A	T	S		H	A	L	T	E	R		H	O	E
E	T	E	R	N	A	L		A	N	E	M	O	N	E
R	E	S	T	O	R	E		I	G	N	O	R	E	D
E	S	T	A	T	E	S		D	R	A	P	E	R	Y

PAGE 206
Find the Ships

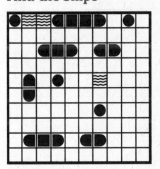

TWO-BY-FOUR
EPIC, HOUR; OUCH, PIER (or RIPE); COUP, HIRE (or HEIR)

PAGE 207
Hyper-Sudoku

2	9	5	7	6	1	4	3	8
3	6	1	9	4	8	7	5	2
8	7	4	3	5	2	9	1	6
9	5	8	2	7	6	3	4	1
1	4	6	8	3	9	5	2	7
7	3	2	4	1	5	8	6	9
4	8	9	6	2	3	1	7	5
6	1	7	5	8	4	2	9	3
5	2	3	1	9	7	6	8	4

CITY SEARCH
BARON

PAGE 210
Circular Reasoning

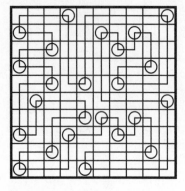

TELEPHONE TRIOS
CENTAUR, PHOENIX, UNICORN

PAGE 213
Islands

IN OTHER WORDS
EVERYDAY

PAGE 208
Themeless Toughie

```
SNAKEOIL S SAMPLE
CAROTENE O OBERON
RICARDOS R RESORT
ALINE NOBEL TRE
PENS PETER TOAN
ERG PASHA LICIT
CUTTOTHEBONE
SWEETER AEDILES
PERSONAGRATA
ARRAN CREDO CSA
REAR SKITS CATS
SIN MUSER CASAS
ENTREE VENERATE
STRAIT EARLOBES
TOYERS STALBANS
```

PAGE 211
Themeless Toughie

```
MOSSHART RHESUS
INCLOVER HALEST
SARATOGA INDIGO
ATOM WAGING SRO
DOOMS NINO EMAG
DOGEAR CBC WINE
STERNUM REJECTS
TRI ERA
CARLOAN DONTASK
ASEA LUC SEWNON
SATS REAR TITLE
ARI NOTBAD TWAS
BUREAU ABETTERS
ALEAST LAKEERIE
SEETHE STANDPAT
```

PAGE 214
Themeless Toughie

```
ELPASO ROSSETTI
DARNED ELECTRON
IRONED ADDITION
TAJ PSYCHE ASTI
OMENS OHARA TIN
RICO DUET SLANG
SETTLERS TWANGS
AILS ROAD
SPARSE RAINDROP
LIBYA TAIL EURO
IRA SHUNS TRILL
PANS ONSALE NAY
UNDERSEA ARMING
PHONETIC BRANDO
SANDBANK SAIGON
```

PAGE 209
Arrow Routes

THREE AT A RHYME
BLURT, CURT, DIRT

PAGE 212
123

1	3	2	1	2	3	2	1	3
3	2	1	3	1	2	1	3	2
2	1	3	2	3	1	2	1	3
3	2	1	3	1	2	3	2	1
1	3	2	1	3	1	2	3	2
3	2	1	3	2	3	1	2	1
2	1	3	2	1	2	3	1	3
1	3	2	1	2	3	1	3	2
2	1	3	2	3	1	3	2	1

BETWEENER
DANCE

PAGE 215
Pathfinder

```
L I R D I N G B A L L
G D E A L P H Y C R O
T P I N E T F A R E O
H Y H S J A L H O V N
C A R T Y P O M A R T
Y C A K O [T] R A I S C
C L E R G R E B N N O
R K C I T A N U L I O
O S H A W X I S E P T
T D E M A I L Z E P E
O M P O L O D N O G R
```

COMMON SENSE
STRONG

PAGE 216
Bead Maze

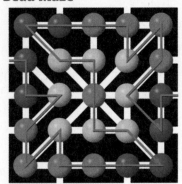

COUNTDOWN
987-654-321 = 12

PAGE 217
Themeless Toughie

C	O	M	P	E	L	S		S	T	A	T	I	S	M
O	C	E	A	N	I	A		P	I	R	A	N	H	A
S	T	A	R	T	E	R		A	R	O	U	S	E	R
M	A	T	T	I	N	G		S	E	N	S	O	R	Y
O	N	A	I	R						M	I	L		
S	E	X	I	E	S	T		R	O	T	U	N	D	A
			P	R	A	E	T	O	R	I	A	N		
S	T	R	I	K	E	U	P	T	H	E	B	A	N	D
O	V	E	R	I	N	S	U	R	E					
A	D	D	E	N	D	S		O	R	I	G	A	M	I
P	I	E								M	A	V	E	N
I	N	A	H	E	A	P		K	I	P	L	I	N	G
E	N	G	A	R	D	E		I	S	O	L	A	T	E
S	E	L	L	O	U	T		D	E	S	O	T	O	S
T	R	E	S	S	E	S		D	E	E	P	E	S	T

PAGE 218
ABCD

B		C	A	D	
C		A	D	B	
	D	B		A	C
A	C	D			B
D	B		C		A
	A		B	C	D

SOUND THINKING
MALIGN, MELON, MILLENNIA

PAGE 219
Sudoku

5	4	7	2	8	1	6	3	9
2	6	3	4	9	7	1	5	8
8	9	1	6	3	5	7	2	4
9	1	2	3	5	8	4	6	7
4	8	6	7	1	2	3	9	5
7	3	5	9	6	4	2	8	1
3	5	4	8	7	6	9	1	2
1	2	9	5	4	3	8	7	6
6	7	8	1	2	9	5	4	3

ADDITION SWITCH
7 1 5 + 1 8 6 = 9 0 1

PAGE 220
Themeless Toughie

L	A	S	T	W	O	R	D		P	R	A	G	U	E
A	N	N	A	R	B	O	R		R	U	N	I	N	S
C	O	A	L	E	S	C	E		O	S	A	G	E	S
E	N	G	I	N	E			A	D	D	S			
			S	I	D	E	D	I	S	H	E	S		
S	A	R	C	A	S	M		B	E	A	T	O	U	T
A	V	E	R	Y		P	L	O	D		U	R	G	E
R	O	B	I	N		L	O	N		S	C	R	E	W
T	W	I	N		N	O	T	A		S	C	O	N	E
R	A	N	G	I	E	R		I	G	N	O	R	E	D
E	L	D	E	R	B	E	R	R	Y					
			K	U	S	H		R	E	G	A	R	D	
B	R	A	Z	I	L		O	R	A	T	O	R	I	O
R	O	W	E	N	A		D	A	T	A	B	A	S	E
R	E	N	E	G	E		E	Y	E	L	I	N	E	R

PAGE 221
One-Way Streets

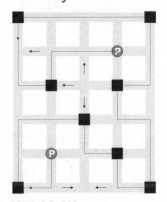

AND SO ON
DIVIDE and CONQUER

PAGE 222
Split Decisions

TRANSDELETION
EMERALD

PAGE 223
Themeless Toughie

T	H	E	P	I	T	S		P	L	A	C	E	B	O
H	A	M	I	T	U	P		H	A	S	O	V	E	R
I	M	I	T	A	T	E		A	D	O	R	I	N	G
M	E	T	A	L		W	A	N		K	A	N	G	A
B	L	T	S		C	E	N	T	S		S	C	A	N
L	I	E		V	A	R	I	O	U	S		E	L	I
E	N	D	E	A	R	S		M	R	M	U	S	I	C
		A	L	I				F	A	N				
H	A	S	T	O	B	E		P	E	R	U	S	A	L
A	R	C		R	O	U	G	H	I	T		P	R	O
S	T	A	B		U	B	O	A	T		N	A	S	A
I	D	T	A	G		A	P	R		C	O	N	E	D
D	E	T	R	A	I	N		A	I	R	L	I	N	E
I	C	E	R	I	N	K		O	N	A	T	E	A	R
M	O	D	E	L	T	S		H	G	W	E	L	L	S

PAGE 224
Think Straight

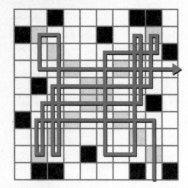

THREE OF A KIND
Intermediate Ma<u>th is</u>, to
<u>me, ans</u>wers to a stack of
<u>way-out</u> examples.

PAGE 225
Star Search

MIXAGRAMS
A B I D E C H A T
G O O S E R E N T
I N F E R P A I D
D E T E R I D O L

PAGE 226
Themeless Toughie

I	N	D	I	G	O		N	E	A	T	I	D	E	A
N	O	O	N	A	N		O	N	P	A	R	O	L	E
G	O	L	A	S	T		T	A	P	W	A	T	E	R
E	D	E	S	S	A		I	T	E	S		O	O	O
A	G	R	E	E	R		N	E	A		D	A	N	G
R	E	S	C	R	I	P	T		R	H	E	T	O	R
			A	A	H	S		O	P	E	R	A		
B	L	O	W	I	N	G	O	F	F	S	T	E	A	M
L	I	V	E	N		E	S	P	O					
E	V	E	N	T	S		E	D	U	C	A	T	O	R
N	E	R	D		P	O	W		R	O	X	A	N	E
D	U	D		A	R	G	O		S	H	I	L	L	S
S	P	O	T	T	I	E	R		T	E	L	L	I	T
I	T	E	R	A	T	E	D		A	R	L	E	N	E
N	O	S	I	N	E	S	S		R	E	A	R	E	D

PAGE 227
Islands

INITIAL REACTION
25 = CENTS in a QUARTER

PAGE 228
Line Drawing

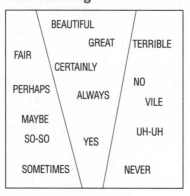

TWO-BY-FOUR
AIRY, MUTT

PAGE 229
Themeless Toughie

A	L	I	M	E	N	T	E	D		H	U	N	C	H
P	E	T	E	R	A	R	N	O		O	P	E	R	A
I	N	E	A	R	N	E	S	T		W	A	L	E	S
A	I	R	S	O	C	K		T	S	E	T	S	E	S
R	E	A	L	L	Y		V	E	E		R	O	L	L
I	N	T	E	L		M	A	D	E	S	E	N	S	E
A	C	E	S		W	A	R	L	I	K	E			
N	E	D		T	E	R	M	I	N	I		C	A	B
			B	O	L	T	I	N	G		M	A	L	A
S	S	V	A	N	D	I	N	E		M	I	C	K	Y
T	E	A	R		E	A	T		R	A	S	T	A	S
E	N	S	N	A	R	L		C	O	N	S	U	L	T
N	O	S	E	Y		A	N	A	S	T	A	S	I	A
C	R	A	T	E		R	E	P	E	L	L	E	N	T
H	A	R	T	S		T	E	N	N	E	S	S	E	E

PAGE 230
Triad Split Decisions

SUDOKU SUM
4 5 9 + 3 6 1 = 8 2 0

PAGE 231
Color Paths

THREE AT A RHYME
CHUM, FROM, THUMB

PAGE 232
Themeless Toughie

M	A	S	S	A	G	E	S		M	O	D	E	S	T
A	L	L	E	L	U	I	A		I	B	E	R	I	A
R	E	A	C	T	I	N	G		M	O	N	A	C	O
K	E	P	T	A	T		A	T	O	I				
			A	S	S	E	S	S	M	E	N	T		
	S	E	N	O	R	A		M	A	T	A	D	O	R
L	I	V	E	D		U	M	P	S		D	I	V	E
E	L	I	T	E		T	O	E		M	E	T	E	S
P	E	N	T		N	E	T	S		I	D	O	L	S
U	N	C	L	E	A	R		T	U	T	O	R	S	
S	T	E	E	L	I	N	E	S	S					
			A	V	E	R		A	W	H	I	L	E	
M	E	A	N	I	E		R	E	G	A	I	N	E	D
A	R	D	E	N	T		O	V	E	R	L	O	N	G
P	E	E	W	E	E		R	E	S	P	O	N	S	E